Adapted for the Screen

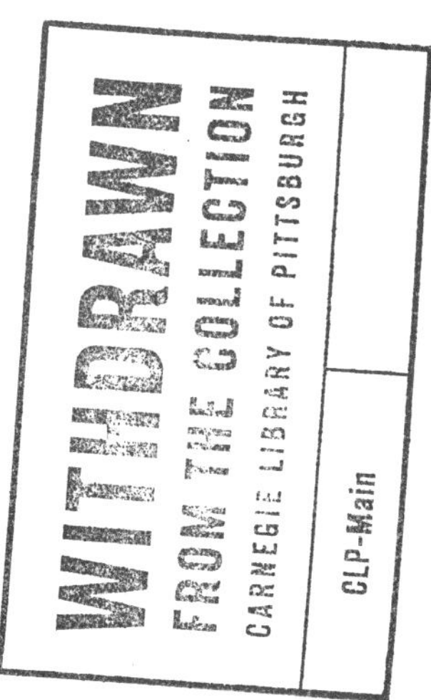

Adapted for the Screen

The Cultural Politics of Modern Chinese Fiction and Film

Hsiu-Chuang Deppman

University of Hawai'i Press
Honolulu

Illustrations in this volume were supported in part by a grant from Oberlin College.

Printed in the United States of America

15 14 13 12 11 10   6 5 4 3 2 1

Library of Congress Cataloging-in-Publication Data

Deppman, Hsiu-Chuang.

Adapted for the screen : the cultural politics of adaptation in modern Chinese fiction and film / by Hsiu-Chuang Deppman.

p. cm.

Includes bibliographical references and index.

ISBN 978-0-8248-3373-2 (hardcover : alk. paper)—ISBN 978-0-8248-3454-8 (pbk. : alk. paper)

1. Film adaptations—History and criticism. 2. Chinese fiction—20th century—Film and video adaptations. 3. Motion pictures and literature—China. I. Title.

PN1997.85.D36 2010

791.43'60951—dc22

2009047052

University of Hawai'i Press books are printed on acid-free paper and meet the guidelines for permanence and durability of the Council on Library Resources.

Designed by Santos Barbasa Jr.

Printed by The Maple-Vail Book Manufacturing Group

Contents

Acknowledgments

"Zhi duan qing chang" is a popular Chinese expression that means "the paper is too short for long feelings." It fits my attempt to thank those who have made researching Chinese film and fiction such an enjoyable task.

I wrote the bulk of this book in 2006–2007 on a research leave from Oberlin College. A Freeman Curriculum Grant and two Powers Travel Grants made possible my archival research in Shanghai, Hong Kong, and Taipei. I also benefited from a 2006–2007 Research Fulbright to Taiwan, and I am grateful to Peng Hsiao-yen for a visiting fellowship in the Institute of Literature and Philosophy at the Academia Sinica.

I appreciate the scholarly advice and camaraderie of Kirk Denton, Christopher Lupke, Michael Berry, David Bordwell, Ying Zhu, Chris Berry, Wendy Larson, Ru-shou Robert Chen, and Whitney Dilley. Katherine Linehan was most helpful in reading an earlier draft of the manuscript. The anonymous reviewers at the University of Hawai'i Press offered invaluable suggestions to the manuscript, and Pamela Kelley gracefully helped bring this project to fruition. I thank Zhang Ziyi for permission to use her image on the cover.

Audiences and colleagues constructively commented on the material in this book during presentations at Shanghai University, Academia Sinica, University of California–Santa Barbara, Eckerd College, National Chiao Tung University, National Tsing Hua University, National Cheng Kung University, Zhejiang University, and Hong Kong University. A condensed Chinese version of chapter 1 was published in *FaAs: Film Appreciation Academic Section* in 2007, and an earlier version of chapter 2 appeared in *MCLC: Modern Chinese Literature and Culture* in 2003.

This book would not have been completed without the steady

support of my friends and colleagues at Oberlin College and the love and encouragement of my family. I thank my sister Hsiu-Miao for her devotion, and every day my daughters Formosa and Ginger teach me new ways of looking at life. Above all, I am short of words to express "long feelings" for my husband, Jed Deppman, who has been my rock and inspiration. This book is for him.

Introduction

Whether adapting fiction into film is an art or a science, Chinese directors are good at it.

Since 1995 all eight of Ang Lee's films have been adaptations, and his results have been nothing short of spectacular: *Crouching Tiger, Hidden Dragon* (2000), *Brokeback Mountain* (2005), and *Lust, Caution* (2007), to name just three. Zhang Yimou's best movies are also adaptations: *Red Sorghum* (1987), *Raise the Red Lantern* (1991), and *To Live* (1994). In 2002, Dai Sijie took the art of Chinese self-adaptation to new heights when he remade his own award-winning novel *Balzac and the Little Chinese Seamstress* into a film. Chen Kaige, Ann Hui, Stanley Kwan, and Hou Xiaoxian (Hou Hsiao-hsien) are a few more brilliant lights in this area.

In spite of this record of achievement, however, there are few comparative studies of Chinese fiction and film. It is easy to find books that offer detailed, sensitive interpretations of film or literature as separate texts, but not ones that put the two together. Why are Chinese literature and cinema still routinely treated as parallel disciplines with distinct aesthetic boundaries?

Over the course of writing this book, I have come to appreciate two reasons why the scarcity of such comparative studies cannot all be attributed to a lack of scholarly interest or academic overspecialization. The first has to do with the inherent difficulty of studying cross-media adaptation of any kind. As theorists of translation and ekphrasis can attest, it is difficult for an observer to establish general principles, rules of thumb, or even minimal best practices for any inter-arts discipline. Besides having many different formal attributes, fiction and film have distinct methods of production (usually an individual writer vs. a collective filming crew), modes of distribution (usually a bookseller vs. a theater), and circumstances of reception (usually solitary reading vs. public viewing.) The more scientific or universally valid a theory of adaptation seeks to be, the more individual cases it must account for across these fields, and the more it must seek a platonic solution to the question of the commensurability of media. This explains why from the 1940s on the Western canon of adaptation theorists—André Bazin (2000, 2005), George Bluestone (1957), Keith Cohen (1979), Dudley Andrew (1984, 1998), James Naremore (2000), Kamilla Elliot (2003), Robert Stam (2005), Robert Stam and Alessandra Raengo (2005), and Linda Hutcheon (2006)—drew so heavily on the theoretical resources of hermeneutics, semiotics, structuralism, translation, and narratology.[1] They were eager to discover an analytical paradigm, a grammar, a nuanced yet neutral vocabulary that could describe the origin and transmission of both literary language and cinematic moving images. They were often frustrated, but their impressive insights on how film directors adapt literary phenomena such as narrative, character, style, and mood have left a lasting impression on me and on this book.

A second reason has less to do with medium per se than with the rich, allusive texture of Chinese cultural traditions. Even when understood to be rigorously distinct from each other, modern Chinese literature and cinema are self-evident examples of what Mikhail Bakhtin would call *cannibalistic* forms: each devours and remixes a wealth of antecedent culture (1992: 33–34). Or, in the structuralist terminology of Gérard Genette, each is *transtextual* because it always already exists in relationships with a vast horizon of other texts (1997:1). This presents adaptation studies with a serious problem, for if a work of fiction or a film is understood to be embedded in an inexhaustible "formal" tradition of its own—not to mention in other political, historical, artistic, or personal contexts—then it is an infinitely rich artifact of culture long before it reaches the transformative dialectics of being "adapted." Thus studies of Chinese adaptation will always run the perilous risk of mixing two infinities.

Given the fact that the cross-fertilization of Chinese film and fiction has radically transformed both fields, however, I believe this is a risk more critics should take. Indeed, an initial attempt or pragmatic primer of some kind, a defense and illustration of at least a few strategies for studying adaptation, is not only warranted but overdue. Here, then, in Table 1 are the examples on which this book is based.

These seven sites, moments, or events of adaptation could be organized and analyzed in many different ways, each with its own integrity and implied assumptions about how cultural materials influence one another or otherwise belong together. A table like this looks very different when it privileges region (China, Taiwan, Hong Kong, overseas), genre (melodrama, martial

Table 1. Movies and Fictions Examined

Fiction Title	Year	Writer	Place	Movie Title	Year	Director	Place
Crouching Tiger, Hidden Dragon	1941	Wang Dulu	China	*Crouching Tiger, Hidden Dragon*	2000	Lee, Ang	US
Wives and Concubines	1990	Su Tong	China	*Raise the Red Lantern*	1991	Zhang Yimou	China
Red Rose and White Rose	1942	Chang, Eileen	China	*Red Rose / White Rose*	1994	Kwan, Stanley	Hong Kong
Intersection	1972	Liu Yichang	Hong Kong	*In the Mood for Love*	2000	Wong Kar-wai	Hong Kong
Balzac and the Little Chinese Seamstress	2000	Dai Sijie	France	*Balzac and the Little Chinese Seamstress*	2002	Dai Sijie	France
A Time to Live, A Time to Kill	1986	Zhu Tianwen	Taiwan	*A Time to Live, A Time to Kill*	1985	Hou Xiaoxian	Taiwan
The Personals	1992	Chen Yuhui	Taiwan	*The Personals*	1998	Chen Guofu	Taiwan

arts, romance, autobiography), or chronology (according either to the year of book or film production or to the historical period represented). One can also very productively arrange studies of film adaptation according to reception history, literary or cinematic movement, prominent themes, narrative structures, or sociopolitical impact. There are many other good options.

In fact, since different combinations of factors can become decisive in almost every individual case of adaptation, I think it is a mistake to try to decide the matter in advance. I believe, a fortiori, that because one cannot fix criteria in a general hierarchy, no abstract science for the study of Chinese adaptation is ever likely to form, and so I have adopted in this book an approach that is responsive, descriptive, and ex post facto rather than predictive, prescriptive, or a priori. Instead of yielding to the temptation to impose default frameworks such as region or genre on the empirical messiness of adaptation—though I did try to represent diversity in these areas—I have contented myself with carefully studying seven films that I rank among the best, most influential, and most interesting examples in the modern history of Chinese adaptation. Blending historical contexts with close readings, I have tried to identify and examine some of the richest and most revealing hermeneutic points of contact and divergence between source texts and films. I use the phrase "cultural politics" as an organizing device not because I think of it as a universal framework or "principle of principles," but because I believe that, loose as it is, it captures much of what I have found to be important and exciting about my chosen examples.

My method is not designed to measure what is "gained" or "lost" in the process of adaptation according to a hypothesized neutral scale, nor does it emphasize platonic or semiotic questions about the commensurability of forms or media. The kinds of questions I ask about each instance of adaptation are different: What are the important factors at play in it? What contexts is it responding to? What is unique or compelling about its style, theme, genre, or narrative? More broadly: what does a given case of adaptation say about Chinese history, art, politics, or culture? To answer such questions it is sometimes crucial to consider form and medium—we will see that genre, in particular, is almost never irrelevant—but often it is just as important to consider representations of gender, race, and class in colonial or postcolonial conditions, psychoanalytic phenomena, auteurial preferences, aesthetic techniques, political history, or anything else that might contribute to the complex cultural politics of Chinese adaptation.

Empirically speaking, gender politics are a prominent feature of many Chinese film adaptations. The topic is on the minds of writers and directors, in their texts and on their screens. In actuality (and this helps explain its prominence), gender politics is almost never *only* about gender politics if this phrase is construed narrowly to mean the sociohistorical condition of women, the struggle for women's rights and liberties, or the problem of political status or sexual exploitation. Instead, in the Chinese context the various problems that the May Fourth Movement synopsized as the "woman question" turn out to be frequent—and therefore often ready-made—allegorical loci for interrogating postures of the artist, constructions of nationhood, Confucian philosophy, class conflict, and too many other topics to list in an introduction. Moreover, just as many films make gender politics an unavoidable topic, others make it class or identity politics. From the class war in post-1949 China to the postmodern theorization of multiculturalism, writers and directors thoughtfully investigate paradoxes of bourgeois morality and tensions between regionalism and nationalism.

The seven chapters in this book represent key episodes in the modern history of Chinese film-literature interaction and, taken as a group, open up new possibilities for exploring cultural politics. To introduce the logic of this book in a bit more detail, I provide here some brief chapter descriptions.

Chapter 1, "Wang Dulu and Ang Lee: Artistic Creativity and Sexual Freedom in *Crouching Tiger, Hidden Dragon,*" treats stylistic and philosophical issues raised in and by one of the world's best-known Chinese films. Lee's transformation of Wang's story sensitively reinterprets narrative situations and character psychology, thereby illustrating the idea shared by many adaptation scholars that narrative is the common ground beneath fiction and film. Bazin, Bluestone, Cohen, Andrew, and others agree that the goal of adaptation is "to simplify and condense a work from which it basically wishes to retain only the main characters and situations" (Bazin 2000: 25). Yet Lee's adaptation also does much more. It not only capitalizes on Jen (an irresistible heroine in fiction who becomes even more irresistible on screen) and on a supremely climactic narrative event (leaping off a bridge into the clouds), it also introduces a transcendental style that enables gender politics to figure artistic freedom.

This argument may surprise readers who tend to identify "gender politics" with issues related to the struggle for "gender equality," an association that has become nearly an equation in much of American feminism. Yet with different stylistic commitments and varying degrees of emphasis, Wang and Lee construct, narrate, and vivify the teenaged martial arts warrior in such a way as to connect the *sexual* freedoms of women with the *creative* freedoms of artists. The physical and psychological obstacles Jen faces as she confronts the constraints placed on her—her sex, rank, ideological inheritance, filial piety, jealous enemies—translate the difficulties negotiated by artists in twentieth-century China. Jen's powerful fighting skills, resourceful imagination, and almost Nietzschean psychological strength open up models for artists seeking new freedoms to interpret, imagine, and narrate.

Chapter 2, "Su Tong and Zhang Yimou: Women's Places in *Raise the Red Lantern,*" compares the aesthetic and ideological connections between two mid-1980s movements: Experimental Modernist Fiction writers and Fifth Generation filmmakers. Just like Ang Lee, Zhang Yimou reconstructs Su Tong's basic plots and characters and reinterprets, for allegorical purposes, the novelist's attitudes toward Chinese gender politics. The story is set in 1920s China, precisely the decade when the May Fourth Movement pursued a critique of traditional Chinese sexual hierarchy, so the representations of women's lives in both works participate in debates over national culture and the ongoing dominance of tradition.

Much more than Ang Lee and other "literary" filmmakers, however, Zhang aggressively reworks, one can even say rewrites, the narrative style, imageries, scenes, and symbolic resonances of the source text. The creative force of his critical realist techniques is apparent in the way he adds an entirely new layer of coherent and interpretable symbols—imprisoning courtyards, cyclical seasonal changes, lantern-raising rituals, among others—to engineer his critique of China's traditional sexual oppression. To show the detailed philosophical and aesthetic differences between Zhang's humanist realism and Su's modernism, I analyze the reasons why Zhang replaces one of Su's most developed patterns of imagery—a well in a back garden, symbolically linked to a vast feminine cosmology—with a very different pattern of his own: a dark room on the roof of a building connected to the phallocentric cultural architecture of male domination. Controversial as this may sound, Zhang's film adaptation is much more culturally conservative than Su's text.

Chapter 3, "Eileen Chang and Stanley Kwan: Politics and Love in *Red Rose (and) White Rose,*" adds race to the complications of gender politics. Writing in a lucid, satirical, yet profoundly humanistic style that one could call "postrealist," Chang illustrates the sexual and ideological confusions of a Western-educated Chinese man, Tong Zhenbao, as he oscillates between two self-images: an exalted manly colonist and an emasculated colonized subject. Chang traces Zhenbao's attempts to impose order and value on his encounters with four women—a French prostitute, a Eurasian student, an overseas Chinese, and a Shanghainese local—and this serial structure systematically lays bare his inherited traditional Chinese attitudes.

In his adaptation, Kwan—one of the most important directors of the Hong Kong New Wave—picks up on Chang's fine-grained study of the power relationships involved in seeing and being seen. Both artists creatively manipulate visual metaphors such as lights, roses, mirrors, and architectural spaces to expose the cultural constructedness of physical and emotional experience. In both versions of the story, this stylistic commitment destabilizes the authority of Chinese male perspectives and offers, in their place, models of cultural hybridity. From a technical point of view, Kwan's fidelity to the movements of Chang's text is not surprising, for among modern Chinese writers Chang is one of the most adept in cinematic language, especially in matters like point of view, framing, dramatic structure, and mise-en-scène. Not only was she a movie aficionado, she also worked extensively as a film critic and screenwriter. By the same token, Kwan's appetite for Chinese literature, especially popular fiction, made him one of the most "literary" directors of his generation.

And yet, while Kwan fully understands the feminist style and strength of Chang's original story, he noticeably streamlines his adaptation by condensing what in Chang is a provocative exposure of racial issues. Political context helps explain these differences: for Chang, the raging wars in the 1940s brought a strong imperative to treat race and sex as equally urgent issues, and her literary analysis of China's "sinochauvinism" reveals a nation whose relations with others, and with its own diverse population, often falls into complex and paradoxical traps of antagonism and self-representation. In particular, her expositions of the crises of the Chinese male subject invite readers to rethink widespread, codified definitions of Chineseness. By contrast, Kwan's overwhelming concern in 1994 was Hong Kong's imminent return to China in 1997. He borrows from Chang the gendered allegory of interactions between a masculine "fatherland" and feminine "mistresses," using the sexual hierarchy to present and critique—sometimes openly, sometimes not—key political issues between Hong Kong and China. Many of these issues, of course, are still being negotiated: democracy, individual freedom, cultural diversity, and social mobility. Taken together, Chang's mixed-media fiction and Kwan's literary adaptation propose a more diverse and symbiotic future for Chinese culture.

Chapter 4, "Liu Yichang and Wong Kar-wai: The Class Trap in *In the Mood for Love,*" examines the everyday life of middle-class couples in the thriving capitalist environment of 1960s and 1970s Hong Kong. A melodrama, *In the Mood for Love* illustrates an aborted romance between two working middle-class people entangled in the hypocritical demands of bourgeois morality. Liu's story, a modernist piece of novella titled *Intersection,* records the interior monologues of two different characters—an elderly male Shanghainese immigrant and a young local Hong Kong girl—as they saunter through the maze of Hong Kong's cityscape and survey the mercantile environment with their restless gaze.

Wong's film bears little resemblance to the original story and his method of adaptation is the most abstract that I discuss here. He uses what some scholars call "intersecting adaptation," a style that seeks to show, as Bazin puts it, that "the film *is* the novel as seen by cinema" (quoted in Andrew 1984: 99). Wong appears to literalize, or radically distill, Liu's novel into nothing—at least nothing visible—other than three frames containing three separate quotes: the opening shot, an intertitle, and a concluding still. Because of the different plots in the story and the film, the seeming random nature of these quotes generates a kind of fusion of literary and cinematic languages: words *as* images. Sweeping away concerns about fidelity, mimesis, or other platonic models for adaptation, this technique metaphorically proposes, as Bluestone explains, "two intersecting lines," where "novel and film meet at a point, then diverge" (1957: 63).

A key to understanding the kinship between Wong and Liu lies in their shared technique of showing how the minds and bodies of their characters are constructed by material goods that come to symbolize their constricting class status. Objects like men's ties, women's purses and dresses, rice cookers, Western steak, Chinese noodles, and so forth dramatize and historicize the intersection between Hong Kong's capitalism and the minds of its citizens. It is ultimately no accident that this abstract technique of adaptation finds its home in one of the world's greatest consumer markets, where bourgeois materialism, middle-class moral constraints, excess, illusion, and disillusionment all help weave the miscegenated social tapestry of Hong Kong.

Chapter 5, "Dai Sijie: Locating the Third Culture in *Balzac and the Little Chinese Seamstress,*" explores a paradigmatic East-West and city-country cultural encounter through the lens of a film director adapting his own bestselling novel. Set in the Chinese Cultural Revolution, both the novel and film describe the experience of two urban teenagers sent to the countryside to be re-educated by peasants. An inside-outsider with a unique perspective, Dai writes in French about his intimate but distant Chinese memories and constructs a dialogic picture of China that has a complex, evolving cultural and class makeup. While Dai's novel highlights, often humorously, divisive and discursive cultural practices—official Communist discourse, antiofficial Western romanticism, and nonofficial local parody, among many others—his film imagines a native land that mitigates class conflicts and nostalgically personifies a magnanimous "China."

Both Dai's fiction and his film study the characters' relationships with the surrounding landscape—a metaphor for China as "native soil"—but they create strikingly different representations. In the novel the first-person narrator internalizes class, cultural, ideological, and sexual conflicts in ways that implicate nature as an accomplice of an oppressive political system that perpetuates the characters' sufferings. In the film, however, Dai's objective camera creates a more measured and conciliatory distance between the characters and their environments: as director he specifically turns to long takes and long shots of natural scenery to highlight the tolerance and beauty of the fatherland.

Chapter 6, "Hou Xiaoxian and Zhu Tianwen: Politics and Poetics in *A Time to Live, A Time to Die,*" moves in the opposite direction from the other chapters, for it is about Zhu Tianwen's adaptation into literature of a 1985 film by Hou Xiaoxian. A political allegory about Taiwan's coming of age in the 1950s and 1960s, Hou uses the perspective of a teenage boy whose family emigrates from the mainland to Taiwan in 1948, right before the Communist Revolution in 1949. The comparison between Hou, one of the most influential Taiwanese/Chinese directors today, and Zhu, a preeminent Chinese/Taiwanese woman writer, highlights the "literary cinematics" of both artists and reveals competing gender and nationalist politics in Taiwan's multicultural society.

Zhu's literary adaptation opens up difficult questions of intertextuality, identified by Genette as quotations, plagiarism, allusions, and other forms of "copresence" among two or more texts (1997: 1–2). The special complexity of cross-pollination in this particular adaptation is due to two circumstances: Hou and Zhu are longtime collaborators in both filmmaking and scriptwriting, and both are avid readers of fiction, sharing a taste for Shen Congwen, Eileen Chang, and others. Despite such commonalities, the two artists produce very different aesthetic experiences, as can be seen in the way they differ with regard to perspective, narrative structure, and temporal construction. Zhu's story creates a form of literary montage that generates a cinematic effect of movement by essentializing a discontinuous temporal structure, while Hou uses an objective camera, long takes, and slow panning shots to approximate still photos and to suggest visual tropes.

Chapter 7, "Chen Yuhui and Chen Guofu: Envisioning Democracy in *The Personals,*" analyzes Chen Guofu's popular adaptation of Chen Yuhui's autobiographical novel *The Personals* (1992) into a film with the same title (1998). The story allegorizes a woman's failed pursuit of love and marriage to illustrate Taiwan's negotiations with its miscegenated postmodern identity as China's "renegade province," Japan's postcolonial partner, and America's Asian-Pacific protégé. These multiple identities reflect the island state's ongoing "de-China-fication," a gradual and almost self-castigating process that began after the Democratic Progressive Party (DPP) was legalized in 1987 and accelerated when the DDP's Chen Shuibian was elected president in 2000. The story invites the reader/viewer to scrutinize the democratic cultural diversity of Taipei in the 1990s, but the two versions use very different techniques to do so. Chen Yuhui's narrative combines fiction with a sociological investigation of human psychology and an anthropological field study, while Chen Guofu's film blends the traditions of narrative cinema with quasi-documentary reportage.

Exploring a postmodern sensitivity to pastiche, multivalent utterances, and an unreliable narrator, Chen Guofu and Chen Yuhui construct speeches and dialogues as if they were self-deconstructive confessions. Chen Yuhui uses narrative vignettes to envision, on the one hand, a democratic picture of marginalized men responding to a marriage ad, and, on the other, a composite picture of a socially alienated woman who tries to understand herself through a series of interviews. In Chen Guofu's adaptation, he responds to Chen Yuhui's dialogues with anatomic close-ups, shot-reverse-shots, and mirrored reflections, all in order to transform the prosaic interviews into a variety of narrative accounts, including soliloquies, conversations, and audio diaries.

Chinese directors have been borrowing and transforming literary texts for a long time. "You are still a thief today," says Yu Jiaolong to Luo Xiaohu in Wang Dulu's *Crouching Tiger,* "so how can I be together with you?" Yu tries to moralize, but banditry is irresistible.

CHAPTER 1

Wang Dulu and Ang Lee

Artistic Creativity and Sexual Freedom in *Crouching Tiger, Hidden Dragon*

Adaptation is...both a leap and a process.

—Dudley Andrew[1]

Viewers of Ang Lee's blockbuster *Crouching Tiger, Hidden Dragon* (2000) are always intrigued by the last scene in which Jen (Zhang Ziyi) leaps off the bridge for no obvious reason. It is not easy to decide whether this is a suicidal act, an attempt to eliminate shame and compensate for misdeeds—in which case Jen may be revealing a repressed Confucian sensibility—or an act of rebellion and escape, a soaring liberation from tradition and patriarchy. In fact to examine this moment, a flashpoint for conservative and liberal interpretations, is to open a window not only on the way Ang Lee has adapted the fiction of Wang Dulu but also the way the film as a whole has helped shape the image of Chinese women in the postmodern global market.[2]

Many mainstream critics see Jen's leap as an expression of guilt. Since the Manchurian princess is complicit in Jade Fox's murder of Li Mubai (Chow Yun-fat) it seems plausible to assume that remorse has driven her to a real suicide, no matter how beautiful or sublime it may be. Rong Cai calls Jen's death "a masochistic act of repentance" and argues that her "female body is punished for initiating and harboring the unauthorized desire that causes the demise of the male hero" (2005: 456). Catherine Gomes finds *Crouching Tiger* to be saturated with traditional Confucian gender politics (2005: 52), and Emilie Yeh and Darrell Davis speak explicitly of a "Confucianizing" tendency running through the films of Ang Lee. They suggest that Jen's leap is a self-sacrificial atonement for "wrongs she has caused Li, Yu, and her family" (2005: 194).

Kenneth Chan is a good representative of those who see Jen's flight as a radical break from convention, "a strong feminist statement" against the dominant patriarchy. Because Jen rejects the opportunity of reuniting and staying with Lo, she can be interpreted as "saying that her relationship with Lo cannot be structured in any way but in accordance with society's (and hence patriarchy's) expectations ..." (2004: 14). In a similar vein, Fran Martin collects "pop-feminist" readings of *Crouching Tiger* that see Jen as one of "the hard-fighting third-wave feminist heroines of globalizing popular media culture" (2005: 157). In 2001, *Time* magazine portrayed *Crouching Tiger* as a celebration of "girl power" and compared it to such popular entertainment as Drew Barrymore's *Charlie's Angels* and the children's animation series *The Powerpuff Girls.* Many viewers familiar with Euro-American media culture align *Crouching Tiger* with a larger postfeminist movement that sees Jen both as a feminist and a feminine action hero.

What is it about *Crouching Tiger* that produces, in roughly equal measure, conservative, Confucianizing, and misogynist responses on the one hand and progressive, liberating, and feminist ones on the other? The question may seem insoluble—a matter of taste—but it may also be a by-product of Ang Lee's complex thinking about gender and politics. This Chinese/Taiwanese director, who was trained and currently resides in the United States, has given long thought to questions of personal and aesthetic freedom in traditional and contemporary China and Taiwan. One of the reasons this film is so compelling is that he has used it to link these questions about gender to the process of adapting martial arts fiction to martial arts cinema.

In a 2005 interview with Michael Berry, Lee remarks that when critics used to ask him to identify a theme that recurred in his films, he would say "people in a changing time." He also gives another answer: he has been exploring "the concept of freedom against social propriety." There are two sides to this, he notes—"someone putting a force upon you" and "you putting a force upon yourself"—and his concluding remark is very suggestive in the context of *Crouching Tiger:* "There is no such thing as absolute freedom. Unless, of course, you jump off a cliff to get away from it all!" (quoted in Michael Berry 2005: 155). Emphasizing both external and internal obstacles to freedom, Lee produces a dialectical and conditional model of subjectivity that validates a spectrum of interpretations of Jen's final, "absolute" act. The film is both a performance and a study of the external and internal conditions on freedom, the former spectacularly borrowed from martial arts fiction and the latter generically embedded as psychological drama. The groundbreaking combination has created a new field for representations of power and sex in Chinese cinema.

Given Ang Lee's distinguished track record in exploring the topic of individual liberty from both sociocultural and generic perspectives, it is no accident that Jen's problematic freedom lies at the heart of *Crouching Tiger.* His 1990s "father-knows-best" trilogy systematically explored individual freedom and social constraints, with *Pushing Hands* (1991) advocating that one maintain cultural independence even when seeking to integrate into a new society, and *The Wedding Banquet* (1993) depicting the pragmatism of two conservative Chinese/Taiwanese parents who quietly accept their son's sexual orientation. *Eat Drink Man Woman* (1994) reconfirmed the idea that everyone at any age should have the freedom to pursue personal happiness, and *Brokeback Mountain* (2005) showed gay cowboys escaping the imprisonment of normalizing heterosexual marriages and embracing a sexual awakening in the conservative American West of the 1960s.

Thematic foci on sexual and other personal freedoms are a part of Lee's broader effort to examine different topics of cross-cultural and transhistorical significance. After the trilogy, Lee took on adaptation projects that bore little connection to his life experience. *Sense and Sensibility* (1995), *The Ice Storm* (1997), and *Ride with the Devil* (1999) represent an array of genres, cultures, topics, and periods: *Sense and Sensibility* is based on a Jane Austen novel that delineates the oppressive cultural traditions of nineteenth-century Georgian society; *The Ice Storm* adapts Rick Moody's novel about cultural confusion and loss in 1970s America; and *Ride with the Devil* is based on Daniel Woodrell's novel *Woe to Live On,* which exposes the paradoxes of race, sex, and politics in the American Civil War. Lee also greeted the new century with adaptations from three more genres: martial arts, sci-fi, and the Western. Along with *Crouching Tiger, Hidden Dragon,* he adapted the popular comic *The Hulk* into a sci-fi thriller with the same title (2004) and reinvigorated the Western with his award-winning version of Annie Proulx's *Brokeback Mountain* (2005). His most recent work is a romantic melodrama: *Lust, Caution* (2007) adapts Eileen Chang's spy romance about a group of patriotic Chinese students in 1940s Japan-occupied Hong Kong and Shanghai.

If we speculatively connect the post-1990 trajectory of Lee's work to the last scene in *Crouching Tiger,* then we glimpse in Jen's leap not only a desire for ecstatic release but also a yearning for a wide range of political, sexual, and creative freedoms. At the same time this overview of Lee's amazing variety of themes, genres, nations, and periods brings forth the one constraint they all obey: they are all adaptations of fiction.

Lee is thus a critical figure to open this book on the art and cultural politics of Chinese film adaptation, for it is almost never possible to separate Lee's auteurial postures from his literary sensibility. And within his oeuvre

Crouching Tiger is a good film to begin a conversation about adaptation because it complexly negotiates the stylistic and ideological influence of Wang Dulu's fiction.[3] The two artists share a narrative penchant for stories about the conflicts and compromises societies force upon individuals, and Lee is specifically inspired by the way Wang narrates Jen's against-all-odds pursuit of destructive liberation. "I went through the five volumes of the original novel," Lee enthuses, "and basically fell for *Crouching Tiger* after reading the description of that last image of Jen Yu flying down. The character of Jen was also very rare in the martial arts genre and really gripped me. Reading the novel, it was obvious that Wang Dulu was into Freud and Greek tragedy" (Michael Berry 2005: 343) This last comment suggests that interpreting Jen's great leap requires simultaneous attention both to psychoanalysis and to the stories of classical tragic heroines such as Antigone or Phaedra, whose complex death wishes arguably prefigure Jen's. As we will see, if Wang's language implicitly recalls the way Freud characterizes the tensions among id, ego, and superego and describes people as suppressing their pleasure principles, then Lee extends this psychological vision by contrasting two of his main characters—Xiulian and Jen—and by explicitly allegorizing their conflict as the friction between ego and superego.

Before we can fully appreciate Jen's actions from a Freudian perspective, however, it is necessary to note some broader aspects of Lee's relationship to Wang. One key tendency of Wang's fiction is that it postulates humanity as self-imprisoning, and this feature is especially visible in his martial arts novels. See, for example, his complete *Crane Iron Series* (*He tie xi lie*), serialized in the *Qingdao Daily Journal* (*Qing dao ri bao*) in 1941 (Sang 2005: 289). According to Xu Sinian, Wang's storytelling departs from the plot-centered narrative structure in traditional martial arts fiction and focuses instead on a "tragedy of personality," in which characters ultimately come to realize that their "enemies are themselves" (Xu 2001: 2).[4] Lee also borrows Wang's related technique of creating complicated, inscrutable, and even antiheroic protagonists. Xu notes that because Wang's protagonists transcend the good-evil duality of traditional martial arts fiction, they add tension and depth to the narrative. Jen, for instance, embodies a form of ambivalent "chivalry" that is neither virtuous nor sinful exactly, and her ambiguous behavior challenges conventional standards of moral judgment. In his adaptation Lee captures Jen's Janus-faced spirit and endows her with the kind of unbounded cultural imagination that enables her to break from the constrictive model of female propriety that dominates traditional Chinese narrative. She ultimately becomes free to find solace in an eclectic mix of myths, fables, and literary tropes.

There are also important ways in which Lee diverges from Wang. The protagonist in Wang's literary version of *Crouching Tiger* (1941) is mainly concerned with romance and marriage and is thus devoted to managing the emotional crisis between herself and the desert bandit Lo. Lee, by contrast, explores Jen's nebulous relations with a wide range of characters, including Li Mubai, whose attraction to Jen could be construed as sexually charged and thus a threat to his own reputation as a righteous knight-errant (Kenneth Chan 2004). Lee also highlights the competitiveness, fragile sisterhood, and even sexual attraction between Jen and other women.[5] As he expands the influence of female antagonists on Jen's worldview, Lee creates a dissonant community that ultimately provides Jade Fox and Xiulian narrative space for individualized, gendered statements (Ang Lee 2002: 274–279).

It is also important to note that Lee's process of adaptation cannot be reduced to his own literary preferences and interpretations, for he relies on many collaborators. Master Yuen Wo-ping (Yuan Heping) was hired to help choreograph the sensationalized scenes of martial arts combat, and James Shamus, Lee's longtime partner in production and scriptwriting, collaborated with two seasoned writers from Taiwan, Wang Huiling and Cai Guorong, to internationalize and "authenticate" the adaptation from Wang Dulu. Wang Huiling's contribution to Ang Lee's filmmaking was especially significant in *Eat Drink Man Woman* (1994) and *Crouching Tiger;* in both cases her scripts strengthened Lee's representations of complex female psychology (Wang Huiling 2006b; Ang Lee 2002: 289–292).

One result is that Wang and Lee generate very different representations of sexual politics. In Wang's fiction, Jen's search for independence generally derives from her inflated sense of self-importance: she is a social deviant intent on protecting her own ambition, rank, and romantic interest. By contrast Lee's emphasis on the "input" from other female characters suggests that Jen resists traditional marriage because she participates in a collective identity, one more gendered than aristocratic and one to which, paradoxically, her nominal antagonists Jade Fox and Xiulian contribute. Jen's leap may be an individual decision, but it emerges from and crystallizes the pressures and desires of many women.

Wang Dulu also uses Jen to pursue a critique of marriage. Almost from the beginning of the story, she sees marriage as a union of patriarchal powers and understands herself, the daughter of an important official, to be a valuable commodity. It is obvious to her that she is being traded by the fathers of two households (Yu and Lu) in order to secure a profitable alliance in politics, but Wang's ingenious touch is to make her not simply a victim or rebel against the established norms but an accomplice in consolidating class hierarchy and perpetuating exploitation of the underprivileged. Invested in the stabilizing structures of power, she oscillates throughout the story between the opposing desires to be a maverick and a conformist.

Her struggle with self and system, which perhaps rises to the level of Aristotelian *hamartia* or tragic flaw, is most visible in her desire for *romance* with a man of nature, uncodified by social decorum and cultural rituals, and *marriage* with a man like herself, a social elite. Wang's Jen starts out as a perfect rebel—intelligent, beautiful, wealthy, dreamy, and talented in martial arts—and just as in any romantic comedy, she finds a lover who is positioned at the opposite end of the social spectrum. Alas, as it usually happens, she quickly realizes that she must transform the unsophisticated and socially deprived Lo into someone like herself to legitimize their relationship. And yet to do so may diminish the couple's romantic flare: they have met and fallen in love, after all, in the Gobi Desert, a vast kingdom on the periphery of law and civilization. That they will quarrel is generically and humanly inevitable; their freedom and love are doomed to disappear as they move closer to the capital.

Unlike much martial arts fiction, Wang's *Crouching Tiger* pays less attention to action scenes than to the emotional outbursts that reveal the characters' despair and uncertainty. In particular Wang crafts complicated scenes of intense negotiation in which hypocrisy, duplicity, and moral ambiguity come into full paradoxical play. The following passage is from the lovers' first reunion after their desert affair. As soon as Jen sees Lo, she beats him up, regrets it, pities herself, blames Lo for his lack of "official" success, then falls into an ambivalent mixture of self-pity and self-disgust:

> After crying for a while, Jen walked over, took his arm, and gently comforted him: "Don't be depressed. You should know that I have had it much worse than you this whole year. I miss you and cry often. I know that it isn't easy for you to find an official post, but you should at least change your image as a bandit and leave that desert. You are still a thief today, so how can I be together with you? I am the daughter of a distinguished noble. Although I practice martial arts, you cannot take me to be one of those women roaming in *jianghu*;[6] I could never leave my father to stay with a bandit for good. If you want to marry me, you must find a way to become a government official. Do you understand? Don't be sad, just leave. No matter what happens, I'll always wait for you!" (Wang Dulu 2001: 286)[7]

With this speech Jen asserts her aristocracy and assumes control of their relationship. She initiates contact, sets the tone, and dictates the rules of the game: their marriage must have the blessings of family and society. If Lo will compensate her suffering by leaving his thieving profession, then Jen will be faithful to him in return.

This proposed contract is hypocritical, however, for although Jen complains about Lo's thievery, she herself will later steal the Green Destiny sword and initiate the chain of events that climaxes with her leaping off the bridge. Indeed, she has little moral authority, and her disingenuousness is further manifest in her speech about an insurmountable existential divide between noble and plebian. She disdains ordinary women who eke out their living wandering through *jianghu,* yet later she confesses her longing for precisely the autonomy that women warriors have often enjoyed in a society outside the constraints of a traditional community. And despite her vow to play the role of a pious daughter and abide by her parents' wishes, she leaves her family to experience the freedom of living among fugitives.

Jen embodies many social contradictions, but the most serious travesty of trust is her false promise of fidelity to Lo. She contrives to marry Lu Peijun—her parents' choice of a husband for her—to assuage the mounting pressures she feels. Although Jen and her husband never consummate their marriage, Lo is nonetheless traumatized by the spectacle of their elaborate wedding ritual. More perplexing, perhaps, is when the Manchurian princess finally reunites with her lover after a long interval, she rejects a happy ending by disappearing into the thin air the next morning. Granted, Lo has not kept his end of the bargain—he has not become a government official—but quite apart from that Jen seems to have simply fallen out of love.

It is tempting to ask whether Lo has become too much like Jen herself, too "cultured," or whether Jen is no longer excited by the idea of a primitive passion, but more is at play in Jen's mixed emotional response than just the opposites-attract formula of romantic comedy. To see the wider stage on which the romance is enacted, and to appreciate Lee's adaptation of Wang's plot and setting, we must enter the esoteric world of *jianghu*. Wang Dulu and Ang Lee both construct *jianghu* as an alternative space for women to find their subjectivity, but Lee goes much further than Wang in evoking the imaginary power of this place where the importance of sexual identity as an essentializing marker is diminished.

The term *jianghu* is embedded in a rich tradition. Literally it means "rivers and lakes" to signal its denizens' escape from the laws of the land, but metaphorically it suggests "an abstract, if not imaginary, realm where mythic heroes dwell and conduct their business based on a meritorious code of honor and righteousness" (Teo 2001a). Not bound by official laws, it is an underground society in which schools of different kung fu practices—*shaolin* and *wudang*, to name two of the most famous—safeguard, but at times also disrupt, the peace of society.

One of the most important attractions of *jianghu* is that being outside of official classifications, it promotes a form of "democratic" equality or meritocracy: regardless of birth, those who are most skilled in martial arts claim ruling authority over others. The Darwinian conditions in which the denizens of *jianghu* live produce a perpetual arms race, for their best interests are always served by seeking the most powerful weapons and secret kung fu manuals. In *Crouching Tiger,* for example, disputes derive from Jade Fox's stealing the kung fu manual of the Wudang School that belongs to Jiangnan He (Li Mubai's master) and Jen's stealing Li Mubai's potent Green Destiny sword. Not surprisingly, the ruling class in *jianghu* is made up of powerful warriors, and among whom the most respected are the *xia,* the knights-errant.

Like the term *jianghu, xia* cannot be perfectly defined. Still—and despite the fact that few scholars have attempted to differentiate male knights-errant from lady knights-errant—it is important to note that moral functions in *jianghu* often divide along gender lines. In *The Chinese Knight-Errant,* James Liu describes the historical and conceptual evolution of the figure of the knight-errant and identifies eight of the figure's most distinctive traits: altruism, justice, individual freedom, personal loyalty, courage, truthfulness and mutual faith, honor and family, and generosity and contempt for wealth (1967: 4–6). Among these characteristics, Liu highlights "altruism," the knight-errant's selfless contribution to society. Liu points out that knightly altruism is so significant that "the word *hsia* [*xia*] ('knightly' or 'chivalrous') has become associated in usage with the word *yi,* which is usually translated as 'righteousness' but, when applied to knights-errant, has quite a different meaning and comes close to 'altruism'" (4). Liu further quotes from Feng Yu-lan to suggest that *yi* "means doing more than what is required by common standards of morality, or in other words behaving in a 'supermoral' way" (4).[8]

But there is room for disagreement about whether selflessness and communal spirit are the most prized attributes of a Chinese knight-errant. In her study of Chinese women warriors, Sufen Lai proposes instead that "the principle of *bao* (reciprocality, repayment) is the most important ethical standard" (1999: 90). She identifies two forms of *bao* in the Chinese context: *bao en* (returning a favor, repaying mercy bestowed by others, and so forth) and *bao chou* (revenge, eye-for-an-eye payback). Lai argues that these two types of *bao* create the context for all codes of chivalrous behavior. Karl Kao finds an English translation of *bao* that captures both sets of meanings—requital—and agrees that it is the main motivation for a lady knight-errant's action (1989: 117).

Although they overlap, *yi* and *bao* establish different moral priorities. *Yi* emphasizes the virtue of altruistic behaviors, because it places communal good over and even against individual fulfillment. *Bao* emphasizes a personal desire for being fair in reciprocating either a favor or a grievance. Characters motivated primarily by *yi* tend to be proactive and concerned for the well-being of society, while those driven by *bao* react to circumstances and think first of themselves. This explains why Stephen Teo (2001a) considers Ang Lee's representation of heroism in *Crouching Tiger* to be "watered down" and "unconventional": the film has such a strong romantic premise that its focus on individual passion interferes with the chivalrous principles of *yi*. Still, it is possible to construe *bao* as deriving from a sense of justice insofar as it shows an individual wishing to return what is given, good or bad, to oneself or one's family.

If we identify *bao* as a central characteristic of a lady knight-errant,[9] then it becomes clear that Ang Lee uses the three main female characters in *Crouching Tiger* to represent different interpretations of it, and the interactions among them to reconfigure and complicate traditional dualisms in gender politics and moral standards. We have seen that Jen is too paradoxical to be considered either "good" or "evil," so it is not surprising that Lee refers to her in interviews and autobiographies as "in some ways" the movie's real villain (2002: 274–275). Critics have often organized their interpretations around the idea that Jade Fox is an irredeemable character on the one hand and Xiulian a righteous traditional woman warrior on the other. But Lee's film, even more than Wang's novel, stresses the complex motifs of human behavior to such an extent that simplistic readings of characters become untenable.

Jade Fox's crime originates in a desire for revenge and hence can be justified by the moral parameter of a lady knight-errant's wish for reciprocation. She kills Li Mubai's master Jiangnan He and steals his kung fu manual because, she claims, she was sexually abused by Jiangnan He for many years. This accusation transforms her action into a justice-seeking vengeance against misogyny and exploitation. Her indictment also exposes the vice and hypocrisy of the leader of a well-respected martial arts school—*wudang*—in *jianghu*. Although Lee's narrative goes no further to verify Jade Fox's charge, no one, not even Li Mubai, denies or contradicts her story. Jade Fox's allegation, therefore, suggests the impossibility of making moral judgments about the conflicts of a previous generation and establishes a plausible parallel between Jiangnan He and Li Mubai. This connection casts a shadow on the male protagonist's moral character, and thereafter the way Li insistently pursues Jen to make her his disciple never seems entirely innocent. Is he perhaps overwhelmed by her beauty and brilliance? Would he, like his master, use his power to take advantage of his female disciple? These unanswered questions, along with the intrinsically ambiguous moral force of *bao,* destabilize the chivalric ethical paradigm.

Like Jade Fox, Xiulian sees *bao* as a key obligation, but rather than trying to punish her enemy, she seeks to prove her own high moral standards. She delays her confession of love to Li Mubai, for instance, because she wants to honor the memory of her fiancé, who died while saving his best friend, Li. She abides by the laws for behavior prescribed by the Four Books and Five Classics—the traditional Confucian teachings—and assumes responsibility for establishing a model for women warriors in *jianghu.*[10] Even so, Xiulian struggles with conflicts between social constraints and personal desire and ultimately loses happiness because she suppresses her pleasure-seeking instincts. Although Li Mubai gives Xiulian a precious guarantee of his undying love before dying in her arms, she fails to reciprocate his words of affection. Ang Lee makes Xiulian's conservative, altruistic personality seem dated and unfulfilling.

Jen's behavior provides a striking contrast to that of Xiulian. She completely rewrites the principles of "reciprocation" by returning mercy with malice: she castigates and lies to her teacher Jade Fox; she fights against her adopted sister Xiulian's goodwill; she repudiates Li Mubai's effort to train her as his student; finally, she returns Lo's affection with a mixture of indifference and anger. Jen's erratic behavior is disruptive, and her id-driven philosophy goes against the moral function of a lady knight-errant, who is expected to enforce the law, not break rules. However, her unpredictable nature suggests a potential malleability that gives other characters (and even the audience and the director) hope for transforming her into a "good person" and perhaps an ethical warrior. Throughout the film Lee's narrative sustains an ever-deferred expectation that makes Jen into a kind of "project" in progress. Through her yet-to-be-defined, in-between character, Lee both critiques and exploits the rigid dichotomy between good and evil in traditional martial arts cinema.

This consideration of Jen's psychology brings us to the Freudian aspects of Ang Lee's attraction to, and adaptation of, Wang Dulu. As we have seen, Lee explicitly interprets Wang as indebted to Freud, and Jen in particular invites description in the terms of id, ego, and superego, the conflicts among which translate rather easily her struggles to reconcile reality and fantasy, repression and liberation. Freud defines the id as an inborn human instinct to pursue the pleasure principle, an unconscious drive that focuses on satisfying the libido. Jen's initial attraction to Lo can be seen as the id prevailing, but the sequence of her confrontations with him register all the classic symptoms of how the ego struggles to balance the goals of the id (gratifying instinctual sexual desire) with those of the superego (imposing an internalized cultural-parental authority). In *Civilization and Its Discontents,* Freud describes the superego as preserving the vitality of civilization: it suppresses the violence of the id and forces the ego to submit to cultural authority either through conscience or a sense of guilt; the latter "expresses itself as a need for punishment" (1989: 84). These classical psychoanalytical definitions have been much debated and destabilized, but they are nonetheless a resource both Lee and Wang use to enrich their narratives.

Lee could not miss the way Jen recapitulates the functions of Freud's superego, nor the way Wang appropriates the symbolic meanings of secondary characters to dramatize the battle among id, ego, and superego.[11] On the one hand Lo and Jade Fox rather transparently represent the unconscious id driving to gratify Jen's libido, but on the other, Jen's family, Li Mubai, and Xiulian embody the repressive power of the superego, the control of Jen's sexual and class transgression through fear, guilt, anxiety, and conscience. Within this Freudian perspective, Jen functions as the ego whose moral ambivalence derives from frustrated mediation between the pleasure and reality principles. Her manic-depressive symptoms are manifest in her conflicting interactions with Lo as well as in her sadistic and masochistic behaviors generally. Lo, then, is Jen's repressed Other, uninhibited and fearless, and his naïveté, willful personality, and instinctual behavior all endear him to her, even as his humble status in traditional society constitutes a fearful cultural barrier—he is just as ignorant and powerless as any ordinary citizen.

It is also important to note that Wang and Lee depart from Freud when it comes to their representation of gender relations in the diagnosis of civilization's "discontents." According to Freud, women are programmed to be hostile to civilization because they "represent the interests of the family and of sexual life." The "work of civilization" is men's business. Men associate largely with other men and "carry out instinctual sublimations of which women are little capable." In the face of this, women find themselves "forced into the background by the claims of civilization" and inevitably become jealous and hostile toward it (1989: 59). Already envious of their husbands' homosocial networks, women must compete for men's attention with the demands of civilization. Resentment ensues.

Wang's story, however, reveals that women play a more complex role in sustaining civilization. Not only does Lo fail to carry out what Freud says about "the instinctual sublimations"—Jen reprimands him precisely for this failure—but Jen herself proves to be so deeply invested in the machinery of power that, rather than being "forced into the background by the claims of civilization," she both protects and transgresses the rules that govern her social status. Her antagonism toward "civilization" is not due to Freudian envy but to the fact that marriage will suspend her physical and philosophical freedoms. To avoid marriage is to leave behind both the sexual obligations and the class privileges of being a social elite. Empowered by her martial arts skills, Jen escapes into *jianghu* to explore the freedoms of being a lady knight-errant.

It is one thing to point out that Ang Lee's *Crouching Tiger* succeeds in creating a compelling narrative structure on the basis of Wang's books. It is quite another to ask technical, formal, stylistic questions about how Lee adapted for the screen such abstract elements as the Freudian algebra that undergirds the characters' actions. I argue that the psychological intensity of *Crouching Tiger* is due in large part to Lee's ability to convey the dissonance that permeates Wang's novels by constructing, especially in scenes of dialogue, an intricate play of close-ups, shot-reverse-shots, and mise-en-scène. Lee's staging is so nuanced and subtle that it cannot be appreciated without careful frame-by-frame analysis.

Although studies of *Crouching Tiger, Hidden Dragon* usually focus on the action sequences, Ang Lee's more distinguishing auteurial commitment is to expository dialogues. Such attention, notes Stephen Teo, allows nontraditional viewers, especially Westerners, to become familiar with "the period, the characters, and even the appearance of the sets" (2005: 202). Lee himself explains that because Western viewers are not prepared to take characters for granted as "generic archetypes," they must be "shown *why* characters fight" (quoted in Teo 2005: 202). This is the reason why Xiulian and Li Mubai open the film with an intricate conversation that synopsizes the film's central themes of love, revenge, and Daoist conviction.

Lee uses three additional dialogues that permit Xiulian and Jen to compare their philosophies on the position of women in society. Some viewers think these drawn-out conversations disrupt the lively pace of a martial arts film, but others conclude that the conversations are not only explanatory, but the contrasting rhythms help create rounded, multidimensional characters. A brief analysis of Xiulian's and Jen's first encounter—an argument about marriage and freedom—helps us understand how Ang Lee makes Jen a sympathetic figure suffering an emotional crisis strong enough to power the film's narrative flow.

For Jen, as we have seen, marriages undermine women's freedom of movement and imagination, and she equates the unmarried Xiulian with the kind of "characters in a book" (that is, martial arts fiction), who are free to travel in the anarchistic world of *jianghu* and express themselves through martial arts combat. Tacitly suggesting that a woman can only realize her potential outside marriage and with the protection of outstanding kung fu abilities, her argument is calculated to appeal to Xiulian. It elicits, however, a supremely disdainful response: Xiulian considers the Manchurian princess a naïve romantic. Rejecting the association of freedom with *jianghu,* Xiulian says *jianghu* world resembles a more traditional society in which being moral, keeping one's word, and abiding by convention are just a few of the rules.

This conversation focuses the audience by raising several questions: First, why is Xiulian so reluctant to acknowledge Jen's basic point? Isn't *jianghu* a place that embraces talented single women? Xiulian seems to be withholding something, and at the same time Jen appears too forthcoming. Why is she opening up to a complete stranger? Her candid self-assessment creates the impression that her *jianghu* fantasy is a transference of her anxiety about marriage. Lee's camera work further deepens the sense that neither character is speaking everything in her mind.

In Figure 1.1, there is an abrupt close-up of Jen's face. This occurs when Xiulian tells Jen that only the Green Destiny sword is able to achieve the full potential of the Wudang School's powerful kung fu techniques. At this decisive moment, as Jen ponders the meaning of Xiulian's words, the camera shows the genesis of her idea to steal the coveted weapon. On the surface the shot seems to highlight the passivity of Jen's face in a traditional

Figure 1.1 Jen: ornately dressed patrician contemplating theft.

fashion, but Lee skillfully uses her downcast eyes to signal resistance to the gaze of the lens and the audience. As a result, viewers become suspicious: what is she hiding? Her conversation with Xiulian hints at a deep calculation in her girlish, performative ignorance, as if her speech acts were disguises for an oversized ambition.

Figure 1.2 brilliantly illustrates Jen's predicament and confirms the calculated visual aesthetic Lee employs. Behind Jen we see a cabinet with shelves that display the decorative items reflecting her family's status. Jen is a visual echo of the cabinet: she wears colorful attire and is adorned with hairpins, jewelry, and delicate makeup, all highlighting her social function and class bondage. More symbolically, the flower in Jen's hair is positioned right on top of the vase on the shelf to create an illusive integration of the two. Jen is momentarily a flower in a vase, cultivated for visual appeal. Lee's thoughtful mise-en-scène thus substantiates Jen's critique of marriage: she sees the marital institution as a social machine that objectifies a woman's existence. And despite her passive appearance, Jen's words convey defiance and resentment: "Although I am getting married, I haven't had an opportunity to live the life that I've always wanted." Her eagerness to pursue alternatives breaks the inert image of her being "arranged" in the vase on the shelf.

Xiulian's background is both simpler and less restrictive. In Figure 1.3, her basic and dull attire integrates her easily into the plain surroundings. Her unadorned hairstyle gives her an agile, unbound, mobile look. Compared with the flattened, ornamental surface of Jen's background, Xiulian occupies an angled position of depth and strength: Lee's camera strategically shapes an oblique distance between the character and the wall, which gives her

Figure 1.2 Jen: integrated into patrician family background.

more room to maneuver. The landscape painting on her left—a symbolic projection of her access to *jianghu*—reinforces Xiulian's connection to the natural world, to which the door behind her seems to provide an easy exit. Without the restriction of marriage, Xiulian moves as she pleases. However, the irony is that *her* language emphasizes not a woman's freedom but the ascetic importance of abiding by the Confucian code of behavior. When Jen complains to Xiulian about the pressure of marriage, Xiulian chides her: "For women, marriage is really important. Women eventually have to be married off." Since she is herself a fugitive from marriage, we find paradoxical Xiulian's assertion of the prescribed path for women. It is hard to resolve the contradiction between her submissive philosophy and the image she presents of a strong, independent, and free woman.

Such inconsistency between image and language recur throughout the film and quietly remind viewers of its interpretive instability. This is especially

Figure 1.3 Xiulian: simple unadorned strength.

Figure 1.4 Jen: leaving room into darkness, unreadable.

apparent in the parting scene in Figure 1.4. Although it is a common fade-out shot, we see Jen and her maid walk into a world without light, full of borders, divisions, and threshholds, the layered frames staging the multiple levels of restriction that confine Jen's existence. It seems like Jen is not seeing but being seen, and her passivity reinforces the idea that she is controlled and packaged by the patriarchy. However, Lee's camera angle allows the audience to see only the backs of the departing characters, and Jen's intentions therefore cannot be decoded. She does not see the audience, but neither can the audience attempt to interpret her facial expression. In fact, she is leading a double life as princess and thief.

Staying behind is Xiulian, who sees Jen off with what appears to be a sympathetic look. In Figure 1.5, the gentle lighting adds a golden hue to her face. Unlike Jen, Xiulian is in full view of the camera, which appears to spotlight her candor and openness. But despite her progressive image as an unmarried independent woman, her conservative ideology makes her a paradoxical figure. Her advice for Jen is surprisingly bookish and misogynistic. She endorses a kind of parasitic vision of women, which undermines her own professional accomplishment as the head of a respected security company. Ultimately, the dissonance between her role as a self-reliant woman and her straitlaced image and conservative ideology raises questions: will she follow her own advice and trade personal freedom for an arranged marriage? Or is she also as inscrutable as Jen and the other morally ambiguous characters?

It is hard to ignore such questions, even though Xiulian leaves us with a strong impression that she is a prudish pragmatist who has no ambition to change the world, and Jen epitomizes the image of a dreamer and idealist. I

Figure 1.5 Xiulian: lighting emphasizes her candor and openness.

speculate that it is Jen's romanticization of *jianghu* that best galvanizes and projects the fantasy that underlies the film's success: like the reader/viewer of martial arts stories, she believes in the kind of self-creation that comes through adventure and freedom. So it is no accident that neither Wang nor Lee can resist Jen. Although she has plenty of shortcomings, her curiosity and passion seem to translate the optimism and creative energy that sustains all artistry, perhaps the art of adaptation above all others.

In addition to constructing a hermeneutic mystery at the climax of the plot, Wang and Lee also use Jen's dramatic final leap to project in one single, rich image the human quest for a full range of freedoms—ideological, aesthetic, individual. Most of all they celebrate the power of narrative imagination, for in both book and film this is essentially what motivates her to jump. Martial arts fiction has instilled in her the desire to emulate "the characters in the book," and we readers and viewers are, in turn, invited to emulate Jen. She wholeheartedly believes she can participate in the martial arts stories she has read, apply them to her life, and exploit them for her own advantage. Jumping off the cliff is her attempt to literalize the fiction, to reimagine, join, and ultimately reshape a powerful narrative sequence.

In both versions, one particular folktale motivates Jen's final leap and provides a template for readers and viewers to envision what will happen to her. In the novel, after Jen has promised in a prayer to leap off a cliff if her father gets well, she goes to a temple in Miaofeng Mountain to prepare herself. There she meets a Mrs. Zhan, who says that she understands Jen's motive, for her own great-grandmother did the same thing. "So long as your heart is earnest," she tells Jen: "God will protect you" (*Zi you shen bao you ni)* (Wang Dulu 2001: 758). Mrs. Zhan goes on to explain that when her great-grandmother leaped off the mountain, she closed her eyes, flew, and felt that her body was protected by the clouds. "When she opened her eyes again, she was home" (758).

Ang Lee reworks this story into a flashback. Right before Jen and Lo part ways in the Gobi Desert, Lo tells Jen that there is a local folktale saying that if one dares fly down a high mountain, then God will grant the person a wish. Once, Lo continues, a filially pious son leaped off a cliff in the hope of saving his ailing parents; he succeeded in restoring his parents' health and remaining injury-free. The conclusion Lo draws for Jen is: "An earnest heart makes your dream come true" (*Xin cheng ze ling*). Later, right before Jen literalizes the story by jumping, Lo repeats this moral statement, and Lee's audience is left with the difficult problem of reconciling Jen's actions with the folktale. Is Jen's heart earnest?

The philosophical and aesthetic differences between Wang and Lee become fully visible only if we compare the ways they construct visual and narrative details in the final scene. Wang's Jen is a rational social being caught up in a network of earthly attachments: she plays the role of filial daughter, taciturn princess, conscientious sister, and caring aunt. Her jump amounts to a public trial of her familial loyalty, for she claims that she must reciprocate God's blessing for the health of her father by subjecting herself to divine mercy. After days of preparation, she brings a team of maids and servants to the temple in Miaofeng Mountain. In the midst of a much-anticipated spectacle, Jen stands alone at the edge of the cliff:

> There were rivers running beneath the cliffs. Clouds and mist made the valley look like a boundless sea. None of the people next to her dared walk closer to the edge, but Jen just stood there, turned her head, and said: "Go home, all of you!" Her voice was tragic but firm. After that instruction she never looked back again. Two maids knelt down and burst out crying. At the same time the maid servants trembled: "My precious lady of the lord! Please don't.... Don't..."
>
> Madame Zhan couldn't stop her legs from trembling. She gave a sign of inquiry, closed her eyes, and mumbled incessantly. The manservant came over and pleaded in respectful tones: "Your Highness. Your being here is very important. Our Lord has already recovered from his illness. The Goddess is aware of your filial piety. Please take care of your precious health and come home with us. You must still care for your nephews and nieces.
>
> Jen did not respond to the pleas. She looked down on the mists and clouds beneath the cliff. Suddenly people saw her take a step and jump. All of the maids and maidservants were stunned and raised their hands up and shouted: "Ah..." The manservant moved forward and tried to grasp her but to no avail. The spectators saw nothing but Jen leaping down! In the blowing wind, one of her hairpins fell on a rock. The silhouette of her snow white and blue figure dropped down the bottomless cliff like a falling flower. The overwhelming clouds and mist made nothing visible (Wang Dulu 2001: 761–762).

The dramatic tension produced in this scene is socially rooted, the product of a network of agents, perspectives, and glances. Jen's composure and determination in the face of death contrast with the spectators' fear and paralysis.

She commands the servants to return home and then never looks back at the crowd again; behind her, in stark contrast, are maids crying on their knees, trembling maidservants, and the frightened Mrs. Zhan.

Consistent with his ongoing challenge to traditional hero/antihero dualism, Wang first makes Jen appear to be a martyr and then proceeds to deconstruct, and perhaps reconstruct once more, the myth of her heroism. The spectators assume that Jen is genuinely trading her life for her father's and that her chances of survival are slim. Wang compares Jen to "a falling flower" to symbolize her fragility in a menacing natural world; the valley devours her, leaving nothing visible but a hairpin, a token, perhaps, of her class bondage. But of course Jen is by no means a simple pious daughter or helpless flower, and the altruistic pretense of "saving" her father only disguises her real motive: to free herself from the control of the patriarchy. She has creatively written into existence an alternative persona, a fictional character, a pious daughter who is ready to sacrifice herself for the patriarchal society. But if, for the public, her leap affirms the collective belief system while killing the believer, then privately it preserves and widens her freedom of movement. As the story later reveals, her meticulous planning pays off: she vanishes into the clouds of mystery only to re-emerge months later to visit her lover Lo in "the Five Mountains in Xiling" (766). Ever mysterious, she then disappears again the next morning, her final destination uncertain.

The whole scene resonates with Wang Dulu's profoundly humanistic vision. Jen's final act of defiance is pragmatic, situational, earthbound, and problematically heroic. Wang's Jen believes that the only path to freedom is self-made, that she has to overcome the obstacles posed by culture and nature to secure her freedom, hence she prepares her escape by carefully coordinating friends and subordinates. In this way Wang suggests that the solution to the novel's narrative enigma—how to account for Jen's superhuman ability to land safely in the valley—depends on her creative powers in the human world.

Departing from Wang's vision of Jen as situational and socially embedded, Lee emphasizes her egotism and independence. In the film there is no hand-wringing crowd anguishing over her demise; instead, Jen saunters freely, by herself, across the screen in her last dance with destiny. Her individualism makes the viewer wonder if she in fact harbors any regrets over the consequences of her action. Does the death of Li Mubai really awaken her sense of guilt? What is her motive in asking Lo to make a wish ("Let's return to Xinjiang together") before she leaps down from the bridge? Does she believe that spending the rest of her life with a chauvinistic robber in the desert represents the best option for her future (or is it her past)?

It all comes down to the way Ang Lee privileges the power of allegorical imagination: Jen is inspired to leap into the unknown because she believes in the transcendental power of the narrative—"a sincere heart makes your wish come true." Unlike Wang, Lee makes nature not a threat but a sympathetic witness to Jen's transformative journey of self-discovery.

Lee romanticizes the relation between nature and humanity in the opening shot of the final scene, when Jen goes to visit Lo in the Wudang School. In Figure 1.6, we see that the colossal mountains swallow up her lonely diminutive figure. Integrating Jen into a chiaroscuro image enables Lee, like Wang, to naturalize the complexity of human emotion, and this picture, combining shade and sun, makes visual Jen's ambivalent moral character.[12] Lee similarly leaves room for interpretation in another shot, where Jen seems to be preoccupied, perhaps with thoughts of atonement or self-indulgence.

Figure 1.6 Jen: dwarfed by Nature, her ambiguous moral character symbolized by light and dark.

Figure 1.7 Lo separated from Jen by insurmountable divide.

In Figure 1.7, it is early in the morning. Lo hurries to the cliff to look for Jen. He sees from afar his lover, who appears the size of a single rice grain, standing alone on the bridge. Surrounded by mountains, waters, clouds, and mists, she looks detached and otherworldly. Although Lo himself is a character living on the edge of the law, he is nevertheless heir of a patriarchal system that speaks of his lover as his possession. "Don't touch her," he tells his fellow bandits in the Gobi Desert: "She is mine." The insuperable gap between him and Jen at this final moment illustrates Jen's refusal to be subject to the rule of another domineering patriarchal figure.

Figure 1.8 shows that as Jen leaps forward like a bird, the dejected Lo does not even attempt to stop her. His passivity accentuates her will to self-determination, for her poised, flying posture presupposes control of her

Figure 1.8 Jen leaps from the bridge.

Figure 1.9 Jen aloft in the clouds.

body and spirit, and perhaps even of his as well. Departing from her earlier, more ornamental apparel, Jen's now gray and white attire almost makes her into another Xiulian and demonstrates her liberation from the bondage of an aristocratic life governed by feudal ideals.

Conversing in a composite and ambivalent mode of reality and fantasy, Lee refuses to tell the audience whether Jen survives. In Figure 1.9, we see her floating in layers of clouds, a setting that gives no specific clue as to time or space and offers the audience only a nebulous sense of conclusion. This seems to be the ultimate goal of what the martial arts fiction and movie have set out to accomplish, that is, to transport the audience to a utopian world where mundane concerns, rules, boundaries, and discontents become irrelevant. The surreal finish makes Jen's fall appear to be a stroll in the air beyond civilization.

If Wang's novel is earthbound and human, then Lee's adaptation is transcendental and superhuman. Lee's Jen needs no detailed planning, folkloric impulse, or martial arts skill to fabricate a happy ending, for her leap is an attractively confident and sui generis leap of hope: otherworldly, mythical, and mystical. Hinting that the boundless tolerance of nature can endure and even erase the memories of errant behavior, quietly echoing a romantic Daoist tale about a young man's sacrifice for his parent, Lee uses this leap to make divine the human imagination and release the image and the end of the narrative to the audience.

Some scholars have interpreted Ang Lee's female protagonists not as free but as anarchic and have gone so far as to accuse his films of projecting an implicit misogyny (Yeh and Davis 2005: 199). This oversimplifies characters like Jen, however, whose challenges to social, political, and gender orders are too complex, subtle, and constructively pointed to be called anarchic. In fact, in Lee's Jen I see a multifaceted effort to articulate not mere anarchy but more positive forms of freedom on several cultural and aesthetic levels. These include the freedom of the artist to engage in creative experiments in genre, the freedom of the viewer to apply different critical paradigms, and the freedom of characters to define themselves and pursue individual happiness and personal fulfillment. Keeping this in mind helps us understand how the controversial ending of *Crouching Tiger*—one that treats both the evolving female consciousness and the artist's changing vision—reflects the competing demands of Ang Lee's expository modes. It also gives a reason why Ang Lee has helped reshape contemporary martial arts cinema. Traditionally a "masculine" genre, martial arts films have undergone both a renaissance and a critical makeover in the early years of the twenty-first century, and

Lee's contribution highlights the complexity of sexual politics and adapts to moving images the psychological depth of Wang Dulu's fiction. Although Jen's "leap of faith" magnifies the interpretive uncertainty of film analysis, Lee's portrayal of her process of self-formation represents a significant breakthrough in presenting viewers with an irresistible vision of female agency and self-reliance.

CHAPTER 2

Su Tong and Zhang Yimou

Women's Places in *Raise the Red Lantern*

If Ang Lee is a wide-ranging director's director from the Chinese/Taiwanese diaspora, Zhang Yimou is a versatile chronicler of mainland China's ideological and social transformations from the 1980s on. It is a China he has experienced from many perspectives: as the cinematographer in Chen Kaige's groundbreaking movie *Yellow Earth* (1984); as the male lead in Wu Tianming's *Old Well* (1986); as the director of sixteen award-winning feature films; as the creative spirit behind the impressive opening and closing ceremonies of the 2008 Summer Olympics in Beijing. Zhang has dazzled the world with his inexhaustible talents and is indisputably a transformational figure.

Studies of Zhang have recently gained popularity due to current global interest in cinematic representations of China. There are a lot of Chinas to see in Zhang's oeuvre, with critics often pointing to his evolution from a cultural critic of an oppressive old China to a humanist observer of changing socialist reality to a populist artist celebrating Chinese cultural heritage. Few, however, have examined how his directorial career has intersected with influential contemporary Chinese writers, despite the fact that Zhang owes much of his acclaim to successful adaptations of Mo Yan's *Red Sorghum* into a film in 1987, Liu Heng's *Fuxi Fuxi* into *Ju Dou* in 1990, Su Tong's *Wives and Concubines* (1990) into *Raise the Red Lantern* in 1991, and Yu Hua's *To Live* in 1993. These adaptations garnered him international awards, showcased a vision of China in which women struggle against sexual oppression, and ultimately enabled him to develop an aesthetic platform and political voice. Zhang's bold adaptations essentialize the visual appeal of literature and communicate his empathy for generations of Chinese struggling for survival.

His 1991 adaptation of Su Tong's 1990 novella *Wives and Concubines* into *Raise the Red Lantern* is especially significant. Here Zhang highlights the intersection of two major mid-1980s aesthetic movements: critical realism in film and modernist experimentalism in fiction. Although very different in their interpretations of how art represents life (a point to which I will return), both movements construct complex patterns of imagery that destabilize the meanings of socialist symbolism. Zhang draws from the strengths of Su's plot and reconfigures the story's narrative codes, notably transforming a key symbolic site in the novel—a defunct well in a back garden—into a rooftop death chamber. This substitution makes Zhang's film an important case study for adaptation. While George Bluestone, Keith Cohen, Dudley Andrew, and others agree that novel and film become comparable if "the narrative units (characters, events, motivations, consequences, context, viewpoint, imagery, and so on) are produced equally in two works" (Andrew 1998: 269), Zhang's new metaphor illustrates the important directorial option of changing the *staging* of the story to maximize the cinematic effect.

To understand the complex stakes underlying this adaptation, one must know that in their representations of 1920s China—a critical period following the May Fourth Movement of 1919—Su Tong and Zhang Yimou often compare the dilemmas in women's quests for freedom with the ideological obstacles in China's search for modernity.[1] Like their May Fourth predecessors Lu Xun (Lu Hsun), Ding Ling, and others, artists in the late 1980s systematically construe women's struggle for power as an important gauge of China's modernization (Lydia Liu 1993; Larson 1993; Brown 1993). The historical echo may seem like serendipity, but 1920s and 1980s China have important things in common. Due to increased East-West cultural exchange, the influence of Western culture in China reached decisive peaks in both periods and, especially important for this chapter, the influx of Western culture encouraged writers and artists to make the "woman question" (*funü wenti*) both an illustration of China's oppressive patriarchal system and an issue in the intellectuals' broader struggle for nation-building. Because this quasi-allegorical alignment is self-consciously manipulated in both *Wives and Concubines* and *Raise the Red Lantern,* the aesthetic and philosophical differences we isolate in Su Tong's and Zhang Yimou's diverging portrayals of concubines must always be understood as inseparable from their representations of China.

Su Tong is a major figure in the generation of artists that emerged in the post-Mao era, and his writing is usually taken as a key example of the "experimental fiction" movement or "'modernistic' experimentalism" that began in the mid-1980s (Lu Tonglin 1995; Lee 1990b, 1993). Leo Ou-fan Lee and Lu Tonglin argue that the works of Su's group have striven to subvert the narrative conventions of socialist realism, that is, the official state-sanctioned arts policy that for half a century thoroughly politicized literary expression in mainland China (Lu 1995: 13). These young writers rejected Communist collectivism and gave voice to the frustrations of the Self trapped in socialist reality, experimenting with poeticized language both to depoliticize their works and to deconstruct realist aesthetic properties: "its reflectionism, its linear narrative and 'present' time frame, its lifelike or positive characters, and above all its close and critical linkage with external social reality" (Lee 1993: 376).

Su Tong's theoretical remarks support these observations. Time and again he praises the adventurous spirit of "real" avant-gardes (*xianfeng pai*) who aggressively challenge the existing cultural order and endorse a Nietzschean dialectic of destruction and creation (Su 1990: 8–11). The way he breaks and reconfigures the Communist/realist reality reflects his ongoing desire to liberate writing from its representational functions. Given the constraints of the socialist realist aesthetic, it is not surprising that Su would look for models outside the Chinese literary tradition, and indeed he embraces a postmimetic Western modernist aesthetic along the lines of Baudelaire, Nietzsche, Kafka, and Woolf:

> What is past? What is history? To me, it is a stack of torn pieces of paper; since it is so torn, I can use my own style to pick it up, patch it up, and fold it up to reconstruct a world of my own. I can either examine or *not* examine reality from a historical perspective; I can either reconstruct or *not* reconstruct reality from a historical point of view. Since I award myself such a distance to approach time and space, my writing creates a very wide-open world. (Su 1997: 38; my emphasis and translation)

In this important manifesto Su frees writers to examine past events with experimental and critical approaches and releases them from the moral burden of representing history as reality. One reason Su and many of his contemporaries—Mo Yan, A Cheng, Zhang Chengzhi, Can Xue, Wang Anyi—advocate free forms is to resist political interference in literary production, especially in the form of the socialist realism and revolutionary romanticism sanctioned by the Communist Party. They are also keen to undermine the traditionalist view of writers producing socially responsible reflections of official ideology and "exemplary" consciences. Su puts his own creative tenets into practice not only in *Wives and Concubines* but also in *Rice, Decadence of the South, Angel's Food,* and *My Life as an Emperor.*

Su reimagines the past in a variety of styles. His accounts of southern Chinese ways of life are saturated with a strong sense of nostalgia that links his writing to the lyrical fiction of Shen Congwen in the 1930s and to the stories of such popular root-searching writers as Zheng Wanlong, A Cheng, Shi Tiesheng, and Zhaxi Dawa in the 1980s (Lee 1993: 377). Noting a shared addiction to excess, expenditure, and self-indulgence, David Wang connects Su's narrative style, topical southernism, and "imaginary nostalgia" to the legendary depravity and enchantment of Jiangnan (1997:15).[2] Freeing human experience from the limitations of political logic, human rationality, and moral responsibility, Su's "southernism," like much of his work, represents a striking modernist correction to socialist realism. Such a free aesthetic helps Su focus his exploration into his characters' complex inner lives, and this human interiority comes to pose an important challenge to directors like Zhang Yimou who are resolved to adapt invisible codes into visible signs and translate the conceptual into the perceptual.

The rise of Zhang Yimou to international prominence brought Fifth Generation filmmakers into the limelight. One of the 1982 graduates from Beijing Film Academy, Zhang and his famous cohorts Tian Zhuangzhuang, Chen Kaige, Wu Ziniu, Hu Mei, and others were the "fifth class to graduate from the school's Directing Department" (Rayns 1991:104; Ni Zhen 2006) and were therefore tagged as the "Fifth Generation." To understand the influence of this "new wave" movement on world cinema and culture generally, and Zhang's adaptation of Su specifically, it is useful to summarize some of the movement's most salient characteristics.

All of the Fifth Generation directors were born after 1949—the year of the founding of the People's Republic of China—and later became disillusioned with the very political system in which they grew up. They all shared the experience of being sent to the countryside to "learn from the people" during the Cultural Revolution between 1966 and 1976, and their firsthand knowledge of impoverished rural communities had an important impact on their works.[3] Although trained in the culture of socialist realism, these directors are all "united against didacticism" (Rayns 1991: 112). Their criticism of Communist policies, focus on creating a distinct "Chinese" cinema, emphasis on the symbolic use of images, and reflection on the "ambiguity" of socialist ideology all make these directors a new generation of "experimentalists" who have not only tested the boundaries of political tolerance but sought to change the culture of conformism.

Already we see that Zhang Yimou and Su Tong have a lot in common. Their rise to fame and popularity coincided with the literary and cinematic movements of the mid-1980s. Both of their movements rejected socialist realism, incorporated Western narrative and cinematic techniques, and were disillusioned by the Communist regime. Perhaps most obvious of all, they both searched for ethnographical features of a "real" China (Rey Chow 1995, 2007: 14–15; David Wang 1997: 11–36).

Judging from the enormous commercial successes in Zhang Yimou's career, one might suspect that his creative values are more driven by the market than by ideas. However, in interviews Zhang has expressed strong humanist and critical-realist concerns for the evolution of China as a modern nation (Mayfair Yang 1993: 300–302). His first movie *Red Sorghum* (1987) was set during the Sino-Japanese war (1937–1945) and highlighted the patriotic alliance of peasants with workers from a winery as they fought against the Japanese invasion. His international fame began with *Ju Dou* (1990) and *Raise the Red Lantern*—two movies that criticize the tyranny of patriarchy and the sexual oppression of women. They were both nominated for Academy awards in the category of "best foreign film." His later movies—*To Live* (1994), *The Story of Qiu Ju* (1994), *Not One Less* (1999), *Happy Times* (2002), *Hero* (2002), *House of Flying Daggers* (2004), *Riding Alone for Thousands of Miles* (2005), and *Curse of the Golden Flower* (2006)—all underscore the beauty and complexity of humanity embodied in people's continuous struggle for survival, love, and national unity. Zhang's steady critique of oppressive Chinese traditions and bureaucratic corruption articulates something of an ethic, as if one of the director's main jobs were to reveal sociocultural injustices and speak for the oppressed.[4]

Thus, whatever one thinks about the way Zhang's "ideological" beliefs mesh with his marketing vision,[5] there is undeniably a strand of May Fourth–style humanism in his work. In a 1992 interview Zhang was explicit about it:

> "Using literature to transmit the Tao" is a habit of thought in literary and artistic creation that has been sedimented in Mainland China for thousands of years. Therefore, the works from the Mainland have a heavily literary quality, and their main objective is to embody a humanistic content. The famous works of the Fifth-Generation directors are basically the awakenings of cultural reflection and cultural awareness in this broad humanistic background. From this standpoint, the artistic methods usually carry a necessarily rebellious spirit. Such a pursuit of ours is not only aimed at the innovation of cinematic language and methods, but also to meet the strong demands of social change. (Quoted in Sheldon Lu 1997: 109–110).

Along with trumpeting social change, Zhang here positions Fifth Generation filmmaking as an essentially adaptive art concerned with the rejuvenation of works with "heavily literary quality." His idea of using art as sociocritical consciousness aligns his films with the realism and humanism of Lu Xun, Georg Lukács, and Erich Auerbach generally, and his choice of such charged words as "awakenings," "reflection," and "awareness" is reminiscent of the May Fourth critical-realist tradition in particular. May Fourth writers distinguished sharply between the self and the collectivity and wrote with a thoroughgoing "perspectivism anchored in the sense of truthfulness to both external reality and the author's internal self" (Lee 1993: 364). In their works the "sincerity of the author" was always a crucial "precondition of the technique of realism" (364). Zhang, too, has both the sincerity and technique to generate a sense of moral clarity and narrative coherence in his movies.[6]

With these brief sketches of Su Tong and Zhang Yimou in mind, I can pose my main questions. If, in Ang Lee's adaptation of Wang Dulu's fiction, we saw how a transcendentalist filmmaker could both intensify and radically reorient the narrative and characters created by an author who was a humanistic social observer, then what will happen when the moralist-humanist filmmaker Zhang adapts the literature of a Nietzschean-modernist-experimentalist like Su? How will the dark ironies, fantasy, otherworldliness, and explosive feminine subjectivities in the text translate to moving images? Will Zhang's conscientious filmmaking meet the challenge of finding effective ways to replace some of the more ambiguous and polemical details in Su Tong's original text with more structured and interpretable symbols?

The plot, which is roughly the same in both works, revolves around the fifty-year-old Chen Zuoqian's attempts to control the feuds among his wives and concubines in a 1920s feudal household. The story is told from the perspective of a young woman, Songlian (Lotus) (Gong Li), who at the beginning of both the story and the film enters the household as the fourth "wife" (or the third concubine). Lotus is a modern girl who has attended one year of college but is forced by circumstances to marry the aging patriarch. Into this conservative family she introduces a fresh rebellious energy and an inquisitive sensitivity to the conflicts between modernity and tradition, youth and old age.

Su Tong frames the various power struggles as an allegory for China's centuries-old battle for gender and intellectual reform (Tonglin Lu 1995, Kang Liu 1993: 23–55). The Chen household is a metaphor for an oppressive old China that has been shaken but not shattered by the progressively urgent demands for women's liberation in the 1920s. In her fight for independence Lotus is in fact "heavily literary," since she recalls two other famous female protagonists: Lu Xun's Zijun in "Regret for the Past" (1925) and Ding Ling's Sophia in "Miss Sophia's Diary" (1928). All three works demonstrate a tightening connection between the nation's modernizing project and a woman's "discovery" of her subjectivity.

And yet, although they are both working in this same basic vein, Su Tong and Zhang Yimou use such different titles, symbolic strategies, and narrative emphases that they produce very distinct dynamics. Su Tong's title recognizes female subjectivity and reveals his experimental modernist approach to storytelling: *Qi qie cheng qun* literally means "wives and concubines form a crowd." The title gives the impression that the story thematizes wives and concubines as a single self-determining narrative subject. And in fact it is the women who actively instigate and shape the family's internecine warfare. Su explains that the novella might well have been more lively and interesting if he had written about how a man is able to mediate among these women to control them, but he was much more concerned with "the ways these four women tie themselves together to the neck of the guy and furiously fight with each other to compete for whatever little breathing air there is within the space" (Su 1997: 38). As a result, the existential struggles of these women—the chaotic, blending multiplication of their subjectivities in a *crowd*—threaten the stability of the feudal hierarchy and overwhelm the patriarch's ideological standing.

Su Tong's modernism combines subversiveness, transgression, fragmentation, and irony. The use of the verb *cheng* (form) in the title is typically deceptive. At first it seems to hint optimistically at a self-to-community transformation, as if individual women from diverse social castes were going to become a makeshift community.[7] But as the novel moves along, *cheng*'s connotations of increasing cohesion and harmony cast into greater and greater relief the ever-expanding rifts among the women, whose bickering is in fact made worse by the addition of each new member. Similarly, the unity and togetherness implied by *cheng* contrasts with the progressive disintegration and dissolution of Master Chen's masculinity. Su's title actually foreshadows the cacophony of feminine threats to the authority of a feudal household, in which, as W.B. Yeats's characterization of modern chaos goes, "things fall apart." When the center cannot hold, mere anarchy is loosed upon the world.

So it is not an innocent act when Zhang changes the novel's title to *Da Hong Deng Long Gao Gao Gua*. Although the official translation of this title in English is *Raise the Red Lantern*, a more literal rendering would be *Big Red Lantern(s) Hang High*.[8] Either way, the title promises a very different interaction between the man/system and his women: the Master, the absent but implied authority behind the title, clearly is supposed to have the upper hand in controlling the action of his female subjects. Hinting at commodification, raising the red lantern not only lights up the desirability of his acquisition but also makes the bodies of his concubines speak evidently, uniformly, and visibly for the hierarchy of power relations.

While these lanterns are largely absent in Su Tong's text, they serve the purposes of the film, as Zhang himself observes (Mayfair Yang 1993: 304), by giving "a concrete form" to women's oppression. The lanterns also add an ironically festive color to the screen, with red becoming a sign of disaster instead of celebration. The director's critical-realist search for narrative concreteness and stylistic clarity of vision has been criticized as a lack of depth, but also hailed for its understanding of "the force of surfaces" (Rey Chow 1995: 150).[9] Most of all it makes a powerful statement about the immutable gender gap in feudal China. In fact, Zhang's title is emblematic of the whole film in that it eliminates the threat that exists in Su's text of a female *crowd*: in the film women are explicitly identified with disposable red lanterns, which can be managed, lit up, or extinguished at the Master's pleasure.

The ways Su and Zhang emphasize body language further develop their different strategies of confronting and dismantling chauvinistic feudalism. For Su, Chen Zuoqian's (Ma Jingwu) body is caricatured as a site of female erotic fantasy: to achieve women's sexual liberation is to colonize Chen's body, consume his masculinity, and attack his virility. Zhang, by contrast, unequivocally makes Lotus's body the focal point of all viewing subjects. The camera's relentless indulgence in close-ups and long takes of Gong Li makes the sexualized concubine a scopophilic symbol for the patriarch's abuse of power.

Controversial, inscrutable, culturally ambiguous in so many ways, concubines occupy an intriguing crossover position in traditional Chinese society. Technically speaking, they are neither servants nor real wives, and their ambivalent social standing forces them to negotiate a space for survival in the feudal household. Su's *Wives and Concubines* is a narrative record of their struggles for position, agency, and other microcosms of power. Throughout the story he makes the partition of Chen's body a habitual exercise of control among the concubines, all of whom earn respect and envy for their ability to stimulate and dominate Chen's sexual desire. Lotus often has to compete with Coral, the third "wife," for Chen's attention. On her wedding night Lotus's meticulous scrutiny of Chen's body makes her the all-seeing subject and the groom the seen object. The bride's unconventionally active gaze exposes the reader to an objectifying dissection of the masculine desire and depletion:

> When the night came, Chen Zuoqian came to Lotus's room to spend the night. Lotus helped him take his clothes off and handed him some nightclothes, but Chen Zuoqian said: "I don't wear anything. I like to sleep naked." ...This was the first time she had a clear look at Chen Zuoqian's body. Chen Zuoqian had a body like a red-crowned Manchurian crane, bony and skinny, and his penis was as taut as a well-drawn bow. Lotus felt a little out of breath, and she asked: "Why're you so skinny?"
>
> Chen Zuoqian climbed onto the bed, crawled under the quilt, and answered: "They've worn me out." (Su 1993b: 16–17)

After privileging Lotus's sight and giving her an active voice, Su Tong turns to free indirect discourse to allow her to textualize Chen's body as "a red-crowned Manchurian crane, bony and skinny." The combination of vision and voice unmistakably exposes Chen's frail masculinity and arranges a complex dialectic of agency and power between the two. The exhibition of the patriarch's body underscores the connection between visibility and vulnerability, for he is no longer virile, but exhausted. His emaciated figure represents not a feudal vision of a master's invincible prowess but a palimpsest crinkled from repeated sexual work. The verbs that characterize Chen's bedtime actions—"climbed" (*pa*), "crawled" (*zuan*)—gives a Kafkaesque impression of his being "underneath" and "subordinate," more like a lizard or insect, perhaps, than a crane after all. These verbs also reduce him to an infantile primitive stage; his dependence on the nurturing of an all-seeing mother figure, one who has "helped him take his clothes off," is clearly satirical.

Chen's acknowledgement of being "worn out" by his wives and concubines foreshadows an ultimate defeat. The all-but-omniscient Lotus witnesses and interprets the transformations of his body:

> As a sexually experienced woman, Lotus could never forget what happened next. Chen Zuoqian's back was already drenched in sweat, but his efforts were still in vain. She was acutely aware that he had a deep look of fear and confusion in his eyes. What's going on? She heard his voice becoming timorous and weak. Lotus's fingers traveled up and down his body like flowing water, but the body under her hands seemed to have ripped apart and gone utterly limp; it grew more and more distant from hers. She understood that Chen Zuoqian's body had suffered a tragic transformation and she felt very strange. (Su 1993b: 69)[10]

This is the beginning of Chen's libidinous downfall. Lotus is "sexually experienced," but he is war-torn, and his impotence registers the ironic fact that the master is not only outnumbered by his mistresses but also unmanned by their sexual aggression. The scene is full of images of disintegration: the liquid imagery of "sweat" and "flowing water" reflects both the futility of Chen's efforts and the dissolution of his masculine authority. His body is "ripped apart" and, as it grows increasingly "distant" from Lotus's, registers the symbolic decline of his sphere of control and the rise of her own.

Coral (He Caifei), the most explosive character in the story, finds a cosmological reason for Chen's ills: "The female principle is too powerful in this garden; it would only be what fate ordains if it injures the masculine principle" (74). Her comment summarizes Su's thematic emphasis on the transgressive idea that "powerless" concubines can bring powerful curses and a haunted past to the Chen household. The ambiguity of the "female principle" (*yin qi*) aptly captures the unmanageable threat of these socially indefinable women, for *yin* traditionally connotes not only femininity but also the invisible and ghostly aura of an underworld beyond the control of rationality.

Zhang's adaptation seeks to capture the intensity of Su's text by privileging not Lotus's gaze but highlighting instead Chen's covetous look at his prize. Unlike Su's exhibition of Chen's body as a parody of waning patriarchal power, the film carefully conceals the patriarch's sexuality. Lotus's body is now the focal point of all sexual attention, for it has become a symbolic site of masculine conquest.[11] Repeated shots of her face and torso entrap her in the carnal fantasy of the patriarch and the audience, chained to the marital bond, the enclosed courtyard, the wedding chamber, and finally the wedding bed. Meanwhile, Chen Zuoqian remains an elusive, shadowy figure whose threatening tyranny is magnified by the hiddenness of his presence: never once in the film does the camera give him a frontal shot to reveal his features fully. His identity is consistently obscured by lighting, distance, camera angles, and metonymical representations of his body.

Zhang's chiaroscuro technique of contrasting exposures with disguises is especially effective in the following five shots, which intensify the visibility of Lotus and the mystique of the Master. The first shot (Figure 2.1) is a long take of Lotus at the beginning of the film; here she is immobilized by both the camera and the circumstances of her life. The persistence of the close-up shows the inertia of a resigned nineteen-year-old college student who has just agreed to be the fourth "wife" of a wealthy fifty-year-old man. She is framed by the camera as a commodity, a woman on the market sold to the highest bidder.

Figure 2.1 Lotus before marriage, framed as a commodity.

Figure 2.2 Expressionless Lotus awaits in the wedding chamber.

In the second shot (Figure 2.2), we briefly see a medium close-up of an expressionless bride on her wedding night, all dressed up in the well-lit chamber. The pattern of her brightly colored wedding gown, as we discover later, corresponds to the pattern of the bed frame and thus confirms the structural bondage between her body and the Chen property.

In the third shot (Figure 2.3) the film cuts to the entry of the Master (Chen Zuoqian) from the right, whose indistinct image, carefully concealed

Figure 2.3 Entry of Master Chen obscured as he enters the wedding chamber.

Figure 2.4 Lotus besieged by lanterns so Master Chen can evaluate his new property.

by lighting and camera angles, conveys a strong sense of judgmental authority. His command firmly dictates that concubines exist "to serve the man better."

In the fourth shot (Figure 2.4) Zhang's camera cuts to a medium close-up of Lotus being ordered to raise the red lantern to help the patriarch evaluate his "investment." The passivity and perhaps shame of Lotus are evident in the way that she avoids making eye contact with the groom and

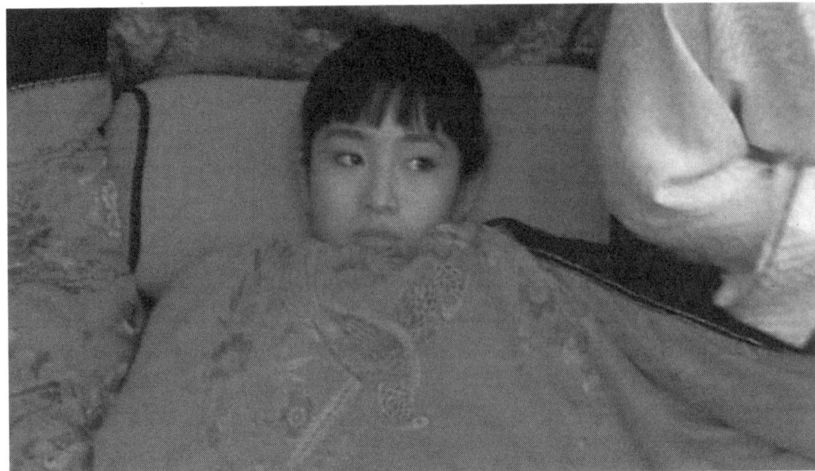

Figure 2.5 Master Chen is a truncated image while Lotus is fully exposed.

the audience. An instructive contrast can be drawn between this shot and Figure 1.1 in Chapter 1, where Ang Lee invests the same demure posture with nascent rebellion. Here, Chen's commentary, commingled with his, and surely the camera's, sexualizing gaze, reveals a strong satisfaction with his ownership and a narcissistic pride in his taste. Although Zhang's exhibitionist close-up has not given Lotus the kind of emotional calculation that Ang Lee gives Jen in her first critical dialogue with Xiulian, his character's self-conscious discomfort nonetheless elicits empathy from the viewer.

Finally, in the fifth shot (Figure 2.5), both characters are positioned in the foreground. However, Lotus takes up more than three-quarters of the frame, while the Master is exposed only metonymically in the scene—part of his arm waving in the air to imply that he is taking off his clothes. The imbalance reinforces the contrast between Lotus's physical vulnerability and Chen's disembodied threat.[12]

The cumulative narrative effect of these five shots is to make the feudal hierarchy of power relations in the household appear unconditionally rigid and consolidated. The shift of focus from the exposure of Chen's body in the novella to the fetishization of Lotus's sexualized image in the movie makes Zhang's patriarch a much more potent and menacing presence. At the same time, the camera's exclusive focus on Lotus's face creates a controversial cinematic language that seems to aestheticize victimhood and vulnerability.[13] His use of such sensual colors as bright red and yellow generates an optical feast for the audience that not only makes oppression visual but also evokes a conventional narrative appeal to "the visible as the ground of its production of truth" (Doane 1991: 1). Mary Ann Doane's psychoanalytical comments on such "surface" shots as close-ups is useful to a consideration of Zhang Yimou's focus on Lotus's face. "The face is that bodily part not accessible to the subject's own gaze (or accessible only as a virtual image in a mirror)," Doane writes, and functions as a "readable text" only "*for the spectator*" (47). Hence frontal close-ups establish a visible link between text and knowability, gaze and ownership. As Susan Steward puts it: "The face is what belongs to the other; it is unavailable to the woman herself" (1984: 125).[14]

This privilege of sight as a form of epistemological control and entitlement is a much more consistent practice in Zhang's movie than in Su's novella, mainly because Zhang is eager to reify a *perceptual* understanding of how the ritual of raising the red lantern amounts to a reaffirmation of the patriarch's authority to objectify women within the system of concubinage. Su, on the other hand, emphasizes the transgressive potential of these women who threaten to bring down the house. The sheer number of the concubines instills a fear in both Chen and his androgynous eldest son, Feipu. Unable to solve the quarrel between Lotus and her maid, Chen in the novel complains: "None of you are easy to deal with; I get a headache every time I see one of you" (Su 1993b: 80). Chen's distress echoes an earlier comment by Feipu: "I'm afraid of trouble, afraid of women; women are really frightening" (65). The unmanageable "woman problem" faced by Su's male characters keeps their physical and mental weaknesses in view and climaxes at the description of Chen's impotence. The anxiety of these male characters is visible but less verbalized in Zhang's movie. The director presents, instead, women's body language, often using stiff, motionless close-ups to convey their sense of entrapment.

On the whole, it is important to consider these differences in the context of Zhang's cinematic strategies, for as an interpreting director he largely abides by a basic narratological principle laid out by Bluestone and other critics: "Where the novel discourses, the film must picture" (Bluestone 1957:47). This assumption sees the film as a spatial art that shows more of the external actions of characters than their thought, consciousness, or interiority (McFarlane 1996: 27–28). In adapting the work of Su, whose text consciously explores the complexity of human inner life, Zhang seems resolved to magnify the narrative divide between the interiority of literature and exteriority of cinema.

The director also seems convinced that this cinematic turn to external action is necessary in adaptation for a film to achieve the same depth of social and cultural criticism as the original text. Recall that the story is about the historical oppression of women, and its climax is structured around the dramatic murder of Coral, the third concubine and a woman of great beauty and defiance. She violates the "house rules" by having an affair with the family doctor, and at the end of the novella Chen and his male servants drown her in a back-garden well. In Zhang's movie, however, Chen's men kill Coral by hanging her in the rooftop chamber. In both the novella and the film, Lotus witnesses the murder, and the family subsequently labels her "mad" in an effort to discredit her. Su and Zhang carefully stage their use of space and vertical perspective surrounding the central images, whether of the well in the novella or of the enclosed tower room on the compound roof in the film, to map out key theoretical differences between the two texts. These two metaphorical spaces, I suggest, not only juxtapose the fluidity of feminine ambivalence with the solidity of the patriarch's iron rule, but also open up very distinct imaginary spaces for the reader and the viewer.

Relocating the site of the execution from a well to a rooftop chamber represents the hermeneutic crux in the adaptation, the one that I believe reflects the most important philosophical and aesthetic differences between Su and Zhang. To elucidate these, it helps to begin by noting that the two locations invite contrasting interpretation as spatial extensions of female (Lotus) and male (Chen) sexuality and body language. The well is suggestive of a female cave that is dark and filled with inscrutable water, whereas the rooftop chamber signifies a phallus erected to defend Chen's masculine honor. Similarly, they illustrate important Chinese cosmological interpretations of sexual difference. The well extends deep into the ground, and in its proximity to the underworld can be associated with "feminine energy" (*yin qi*). By the same token, the rooftop chamber sternly reaches out to the sky and the sun, symbolic embodiments of "masculine energy" (*yang qi*). The contrast between these vertical perspectives makes the move downward in Su's story and upward in Zhang's movie very apparent and opens up a potentially infinite series of intriguing polarizations: femininity and masculinity, depth and height, invisibility and visibility, earth and sky, fluidity and solidity. At the same time, we never forget that Su's well and Zhang's chamber are both sites of death, walled-in, cell-like spaces of alienation and confinement. Symbolically, they are Foucauldian institutions that discipline, punish, and ultimately uphold the hierarchy of gender relations by enforcing the moral integrity of the female body.

In Su Tong's novella, the well plays many roles.[15] It is an impersonator, for it embodies Lotus, Coral, and other anonymous, drowned concubines who have been punished for their sexual misdeeds. In one of their idle chats near the well, Lotus asks Coral if she knows who has died in the well. Coral responds: "Who else could it be? One of them was you, and one of them was me" (Su 1993b: 73). Coral's banter hints at the well's magical touch: it is an enchanter that bewitches Lotus and transforms her into an unwilling member of the disenfranchised underground female community. Whenever Lotus goes near the well, her mind begins to wander, and her spellbound body is immobilized: "It was as if her whole body were held fast to the side of the well, willing but unable to tear itself away" (54). Finally, the well is also a narrator, for its watery flow seems to recount stories of the other world. Lotus often hears "the water bubbling up deep inside the well, carrying to the surface the voices of some lost soul" (74).

The meanings of the well are complex, felt as much as understood. The occult "mission" of the place makes it synonymous with illegitimacy and infamy, much like the status of the disposed concubines. The secrecy of its nether regions is threatening: what hides in the cave are dark reflections of infidelity, transgression, and murder, the revelation of which can instigate new conflicts. The unfathomable depth of the well makes it an indecipherable place of mystery, a site to store the tantalizing rumors that amount to unofficial biographies of nameless victims.

Thus the full consequences of Zhang Yimou's symbolic substitution become visible only if we appreciate the complex network of interrelated meanings Su creates with the well. Beyond those already mentioned, the most important ones emerge in Lotus's encounters with it. When she first enters the Chen compound at the beginning of the novella, for example, she goes there as if to a baptism:

> Lotus walked over to the edge of the well and spoke to Swallow, who was washing yarn. "Let me wash my face. I haven't washed my face in three days."
>
> Swallow drew a pail of water for her and watched her plunge her face into the water; Lotus's arched-over body shook uncontrollably like a waist drum played by some unseen hands. (12)

This seemingly innocuous exchange between Lotus and the maid Swallow (Kong Lin) foreshadows two of the most important conflicts in the story: the domestic squabbles between these two women, whose vicious bickering is emblematic of the concubine's existential and class insecurity (Lotus feels that her position as a mistress is threatened by Swallow's aggressive courting of Chen), and the enunciation of the ambivalent function of the well (it is simultaneously a cleansing device and a sorceress's crystal ball). On the one hand, Lotus's act of washing is a metaphorical cleansing of her past; marrying Chen gives her hope of eliminating two stigmas—the bankruptcy of her middle-class family and the subsequent suicide of her father. Washing away her previous identity, however, also means giving up her education and autonomy. As a college student at a time when few women attended college, Lotus is filled with the ideals of women's liberation.[16] But all of her dreams about freedom, revolution, and education vanish after the marriage. During her washing, the act of "plunging" (*mai*) brings to mind the violent images of abyss and self-abandonment; the identification of her body with "a waist drum" further highlights Lotus's loss of sovereignty, for now she is nothing but an instrument being "played by some unseen hands."[17]

These unseen hands, very interestingly, do not belong to Master Chen; instead, they bear a synecdochal relationship to the murdered concubines, who make Lotus their collective voice of vengeance. In her approach to the forbidden ground of the well, Lotus "seemed to see a pale white hand, dripping wet, reaching out to cover her eyes from the unfathomable depths at the bottom of the well" (54). The blinding of Lotus by the imaginary, soaking hand helps the story subvert the ostensible privilege awarded to "sight" as a mode of knowing in scenes like the wedding night. This is a very important, transformative moment in which Su Tong's narrative transports Lotus from the masculine domain of the rational and visible to the feminine sphere of the fantastic and the obscure. The passage enables the protagonist to set herself apart from the homogeneous production of the patriarch's "truth" and to explore the unwritten history of the repressed ancestresses, for now she is able, in new ways, to *see* with her mind's eyes, *hear* with imaginative ears, and to *feel* with intangible hands. Such sensuous adjustments foreground Lotus's agency as a witness to, and echo of, the lives of the women who were sacrificed on the altar of patriarchal power.

If, for Chen Zuoqian, the well functions as a mirror of his deadly authority, then for Lotus it functions as a window onto a radically expanded sphere of female community, a kind of frightening yet attractive location populated with previous generations. In her repeated confrontation with Chen Zuoqian about the well's ambivalent function, Lotus identifies herself as a tragic seer: "No one told me. I saw for myself. I walked over to the side of that well and immediately saw two women floating on the bottom; one of them looked like me, and the other one also looked like me" (36). The uncanny replication of Lotus's image translates both the sense of resignation that attends foreknowledge of one's fate—*I could die here, just like these women, perhaps I am already dead*—and the spirit of rebellion that comes from truth independently learned and held: "No one told me. I saw for myself."

Su Tong's ambivalent use of the well as an instrument of oppression and a tool of opposition participates in a larger cultural polemic about the "woman question." In the period following the May Fourth Movement, writing on gender inequality evidenced a male-centered concern about women's liberation. Such writings, critics contend, often self-servingly constructed "a new [male] subjectivity" at least as much as they uncovered the social and cultural significance of the "new woman" (Chan Ching-kiu 1993a: 13). As a result, writers of reform literature during this period were, as Yue Ming-Bao notes, often "preoccupied with the construction of a cause-effect narrative pattern that would present women as victims vis-à-vis society as the victimizer" (1993: 52). It is almost always a male intellectual who narrated these stories, Yue points out, and he almost always recounted "the tragic fate of a lower-class, uneducated woman, and often nameless woman, whose sad existence reinscribe[d] her historical status as an object" (52).[18] In my view Su breaks almost completely from this monologic narrative structure. He certainly highlights the objectification of women, but he does nothing to advance the male narrator's politics.

On the contrary, and unlike his May Fourth predecessors, Su enables his female characters to be both narrative subjects and independent thinkers.[19] Lotus *is* the educated Self whose mind Master Chen tries to decipher and colonize. During their first date Chen "thought to himself that since [Lotus] was a college student she would naturally be different from most vulgar young women"; moreover, she "possessed a kind of elusive yet beguiling power" (Su 1993b: 20–21). This recognition of Lotus's intellectual vigor has important implications: it challenges the privilege of a masculine order that makes man the only subject of metaphysical inquiry, and it confirms Lotus's ability to articulate, interpret, and ultimately expand the range of her own thought and emotion. Hence the existential identification of the well with Lotus suggests an ambitious feminine quest for self-representation. This quest, daring in its vision and persistence across the narrative, transforms the well from a manifestation of feudal power into a womb, an alternately barren and fertile one, and derides the patriarch's desire to reproduce himself physically through offspring and symbolically through cultural practice.

Defiantly searching to escape from oppressive reality, Su's Lotus returns frequently to the well, and sometimes it offers her a vital link to the underground female community:

> The walls of the well were covered with moss. Lotus bent over and looked down into the well; the water was a bluish-black color, and there were some ancient dry leaves floating on the surface. Lotus saw the broken reflection of her face in the water and heard the sound of her breathing being sucked down into the well and

> amplified, weak yet oppressively deep and low. A gust of wind rushed up; Lotus's skirt billowed out like a bird taking flight, and at that instant she felt a coldness as hard as stone rubbing slowly against her body. (22)

This encounter illustrates the esoteric power of the well and shows Lotus's involuntary, momentary immersion into its enigmatic world. A forsaken and forbidden place, the well tempts Lotus to penetrate into its "bluish-black" water—perhaps blood is mixed in?—and to establish primordial contact with a mysterious community of displaced women. There are no words of knowing or learning in the passage, for everything enhances the intense physicality of the experience: Lotus *sees* her broken reflection, *hears* her amplified breathing, and *feels* her body being chilled, all in a setting of moss, water, leaves, and wind. Readers are forced to do the interpretation: what, especially, is the "coldness" carried by the wind, with its hints of Ovidian metamorphic petrification, and why does it approach her as a mock sexual aggression, billowing out her skirt and "rubbing against her body" as "hard as a stone"? Is it the touch of anonymous dead women, the indifference of nature, a foretaste of her own death, an insight into her predicament in the Chen family? The fleeting, mysterious, frightening contact hints at a perspective well beyond the tyrannical rule of the family. Perhaps when Lotus sees the broken reflection of her face, she does so with the insight that it mimics the interrupted life of the drowned concubines? Readers may also suspect that her status as an educated and outspoken critic of how women are mistreated by the Chens has opened her to a potential fusion with vengeful forces.

All along, the mysterious well harbors the potential for clandestine communication between the dead and the living, and eventually Su exhumes the ancestral voices, seductive, equivocal, and foreboding:

> Blowing in the wind, [the withered wisteria vine] emitted some sort of desolate murmur; the well was still eerily calling her. Lotus covered her chest. She felt as though she was hearing an apocalyptic voice from out of the void. Lotus walked toward the well. She felt incomparably light, as though walking in a dream.... She felt herself lean over helplessly and stare into the well, like the stem of a flower broken by the wind. In another moment of vertigo she saw the water in the well suddenly bubble up as the sound of a vague and very distant voice penetrated her ears: "Lotus...come down here, Lotus. Lotus...come down here, Lotus." (53–54)

Figure 2.6 Ancient Chinese scripts on Chen compound wall tower over Lotus.

Now the alluring babble of the well gives Lotus a different outlook on life, one that is less confined to rules and reason and more attuned to the bliss of an imaginary escape. From the vine's desolate murmur, to the well's eerie invitation, to the apocalyptic voice from the void, and finally to the enticing call of other concubines, Lotus faces all these indistinct and indefinable urges to connect herself to the domain of the unknown. The density and obscurity of Su's imagery render the well an opaque space in which myriad reflections of a woman's self can break loose.

If Su Tong consistently uses the well to create a feminine space of a dark, defiant fantasy, then Zhang Yimou's film is just as committed to erecting a masculine house to emblematize an irreversible gender hierarchy. His cinematography emphasizes the claustrophobic confinement of the Chen compound and substitutes for the infinite depths and inwardness of a well the imposing verticality and ordered space of a building. This revision is evident very early in the movie. As we see in Figure 2.6, when Lotus first enters the Chen compound, behind her is a wall covered with large Chinese characters written in an ancient style. This shot symbolically conveys how she is married into a system of rules, orders, signs, and conventions. The image also shows that Zhang Yimou has an important intellectual and aesthetic investment in the structure of the mansion. He explains the cultural significance of this visual representation:

> I was so excited when I discovered the walled, gentry mansion [where *Raise the Red Lantern* was filmed], which is hundreds of

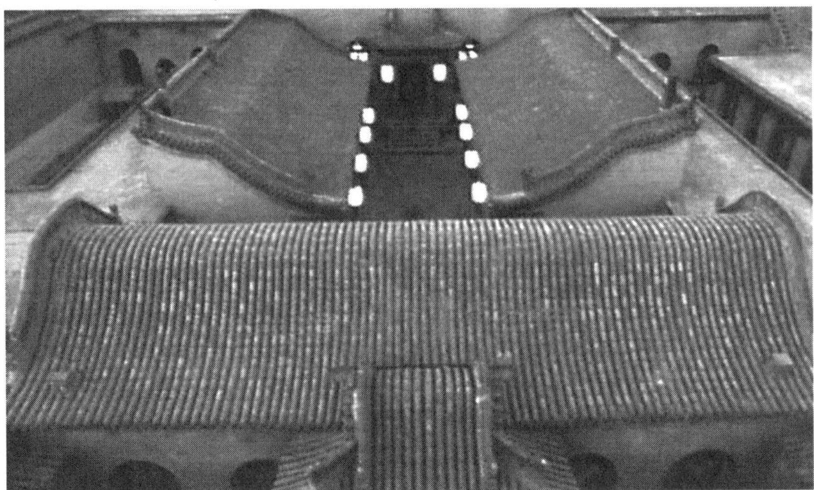

Figure 2.7 The enclosed Chen compound.

Figure 2.8 The imprisoning wedding chamber.

> years old in Shanxi Province. Its high walls formed a rigid square grid pattern that perfectly expresses the age-old obsession with strict order. The Chinese people have for a long time confined themselves within a restricted walled space. (Sheldon Lu 1997: 108)

His camera eloquently expresses the psychological and physical torments of the concubines in a sequence of shots that highlight a systematic captivity of their minds and bodies. In the four shots following her entry into the compound, Zhang juxtaposes the courtyard with the wedding chamber to underscore the oppressiveness of the new bride's cell-like existence. In the first shot (Figure 2.7), the high-angle long take of an enclosed quarter offers a *concrete* view of the bride's physical surroundings: the courtyard is encircled by imposing bluish roofs, the claustrophobic space and color of which strike

Figure 2.9 Long take of Chen courtyard at chill blue dawn.

Figure 2.10 Confining marriage bed the morning after.

one as menacing in the approaching dusk. In the second shot (Figure 2.8), the film cuts to the wedding chamber where the bride is waiting passively for the groom. The physical appearance of the imprisoning courtyard is now replicated in the body of the bride, fastened to the square of her wedding bed frame. It is here, as mentioned earlier, that Zhang visually reinforces the link between the bride and property by making the pattern on Lotus's dress closely mirror the patterns on the bed frame.

Figure 2.9 is a long take of the courtyard that shows the gradual dawning of a new day. The visible transition from the festive lantern nightlight to the more "rational" daylight invites the viewer to reckon with the meanings of Lotus's new life as a concubine. Zhang uses a consistent bluish color scheme to cast a predictably gloomy future for the bride. In the final shot of this sequence, Figure 2.10, we are in the chamber again, but this time the centrally located bed is much more imposing. The bed curtains obscure the audience's view of the bride and groom and mime the courtyard structure, again generating a mood of entrapment. While Zhang does not delve into a character's state of mind with flashbacks, dream sequences, or other thought-processing images, he is very effective at constructing and exposing the emotional bond between the protagonist and her surroundings. The confinement of Lotus within the hierarchical environment further suggests both the mental and physical consummation of her marriage: she is now a part of the Chen property and her value has been exactly determined.

All these shots show that the new bride is left with little breathing room and confirm Rey Chow's observation that for Zhang, a woman is "very much a typical sexual body that is bound by social chains and that needs to be liberated" (1995: 143). Nowhere are these "social chains" more clearly manifest than in Zhang's use of architecture as an oppressive apparatus. As the movie progresses, the director achieves even greater efficacy when he makes the rooftop room into the quintessential symbol of masculine power.

The open, sprawling structure of the roof may seem to contrast with the walled-in constraints of the courtyards and may give an illusory sense of freedom. Topographically the roof, being closer to the sky, suggests a possible channel for humans to communicate with the divine and therefore to assert or interpret the authority of divine judgment. Similar to Su Tong's back garden, Zhang's roof is forbidden ground for the women in the house, and the fact that Coral and Lotus repeatedly visit there only confirms their shared defiance. Not surprisingly, the roof becomes the locus for all punitive action.

Some critics disagree with Zhang's effort to make the roof a space of controversy. "In traditional Chinese cosmography," Dai Qing argues, "the

Figure 2.11 Long shot of sprawling Chen mansion as Lotus approaches tower.

Figure 2.12 Lotus dwarfed by phallic roof tower.

sky was sacred, and, by extension, so was the roof or 'top' of any building. It is thus inconceivable that any family, no matter how powerful, would risk incurring the wrath of heaven by carrying out a private execution on the rooftop" (1993: 335). To some extent one might suggest that Zhang shares with Dai this understanding of the roof's sacredness: the reason he has all the "criminal" acts take place at a site traditionally deemed sacred is precisely to reinforce the perception of impropriety. For a concubine to go up on the roof poses a problematic challenge to the hierarchical structure of the feudal system; the very act of climbing up performs various kinds of border crossings and turf invasions.[20]

Zhang intensifies his ambivalent use of the roof as a seductive and forbidden space by placing a phallic chamber there that extends into the sky and symbolizes the patriarch's power. In Lotus's first encounter with the room, Zhang carefully creates an aura similar to that of a temple visit; her solitary sojourn to the site of crime and punishment cultivates an aesthetic of mystery and curiosity. Standing alone, Lotus confronts the protruding edifice as she searches for an escape from the physical and psychological constrictions of her quarters. In this particular shot (Figure 2.11), the sprawling Chen compound takes up more than three-quarters of the frame and overwhelms the presence of both the sky and Lotus on the roof approaching the mysterious site. The spatial distribution in the frame shows how the feudal patriarch, perhaps more than divine forces, is the architect of a woman's destiny. She is controlled by *his* environment more than by fateful predestination. In the next shot (Figure 2.12), Lotus stands right next to the chamber, whose imposing, colossal structure overawes its visitor. These two shots confirm the image of the tower as a symbolic establishment that trumpets the reigning authority of the master.

More significant still is the final scene on the roof, during which the execution of Coral makes the room not only a death chamber but also an ultimate defense for masculine honor. In this long shot (Figure 2.13), the audience's viewpoint coincides with Lotus's perspective. We see from afar the flow of men streaming in and out of the tower room to assist in Coral's "suicide." The overcast sky and the snow-covered roof create a tragic mood of sacrifice: Coral is an offering to the egoism embodied by the tower. In the final few shots of the roof scene (Figure 2.14), Lotus's viewpoint guides the audience to confront the nightmarish reality of murder. Her heavy breathing, coupled with the jerky movement of the camera, cues an exclusive emphasis on her subjective view of the chamber, clearly staged as a menacing phallic symbol that fills up the whole screen. As she gets closer and closer to it, the oppressiveness of the building becomes more and more pronounced. Finally, there is a cut to a long shot of the tower room, with Lotus suddenly screaming "Murder! Murder!"

This climax indicates the dramatic transformation of Lotus from a *seen* sexual object throughout most of the film to a *seeing* subject at the conclusion whose vision is, nonetheless, more alienating than self-empowering. Zhang's mise-en-scène stages Lotus as a discredited loner, ironically margin-

Figure 2.13 Lotus's distant view of tower as Coral is murdered.

Figure 2.14 Lotus approaches the tower murder chamber.

alized by her hard-fought insight into the feudal oppression of women. Su, in contrast, draws attention to Lotus's link to the *other* female community, the one buried in the garden well, a historical cliché that evokes images of collective revenge and suffering.

Ultimately Zhang's adaptation exposes and criticizes the brutality of the system but does not intervene, as Su Tong does, within the narrative to challenge the dominance of the feudal space. These distinct approaches to the exploitation of women reflect profoundly different conceptions of the relationship between art and society. For Su, writing has an attractively subversive, even nihilistic potential not only because it can problematize sociohistorical issues like gender inequality but also because, in doing so, it can release fiction from being subordinate to reality by reimagining and collapsing historical periods. His works, in turn, arrive simultaneously as adaptations of received historical narratives about China and questions put to any new ones. Zhang, on the other hand, treats film more instrumentally, as a medium of social change, and considers critical realism to be the most effective way to reveal the "backwardness" of "a 'China' that is supposedly past but whose ideological power still lingers" (Rey Chow 1995: 144). On the whole, Su's cynicism about deep-rooted cultural corruption works to discredit the revival of any moralist vision, whereas Zhang's realist faith in the power of critical consciousness commits him to helping shape the narrative coherence of a changing Chinese society.[21]

In the end the different aesthetic strategies produce two visions of Chinese modernity embedded in the characters' bodies. In Su's story, the progressive deactivation of the patriarch's body symbolizes the dismantling of an aging feudal system within which women begin to be heard rather than just seen. In Zhang's movie, however, the relentless display of Lotus's body spectacularizes the oppressiveness of an old bartering system in which the objectification of women's sexuality intimates a criticism of China's lack of progress. Critics will differ on the extent to which these different approaches to the "woman question" can be attributed to the artists' chosen media. If we agree with Sergei Eisenstein that cinema is "a spectacle calculated for a spectator" whose purpose is to influence the audience in a "desired direction" (1988: 39), then the filmic representation of fiction will naturally tend to reconstruct stories in ways that dramatize their visual and emotional interest. Su's experimental literary aesthetic offers his female characters implicit latitude for negotiating ideological and physical independence, while Zhang's critical realism emphasizes the explicit, tangible obstacles to feminine rebellion. Su's modernist experimentalism can maintain an ambiguity about how subordinate victims really were to victimizers, but Zhang's film decisively shows how Chinese women in the 1920s deserve to be watched, understood, and pitied.

CHAPTER 3

Eileen Chang and Stanley Kwan

Politics and Love in *Red Rose (and) White Rose*

Like directors Ang Lee and Zhang Yimou, fiction writer Eileen Chang (Zhang Ailing, 1920–1995) can be considered a blockbuster artist. Chang Fans (Zhang Mi) are spread across the globe and reach deep into diverse Chinese-speaking communities. Her stories appeal to both laymen and scholars because they depict rich and revelatory encounters between tradition and modernity, man and woman, East and West. They often feature blended—or what I call *postrealist*—styles and narrative strategies to critique sinocentrism, with many of her tales satirically deconstructing essentialist or chauvinist versions of the one-China ideal. From Fu Lei's criticism of her satirical approach (1944) to C. T. Hsia's high praise for her deft control of character psychology (1961) to Rey Chow's exaltation of her narrative innovation (1999), Chang has remained as pivotal and riveting a literary figure as Lu Xun, Shen Congwen, and Ding Ling.

Although critics have looked at Chang from many perspectives, they have not done justice to her connections with film. And yet she has had a significant influence on Hong Kong's New Wave (1979 to 1980s) and Second Wave (1990s to 2000s) filmmaking, two movements that have produced some of the world's best movies in recent decades. Within these movements, directors Ann Hui (Xu Anhua) and Stanley Kwan number among Chang's most loyal and sensitive interpreters, producing adaptations that illustrate her narratives of China's cross-cultural interactions and respectfully rendering her feminist politics and postcolonial aesthetics. Of all the films inspired or influenced by Chang's writing, I consider Stanley Kwan's *Red Rose/White Rose* (1994) to be one of the best at translating her ironic representations of Chinese misogynism and nationalism. Borrowing Chang's association of seeing with an emasculating act, Kwan uses mirrors to reveal the insecurity and confusion of his characters and to prove that looking is ultimately coded by gender and race.

This chapter discusses the ways that Chang and Kwan expand the metaphorical structure we saw in Chapter 2—gender relations as a locus for presenting power dynamics in twentieth-century China—by adding racial tensions that illustrate the complex colonial relations among China, South Asia, and the West. Chang's short story, "Red Rose and White Rose" (1991; first published in 1944) is about a Chinese man's sexual relations with women of diverse racial backgrounds and varying degrees of cultural otherness, and both the fiction and film versions use this plot mechanism to explore the paradoxes of China's conflicting identity politics, where "Chineseness" is often paradoxically constructed as both exclusionary and composite, local and universal. Caricaturing this "China-as-One" idealism, Chang and Kwan dramatize and satirize the ways that desire for centralized power tends to unite sexism and nationalism while suppressing difference. Since they share a fine-grained strategy of deconstructing various sites and modes of human vision—the physical, imagined, and symbolic acts of seeing self and others—it is revealing to compare the way their works stage individual scenes. Formalist readings open a window on both the evolving sociohistorical context and the adaptive mechanisms in play when Kwan translates Chang's experiments with tropes, voices, and stereotypes into close-ups and mises-en-scène.

A brief biographical introduction to Chang and Kwan will help contextualize the origins of their art. Born into a prestigious family in Shanghai in 1920,[1] Eileen Chang attended Hong Kong University from 1939 to 1941. Her college education was interrupted by the Pacific War (1941–1945), and she was forced to return to Shanghai in 1942. Despite her short stay in Hong Kong, Chang gained a "New World" perspective that broadened her literary outlook on issues of class, race, and nation. Later she rose to fame after publishing, between 1942 and 1944, in such journals as *Violet* (*Zi luo lan*), *Magazine* (*Za zhi*), *Heaven/Earth* (*Tian di*), and *Signs* (*Wan xiang*). After the Communist takeover of China in 1949, Chang left for Hong Kong again in 1952 and then moved to the United States in 1955. In the subsequent decades, Chang's popularity soared in Hong Kong, Taiwan, and overseas Chinese communities. Her sensitivity to the cultural, political, and racial conflicts between the center and the periphery deeply resonates with the diasporic Chinese societies that have both embraced and struggled with the shifting definitions of the "one China" policy.

Chang expounded her vision of an evolving, composite "New China" not only in fiction but also in essays, film criticism, and film scripts. In 1943 she published her first English essay, "Chinese Life and Fashions," in the English edition of a monthly German magazine *The XXth Century* (*Er shi shi ji,* edited by Klaus Mehnert). After this debut came a series of film commentaries, all published in 1943, which covered such wide-ranging topics as "The Opium War," "Mothers and Daughters-in-law" and "Chinese Educating the Family" (Tay 1994b: 43–44). Chang's film criticism, William Tay observes, reveals her unique "insights into the interpersonal relations in Chinese society" (44). Even more important, perhaps, is Chang's exposition of the political and cultural meanings of women's changing domestic roles. Two film scripts, *Endless Love* (*Bu liao qing*) and *Long Live the Wife* (*Taitai wan sui*),[2] both directed by Sang Hu in 1947, show women criticizing marriage as misogynistic. She later wrote five more film scripts for romantic comedies, all of which highlight the awakening of a feminine consciousness and were directed by Wang Tianlin between 1961 and 1964 for Hong Kong's Dianmao Film Production Company.

It is not surprising that Chang's film commentaries and scripts have important stylistic links with her fiction. Her narratives are so rich in imagery and dramatic "close-ups" that many critics have noted her distinct visual poetics; C. T. Hsia, for example, enthusiastically salutes her fiction for having "the richest imagery of any contemporary Chinese writer" (1961: 395). This assessment by perhaps the world's leading scholar of Chinese literature at the time gave Chang a visible aesthetic identity and made her one of the most studied modern Chinese writers. Along with her evocative imagery, Chang's cinematic narrative strategies have gained critical acclaim. Leo Lee suggests that the "sensuously local and immediate" world of Chang's fiction often relies on cinematic techniques to make readers see her description in a fashion analogous to "a sequence of shots by a movie camera" (1999: 277). For Lee, Chang's filmic writing is a kind of shot-by-shot detailing, a style perfectly suited to highlighting the fragmentation of Chinese modern life and the reconfiguration of city spaces (271).[3]

Rey Chow characterizes Chang's writing as a new "pictorialism," a technique of repeating visual details (1999: 158). This practice creates "a particular politics of style" to account for the changing conditions of a capitalist environment like early twentieth-century Shanghai (158). Chow suggests that Chang's literary application of cinematic techniques maps out the cultural mélange of Shanghai as a global city of confluence, one whose sophistication and complexity can best be captured in the interdisciplinary experiments of narration. In such a place and time, what must be expressed are "the encounters among different cultures and peoples, and the abundance of commodities from foreign lands" (158). These become "daily affairs" and so "the entire twin problematic of how to see in writing and how to narrate in visuality" must adapt by intensifying, as Chang intuited, "exponentially" (158–159).

These and other scholars have articulated Chang's cultural and narrative sophistication but have not gone so far as to draw specific connections between her intensities and filmmakers. While the study of Chang's work continues to evolve and gain momentum in the twentieth-first century, there is much to do in this area.[4] I begin this process here with Stanley Kwan because I believe that he puts forth one of the most dynamic readings of Chang's feminism, cinematic quality, and commentary on colonialism.

Born in Hong Kong in 1957, Kwan has dedicated his career to exploring the changing roles of women, various definitions of sexuality, and the ambivalent postcolonial political identity of Hong Kong. Kwan apprenticed under such prominent Hong Kong New Wave directors as Ann Hui, Patrick Tam, Ronny Yu, Yim Ho, and Leong Po-Chih, and then parlayed this experience into personal fame as one of the most accomplished Chinese directors of our time. Critics appreciate Kwan's popular films for the provocative way they start conversations about feminism, postcolonialism, and postmodernism (Lin Wenqi 1997; Cui 2003). From his celebrated debut, *Women* (*Nü ren xin,* 1985), to his award-winning films *Rouge* (*Yan zhi kou,* 1987), *Center Stage* (*Ruan ling yu,* 1991), and *Red Rose/White Rose* (*Hong meigui, bai meigui,* 1994), to his important documentary *Yin & Yang* (1996) and his famous exposé of Chinese gay culture *Lan Yu* (2001), Kwan has been characterized by critics first as a "women's director" and then a "gay director." These labels, however, do not fully account for the expansiveness of his humanist and egalitarian vision, which questions all forms of unbalanced power relations among social, racial, and sexual groups. Kwan has explained in interviews about his filmic passion: "Basically, my stance is that if I am moved by a project, a story or a group of characters, I will film it no matter what" (Kwan 2002). What moves Kwan, in particular, is the tyranny of an identity politics that prescribes stringent self-other boundaries of all kinds.

Even this brief synopsis of Chang and Kwan is enough to show that they represent an ideal test case for adaptation studies. Both are well versed in literature and cinema, and both carefully manipulate and differentiate their chosen medium by constant reference to the other. Four of Kwan's most successful films are adaptations from popular novels: *Rouge* (1987) from Lilian Lee's novel; *Red Rose and White Rose* (1994) based on Eileen Chang's short story; *Lan Yu* (2001) from the popular cyber fiction *Beijing Story,* and most recently *Everlasting Regret* (2005) from Wang Anyi's award-winning novel. All four films fall quite noticeably into the category of melodrama, a dominant form of expression in Chinese cinema since its inception in 1905 (Ma 1993; C. Berry 2003b).

In making film out of literature Kwan's use of melodrama is particularly significant because, as its Greek origin indicates—*melo-drama* means "a stage play accompanied by music" (Dissanayake 1993: 1)—a certain Chinese translation of the genre—*wenyin pian*—also suggests a mixture of narrative media. "The terminology 'wenyi' is an abbreviation of *wenxue* (literature) and *yishu* (art)," Stephen Teo (2001c) explains, "thus conferring on the melodrama genre the distinctions of being a literary and civilized form (as distinct from the *wuxia* genre, which is a martial and chivalric tradition)." In fact, melodramas in Kwan's adaptations indicate more than the blending of different forms; they serve very specific thematic and social functions. To understand these, it helps to look briefly at the contribution of modern melodrama to cinema.

In *Melodrama and Asian Cinema,* Dissanayake points out three important features of melodrama as a narrative form. First, it gives "prominence to the experiences, emotions, and activities of women" (1993: 2) and hence has been influential in shaping and understanding the development of women's consciousness. Second, the genre eliminates "the received categories of high art and low art, elitist aesthetic and popular entertainment," and its "antirealistic orientation" suits it to forms of postmodern thinking that are suspicious about the play of ideology in cultural construction (2). Third, melodramas illuminate the deep structures of cultures because they concretely represent any culture's "diverse casts of mind, shapes of emotion, vocabularies of expression, imaginative logics, and priorities of valuation" (2).

If the melodrama can be a versatile, expressive, and even progressive genre, then Kwan's adaptations can achieve the populist goals he shares with Eileen Chang. In his hands, in fact, the melodrama produces tantalizing counterpoints between 1940s Shanghai and 1990s Hong Kong—very different times and places—and sheds light on the major changes in Chinese cultural politics in the last half of the twentieth century. But a careful comparison of the artists' works also reveals that Kwan consciously reconfigures Chang's critique of sinocentric sexism by redirecting the writer's concern with racial hybridity towards highlighting a pressing issue of his own day: the cultural hybridity of diasporic, regional, and national Chinese identity.

Chang's story opens in the 1930s with a brief introduction to the life and character of the male protagonist Tong Zhenbao (Winston Chao). An industrious, ambitious "new youth" from a poor working family, Zhenbao earns a scholarship to study in Edinburgh, Scotland. His lackluster life is slowly transformed by a self-indulgent preoccupation with love and sex.

Zhenbao has his first sexual experience with a French prostitute (Sabine Bail) in Paris and is later introduced to love by a Eurasian girl named Rose (Shi Ge). After returning to Shanghai, he is appointed to a high-paying position at a foreign-owned textile factory. The security of his job not only helps him enter into the life of middle-class executives, but it also emboldens him to begin a passionate love affair with Wang Jiaorui (Joan Chen)—a British-educated Chinese Singaporean—who is the wife of an old friend Wang Shihong (Shen Tong Hua). Eventually choosing career over romance, Zhenbao breaks up with Jiaorui and marries a frigid but submissive girl, Meng Yanli (Veronica Yip). The absence of sexual attraction between the couple makes Zhenbao feel cheated by life, so he starts to visit prostitutes regularly to reward himself for the sacrifice he has made for his family and society. The story ends, however, with his renewed commitment to playing the roles of an honorable husband, responsible father, and respectable citizen.

The film plot is very similar. As a result, critics often criticize Kwan for a lack of creativity because he stays too close to Chang's original text (Shih 1995; Duan 1995). But other scholars dispute such assertions. They argue that Kwan, despite his obvious respect for Chang's writing, has made important ideological revisions to her narrative position. Joyce Chi-Hui Liu, for example, defends Kwan's adaptation and sees his film as adding an important historical context to Chang's "apolitical" story (2002: 146–149). Lin Wenqi (1997) contends that Kwan's fidelity to plot in fact pays homage to Chang's ironic critique of the male-centered Chinese ideals for modernization. Kwan's postcolonial skepticism, Lin suggests, ultimately creates a (counter) national allegory to voice Hong Kong's anxiety about 1997 and China's rising nationalism. I agree with both Liu and Lin that Kwan's work in fact reflects Hong Kong's unique political predicament. His filmic adaptation highlights its own *structural* mimesis of the source text in a way that parodies Hong Kong's adaptive political reconnection with China.

Chang's narrative structure is, first of all, ironically paradigmatic. The story chronicles four critical encounters between Zhenbao and his paramours: an anonymous Parisian prostitute, a Eurasian product of miscegenation, an overseas Chinese, and a local Shanghainese. This sequence demonstrates Chang's feminist and postcolonial resistance to the nationalist vision of homogeneity, for she use the four women to embody the algebra of possibilities for a more liberal, diverse, and equal China. Thus it is crucial to see that although this series seems to suggest that Zhenbao progressively approximates his own race, class, and cultural identity in his choice of paramours, in fact he fails each time either to domesticate or identify with any of his partners. His failed "progress" ironically dissolves the self-image he is so keen to construct, and his male ego increasingly disintegrates.

Kwan accentuates Chang's mockery of this failed essentialist vision by drawing attention to his adaptive use of Chang's visual metaphors. Lights, mirrors, roses, architecture, furniture, and food are some of the elements that Kwan employs in innovative interpretations of how Chang sees the different faces of a changing modern China. By fine tuning and sometimes subverting the traditional sociopolitical and gendered meanings of these metaphors, both artists effectively parody the characters' emotional discontents: too much light in Paris becomes blinding, not enlightening; while his posturing before mirrors diminishes, rather than magnifies, Zhenbao's sinocentric ego; the whitest of all roses later embodies not purity but sterile degeneration; the Western-style house turns out to be a Chinese tomb, not the garden of Eden. Such a deconstructive technique translates a particular postcolonial attitude toward China's politics, for it reveals the paradoxes of the nation's master-slave complex. On the one hand, China sees itself as the feminized Other victimized by the imperialistic West, but it also asserts the role of a masculine Self whose sinocentrism feminizes a South Asian Other.

In Chang's story all of these emotional complexes begin with Zhenbao's sexual encounter with the Parisian prostitute, a simultaneously trivial, but seminal event that has an important historical context: it functions as a review of the ways that China's journey to the West can evoke both inspiration and humiliation. Writing in the wake of the New Literature produced during the May Fourth Movement, Chang was keenly aware of China's urgent desire for reform. "Without the benefit of an intimate contact with the civilization of the West," Hu Shih famously asserted, "there could not be the Chinese Renaissance" (quoted in Chow Tse-tsung 1960: 55). The subtext is of course a scathing attack on Chinese culture and tradition, associated by intellectuals like Hu Shih with death and decadence. It was in this call for the birth of a new culture and new nation that many of China's youth were eager to support the idea of "wholesale Westernization" (*quan pan xi hua*). Rapid modernization was the goal, but disillusionment naturally arose when, as a more somber Liang Qichao cautioned it would, the idealism faltered (Chow Tse-tsung 1960: 322–323; Lin Yü-sheng 1979).

Reflecting on this unsettling cultural trend, Chang's story caricatures the ambivalent exploration of many educated Chinese men of the Western body of knowledge. In a carefully written sequence that exposes frustrated Chinese male desire for sexual conquest in Paris, the city of lights, she begins with a subversion of the metaphoric connection between light and enlightenment. The adventure starts with Zhenbao's walk around town on the last day of his visit; he is searching for a momentous event to cap his trip. "The street lights had already been turned on, but the sun was still hanging above the head" (Chang 1991: 59).[5] This double-lit, overexposed world first blinds Zhenbao to the extent that he is unable to find his direction. His disorientation is further aggravated by the Christmas carols that someone is playing on a piano with one finger in the quiet summer afternoon. "When the sun was still shining so quietly and fully on that long summer street, the Christmas music seemed so unseasonable that it made one feel almost as if he had fallen into a disordered dream, topsy-turvy, so absurd that it became laughable" (59). These temporal abnormalities disrupt the order of events that Zhenbao has planned for himself. Like Jen's leap in *Crouching Tiger* and Lotus's visit to the forbidden well/roof chamber, Zhenbao has conceived of his visit to Paris as an intellectual breakthrough that will help him demystify the West. However, not only does too much literal light (both sun and streetlights) disorient him, but the unseasonal music also seems to mock his ambition of being there at the right time and learning the right things. Christmas carols on a summer afternoon serve to remind him that he is there either too soon or too late.

Zhenbao's confusion of times creates an anxiety about disorientation. Chang captures this intellectual stupor in the protagonist's subsequent encounter with a Parisian prostitute, whose sexual attraction is metonymic: she "wore a red slip underneath her black lace dress. He liked red slips" (59). The allure of the woman has been reduced to a symbolic, colorful object, and the succinct description highlights the reductive simplicity of the Chinaman's relation to the fantasized Western body. This objectification further underscores Zhenbao's fetishistic desire for possession: sleeping with a European woman in an exotic city inflames his anticolonial fantasy, one shared by many Shanghainese/Chinese in occupied territories in the 1940s.

Chang weaves sexism, colonialism, and vision together so carefully throughout the story that one must read closely to understand its richness, particularly as a source for film adaptation. The following two passages exemplify her technique of invalidating the knowledge and pleasure associated with the act of seeing. In the first, she uses the disruptive power of two invisibilities—odor and anxiety—to disrupt the sleek power structure of the gaze. A much-anticipated Parisian sexual breakthrough is marred by a prostitute's stench and self-consciousness:

> Many years later, whenever Zhenbao recounted this event to friends, he often made fun of himself with a sense of lighthearted melancholy. "Before going to Paris, I was still a virgin! I should

> have gone back there to commemorate that deflowering." In retrospect, this should have been a very romantic experience, but for some reason he simply could not clearly recall anything vaguely romantic. Instead, it was the irritable part of the experience that gave him a lasting impression. Foreigners often had a little bit more of body odor than Chinese, and this woman was very concerned about it. He saw her frequently raise her arm and tilt her head to smell herself. Her clothes and armpits were soaked with perfume. The combination of cheap fragrance, body odor, and sour sweat created a most unforgettable stench. But what he resented the most was her uneasiness. After coming out of the bathroom with nothing on but a slip, she raised one arm high against the door, tilted her head to smile at him, and he knew right then that she was again sniffing at herself subconsciously.
>
> A woman like this, and even a woman like this, on whose body he had just spent his money, still could not let him be her master. The thirty minutes he spent with her turned out to be the most humiliating experience of his life. (60)

This encounter spoils the Chinese male sexual fantasy about the Occidental body and ridicules the imperialistic and misogynistic tendencies in Zhenbao's mission of reclaiming China's patriarchal dignity. The passage opens with a sense of emasculating regret—Zhenbao's sexual innocence has been irretrievably lost in a commercialized battle of the sexes—and Chang's irony attacks his sinocentric logic on several levels, starting with the "should-have-been" logic: yes, he should have had a romantic, exotic, and triumphant experience, but only if the woman had been a valuable sexual commodity willingly submitting to him. The escapade should have been straightforward, but despite his effort to objectify her body Zhenbao could master neither her mind nor the images of otherness she embodies.

In fact the prostitute presents quite a surprise for both Zhenbao and the reader, for not only is she unromantically aging and smelly, sniffing herself like a dog, but she is also anxiously aware of her own undesirability. For the reader the single most uncanny moment may be when her self-questioning look starts to give rise to Zhenbao's own self-disempowering gaze. Chang manages to turn the prostitute's self-consciousness into a form of female subjectivity that challenges Zhenbao's will to domination—"what he resented the most was her uneasiness"—and her anxiety into a parodic mirror of his own. She knows herself to be undesirable merchandise, and this encounter can offer Zhenbao no erotic-imperialist-romantic journey to the West.

In a scene describing the way the Parisian prostitute pauses in the middle of putting on her dress, Chang pursues the unsettling power of self-reflection in an even more deliberately cinematic way. Here her looking-glass becomes a camera, a technique that creates extreme close-ups and renders a radical perspectivism:

> At that instant he saw her in the looking-glass: She had lots of fluffy, yellowish hair. When her hair was pulled back tightly by her dress, what was revealed in the mirror was a thin long face. Her eyes were bluish, but that dot of blueness migrated to join the blackish circles converging just below her eyes; as a result, her now discolored eyeballs became translucent glass balls. That was a grim, cold, masculine face, an ancient soldier's face. Zhenbao was terribly unnerved by the sight. (60)

Few writers could make the process of unmasking as terrifying and yet as uninformative as Chang does. The series of synecdoches—from fluffy head to long face to blue eyes to discolored eyeballs—fragments the prostitute's visage, and the disintegration of the viewer's perspective magnifies her monstrous appearance.

In this sequence Chang achieves two important narrative goals including, first, the feminist strategy of resisting the eroticization of woman-as-spectacle. Her technique is subtle enough to have misled critics; several have interpreted her descriptions of women as rejecting "female subjectivity" (Joyce Liu 2002: 147). In my view, however, Chang's desexualization of the prostitute liberates the woman from her imprisonment in "to-be-looked-at-ness." If anything, Chang's style works to release women from the dominant economies of fetishization, voyeurism, and the female body to which so many psychoanalytical feminist studies have been dedicated.[6] Second, the destruction of Zhenbao's "big picture" enables Chang to illustrate and criticize the microscopic provincialism that has plagued many Chinese elites: after the burst of the theoretical bubble about "wholesale" Western modernization, many held on to remnants of patriarchal culture to secure their class and sexual dominance in a more familiar and controllable environment. Hence Zhenbao's doubtful moral lesson from his experience is to "construct a pocket-sized righteous world in which he can be the absolute master" (Chang 1991: 61). In other words, only by reconstructing a portable, reductive old China can a male elite reassert the power of his vision and recenter the image of himself.

Kwan's filming of the allegorical sexual encounter between East and West mimics Chang's critique of this Chinese male elite's egocentric self-

Figure 3.1 Aging Parisian wall is an isolating barrier.

Figure 3.2 Zhenbao ascends stairs to red light district.

reflection. Kwan's camera often moves as lyrically and dispassionately as Chang's narration to showcase China's contradictory and abortive desire for Westernization. The essential difference is that his mise-en-scène gives more exposure to Zhenbao's narcissism and vulnerability than does Chang's third-person description. Kwan makes Zhenbao's appearance a questionable sight that balances the prostitute's commodified body. The cinematic presentation of Zhenbao's physical details visually literalizes Chang's language.

Kwan's opening sequence immediately calls attention to Zhenbao's being out of place. The film begins with a horizontal shot of an aging bare wall to establish an image of barrier and a tone of desolation (Figure 3.1). This wall hints at the impenetrability of the old European world that the

Figure 3.3 Smiling Parisian prostitute.

Figure 3.4 In the prostitute's tatty room, Zhenbao reflected in mirror.

audience and Zhenbao are about to enter. Slowly the camera pans to the left and tilts down to capture a straight, dark lamppost that parallels the stiff image of Zhenbao walking up the stairs (Figure 3.2). Dressed in an unseasonable black suit, Zhenbao looks more like a prospective businessman than a young tourist searching for excitement. Disoriented and startled, Zhenbao is attracted to a hotel by a neon light that shines like a beacon right next to a medium close-up of a woman's inviting smile (Figure 3.3).

From the forbidding wall to the ascending motion up to the red-light district, Kwan shows that the path to the West is treacherous: not everything behind the barrier will be sex, knowledge, and freedom.

The subsequent cut to the hotel room evokes a claustrophobic fear of ignorance. Like Chang, but with the immediacy of cinematic images and elaborate construction of mise-en-scène, Kwan uses the mirror as a psychologizing device to offer the audience a different "look" at the characters' emotional reality. Wearing a calm expression and with perfectly groomed hair, Zhenbao outside the mirror looks unfazed by the dated hotel décor: fading wallpaper, a discolored flowery sofa that does not matched the festive gaudy maroon curtain in the background, and a large lamp in the foreground (Figure 3.4). These objects and colors orchestrate an oppressive sense of overt, visible shallowness. However, the scene changes considerably in the image *inside* the mirror, which shows the man not only sitting on the edge of a bed—the most dominant piece of furniture in the reflection—but also staring at a loose strand of his hair, a sign of his involuntary loss of self-control. Displaying a fear of impending doom, his face reveals an anxiety about what the bed—a test of his masculinity—may later reveal.

Kwan quite convincingly exploits the discrepancy of the two views. The movement of his subjective camera focuses only on Zhenbao's mirrored image, which identifies his viewpoint with that of the audience (Figure 3.5). He then carefully adds the details of a bathroom scene to Chang's original story in order to dramatize Zhenbao's voyeurism as he watches the prostitute's preparatory cleansing of herself.

Working with the traditional framing of voyeurism and the classic situation of woman-as-spectacle, Kwan converges in a sequence of what Laura Mulvey has famously called the "three different looks associated with cinema," those of the camera, the audience, and the character (2000: 46–47).

Figure 3.5 Zhenbao's mirrored image waiting anxiously for the prostitute.

The complete darkness of the foreground mimics the power and theatricality of the possessive male gaze in a predatory position. In an effect that can only surprise viewers conditioned to eroticized women, however, Zhenbao's voyeurism is profoundly emasculating. Like Chang, Kwan challenges the fundamental cinematic principle of scopophilia, and all but forces viewers to ask: what happens when the male character and the audience find no pleasure in looking at a woman's body? Can one completely neutralize the phallic power of the look? A shot-by-shot analysis of the scene is thus useful here for two reasons: it reveals Kwan adapting Chang's fiction into a groundbreaking treatment of the relation between the camera and a woman's body and, more broadly, shows how a classic scene can be used to question cinema's fundamental assumptions about "seeing" as "empowering."

Kwan's genius is to vivify Chang's literary technique by reversing one of its basic premises. In Chang's story, the self-conscious behaviors and tormented psyche of the prostitute disrupt the sexual fantasies of the male gaze. Kwan, realizing that in the cinema such activity would only concentrate and consolidate the objectifying gaze, brilliantly reconstructs the prostitute as a completely apathetic and indifferent. The scene begins by exposing her body in a routine and professionally unerotic fashion (Figure 3.6). With her back facing the audience, mimicking a vulnerable female position of being seen without seeing on screen, she sits unceremoniously on the bidet. Her naked bottom seems integrated with the texture of the dreary drapes in the background, a blend of age, inexpensiveness, discoloring, and secondhandedness. Her indifference to self-conscious grooming and self-maintenance reflects an utter disdain for the look, whose power to control and evaluate has now been impaired. Remarkably, Kwan's camera refuses to produce a picture of a seductive body; instead, it moves from a derisive overview of the woman-as-undesirable-package to a close-up of Zhenbao's anxious hands meticulously folding up his jacket (Figure 3.7). Kwan has taken the self-conscious sniffing of Chang's prostitute and transferred it to Zhenbao; he is the one obsessed with details and neurotic about his appearance.

As he contrasts the woman's apathy about "being looked at" with Zhenbao's anxiety about it, Kwan brings to light the shifting power dynamic between the sexes on the screen. The exposure of a woman's body no longer guarantees a mechanical, eye-pleasing delight, either for the character or the camera. This becomes even more apparent in the following shot-reverse-shot sequence with which Kwan highlights both the emotional and physical contrast between the two characters: while the prostitute's disheveled hairstyle, crumpled slip, and heavy body reveal a certain disdainful indifference

Figure 3.6 Nonerotic body as prostitute cleans herself on the bidet.

Figure 3.7 Zhenbao's anxious hands.

(Figure 3.8), Zhenbao's greased hair, meticulous attire, and mild manner emblematize his class, education, and austerity (Figure 3.9).

Emerging from the bathroom, the prostitute suddenly becomes more active, and this seems to realign the traditional gaze-structure: she is to be looked at again, exposed, and known. And yet this seemingly conservative move instantly proves emasculating as well: her teasing swagger gives her the upper hand. Their embrace, split into two images again by the mirror behind them, underscores the woman's phallic command of the situation (Figure 3.10). By design, Zhenbao inside the mirror and outside is marginalized on the edges of the frame. Facing the approaching body—multiplied

Figure 3.8 Disheveled prostitute sniffing under her arm.

Figure 3.9 Zhenbao's appearance emphasizes his class and education.

by the mirror and massed in the center of the frame, Zhenbao appears to be doubly lost.

Kwan's use of the mirror makes ironic both the magnified male ego in Chinese culture and the traditional complicity of cinema in eroticizing women's sexuality. His image resists the gratification of a male gaze, whose power of control has now been frustrated by mockery and impassiveness. At the end Kwan punctuates the encounter with a crane shot of the staircase, which simulates the circular pistil of a rose and signifies the psychological imprisonment of a romantic trap, a *vagina dentata* of pink and evil (Figure 3.11).

Through scenes like this Kwan proves himself to be one of the best possible readers of Chang. His literal presentation of Chang's figurative language preserves, and even italicizes, the critical spirit of her irony: this "rosy" picture refers not just to a romance of sexual love but, more importantly, to a romance with the self that can come with the circumstance of being male, Chinese, and middle-class. Chang's first-person narration and Kwan's subjective camera both effectively demonstrate the limitations of Zhenbao's perspective, which, despite its flirtation with a globalizing outlook, is boxed in by the faded glory of the patriarchal mindscape.

The story of Rose serves as an important interlude that anchors Chang's and Kwan's different interpretations of China's sexual and racial politics: in the novel Rose is a Eurasian, but in the film she is an overseas Chinese. With

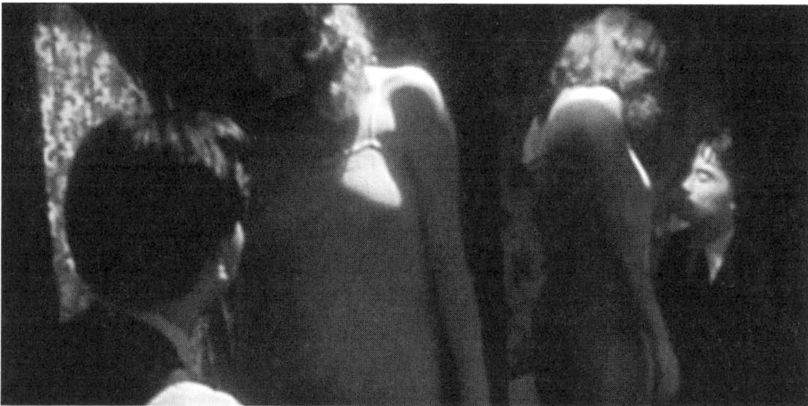

Figure 3.10 Zhenbao marginalized both inside and outside the mirror.

Figure 3.11 An aerial view of the staircase symbolic of a romantic trap.

this revision Kwan shifts narrative attention to issues of morality on marriage and sex and hence obliterates Chang's reasoned critique of China's race relations. Kwan's Zhenbao refrains from accepting Rose's sexual advances because he does not plan to marry her. Chang's Zhenbao, however, rejects Rose because her complex racial makeup—British Cantonese—makes him unable to categorize her.

Kwan's selective "reading" is echoed in other studies of the Rose complex, for most critics tend to focus on Chang's gender politics and overlook her analytical presentations of race issues. Examining Chang's use of metaphor and metonymy, Rey Chow, for example, suggests that Rose "is not simply a name but an objectification of a kind of a primary, unforgettable encounter, the emotion of which is not fulfilled until later. 'Rose' cannot be given up and will need to be repeated with variations" (1999: 163). In the sequence of repetitions, Chow sees "Rose" as "the value-producing mechanism of metaphor, the mechanism that equates rose with a particular woman, then with multiple women, and finally with all of femininity" (164).

Persuasive as far as it goes, this interpretation, I believe, focuses too exclusively on the allegorical meanings of the girl's gendered role. To appreciate the texture of Chang's deconstruction of Chinese essentialism, it helps to nuance the account by looking carefully at the race relations woven into Rose's mixed origin. She is both a woman and a Eurasian, and her identity as an ethnic, political, and moral hybrid makes her a unique literary symbol. Chang uses Zhenbao's rejection of Rose, the product of miscegenation, as a way to articulate her ongoing critique: China, despite its intellectual aspiration for Westernization, clings to the ideal of constructing a homogeneous "one-people" nation.

The prototype of a worldly, post-Obama citizen, Rose is the daughter of a respectable English merchant who has lived in Southern China for years and married a Cantonese woman out of "a temporary emotional outburst" (Chang 1991: 61). The association of Rose's existence with a momentary suspension of reason advertises her as the consequence of a miscalculated romance. Born outside of normalcy, Rose has an air of affectation and mannerisms that overcompensate for her genetic "impurity." "Because Rose was not a pure Briton, she acted more British than any British" (61). Even her physical attraction is caricatured as a form of artifice on display, for her "dainty legs" are "as refined as a mannequin's wooden legs in the shopping window" and "her delicate skin shining like the sanded, oiled wood" (62). These processed, manufactured images make the meaning of her appearance always *analogous to something else,* be it a Caucasian Briton, a mannequin, or a polished piece of woodwork.

Rose's analogical appearance makes her an approximate, incomplete, or virtual object of desire. Her life is what Homi Bhabha might call "a mimicry," and she herself "a subject of a difference that is almost the same but not quite" (Bhabha 1994: 86). Bhabha's critique of mimicry as an ironic imitation of a colonial subject is relevant to our understanding of how Zhenbao's eventual rejection of Rose can be interpreted as *both* a nationalistic refutation of colonial coercion and a traditionalist dismissal of nonconformity. Rose's attractiveness remains as much a disembodied unreality as the problematic marriage between a colonial master, her father, and the colonized object, her mother. In other words she is educated to imitate an idealized British subject in the same way that a mannequin is constructed to model the ideal of an attractive human body. The wood metaphor suggests the impossibility of a successful cultural transplant, for she can never grow or evolve on Zhenbao's home soil. In Zhenbao's parochial view of the world, Rose's hybridity puts her in a neither-nor position: she looks too British to be Chinese and too "Oriental" to be British. By the same token Chang further parodies the "visible" connection between ethnic miscegenation and ethical indeterminacy: Rose's "look" gives her a dubious reputation as a naïve, yet easygoing girl with men. She is too liberal to be a chaste wife and too innocent to be a mistress.

More than other writers of her generation, Chang creates characters like Rose to tease out the racial and ethical complexity of a new metropolitan world order in which the anxiety of displacement often emerges from this ambivalent look of in-betweenness. Rose's resistance to classification makes her a formidable threat to the stability of a patriarchal order—a system Zhenbao publicly denounces and yet secretly adheres to. Chang's narrative gradually reveals Zhenbao's hypocrisy by exposing the colored lenses he wears to categorize women in a duality of red and white, passion and chastity, a binary grouping that underscores the contradiction of Zhenbao's vision and, by extension, Chang's critique of China's rigid view of the world.

Kwan echoes Chang's critique of this dualistic worldview in a much more subdued and abbreviated representation of Zhenbao's "Rose complex." Despite the allegorical significance of the second encounter, Kwan condenses Zhenbao's British excursion to one brief scene in which the director exposes the Chinaman's sexual repression: he has to overcome his physical attraction to the indefinable Rose to claim moral triumph of mind over body. In the scene depicted in Figure 3.12, Kwan's camera visualizes the protagonist's struggle with self-control by compartmentalizing the entanglements of their various body parts—faces, hands, thighs, and trunks. This

Figure 3.12 Entanglement with Rose presented with overlapped body parts.

piecemeal view of their passion is further filtered through the windshield reflection, which generates narrative effects of obscurity and incompletion. In the dimly lit location, Kwan's framing choice undermines the voiceover's comment on how this encounter helps Zhenbao achieve the moral clarity to become an ethical leader in Chinese society.

A more sophisticated example of Kwan's poetics of adaptation is the way he uses Chang's fictional character Jiaorui, a Chinese Singaporean and the third "lover," to explore one of the most contentious issues facing China: defining *Chineseness.* Having grown up in South Asia, Jiaorui goes to England for her education and then moves to Shanghai for marriage. Her complex cultural background begs the question: is she Chinese, non-Chinese, un-Chinese, or sub-Chinese? In an age of globalization, the case of Jiaorui tests the theoretical limits and possibilities of what it means to be an overseas Chinese woman in China.

Before examining the symbolic meanings of Jiaorui in the work of Chang and Kwan, it is useful to contextualize the debates over the notion of Chineseness. In an influential volume edited by Tu Wei-ming, *The Living Tree: The Changing Meaning of Being Chinese Today,* he argues that it is important to create an alternative universe—a "cultural China"—and to define Chineseness as a fluid, "layered and contested" discourse, rather than a rigid, essentialist concept that categorizes Chinese as "belonging to the Han race, being born in China proper, speaking Mandarin, and observing the 'patriotic' code of ethics" (1994: vii). This new symbolic space challenges the hierarchy between the political center (China, Taiwan, Hong Kong, or Singapore) and the diasporic periphery, which includes transnational overseas

Chinese communities. In his effort to "decenter the center," Tu highlights the need to redefine "the periphery as the center" and to modernize the dated worldview of a bordered national space (viii).

Despite his critique of the politicized and exclusionist standpoint of Chineseness, Tu's "cultural China" nevertheless constructs a kind of Andersonian imagined community (Benedict Anderson 1991) that essentializes Chinese ethnicity as a cultural identity on the one hand and totalizes the different experiences of overseas Chinese on the other. As Allen Chun points out, a more meaningful way to "decolonize the fiction of ethnicities authorized and institutionalized by the center" is to question "the legitimacy of existing identities" and their politics (1996: 125). By the same token, Ien Ang comments, "a wholesale incorporation of the diaspora under the inclusive rubric of 'cultural China' can be an equally hegemonic move, which works to truncate and suppress complex realities and experiences that cannot possibly be fully and meaningfully contained within the singular category of 'Chinese'" (1998: 233). In light of these critiques, one may well ask how can one avoid ethnically centered, culturally driven, and discursively constructed notions of Chineseness? How does one theorize a more diverse, diffused, and equal partnership among the many different Chinese communities?

One answer lies in Chang's humanism. Her vision embraces the diasporic experience of indefinable in-betweenness—between languages, between ethnicities, sometimes even between good and evil—as a means of constructing a more creative, transnational space to accommodate a new, more symbiotic Chinese culture. A case in point is Chang's construction of Jiaorui, whose complex ethnic background and movement (from Southeast Asia to Europe to East Asia) enable her to exist in and among cultures and to resist various kinds of limiting categorization. Jiaorui's flexibility and peripheral status prefigure Chang's globalist model for a new woman's mobility, liberation, and self-expression.

Like the first two women, the prostitute and Rose, Jiaorui embodies a dangerous other. For Zhenbao, the intellectual agency of Jiaorui's Western education seems incompatible with her Southeast Asian origin. The indeterminacy of her status makes Zhenbao first speak of the married hostess with a conflicted combination of awe and scorn: Jiaorui "appeared to be the reincarnation of Rose, who had since become someone else's wife" (Chang 1991: 69). The word "reincarnation" hints at Jiaorui's inexplicable otherworldly mystique, while the role of "wife" brings her back to the earthy domain of the familial to criticize her strangeness: overseas Chinese are said to have the worst of the two intersecting worlds, Jiaorui's husband Shihong assumes, "for they not only inherit shortcomings from the Chinese but also acquire bad habits from the Westerners" (69). Inscribed in the contempt for Jiaorui is a fear of her transregional status as an amorphous Southeast Asian "native" whose cultural origin can neither be located nor domesticated.

Shihong's dismissals of Jiaorui as one of "*those* overseas Chinese" (*huaqiao*) exemplify what Rey Chow characterizes as sinochauvinism—a "historically conditioned paranoid reaction to the West" that can easily be flipped over and turned into "a narcissistic, megalomaniac affirmation of China" (1998: 6). Jiaorui is constructed by her Chinese husband and lover as a flawed ideological replica, a bad imitation of both the Western other and Chinese subject. An a priori failure herself, she magnifies the Chinese male ego.

In Chang's text, however, Jiaorui does not surrender to these foregone conclusions. On the contrary, she personifies a feminist and postcolonial challenge to institutionalized scripts and her quality of being out of place, in particular, enables her to question the domesticating writing of women and to redraft her role as the Chinese other. Making the dissection of her name symbolic for a critical anatomy of traditional Chinese culture, Chang enables Jiaorui to destabilize the composition of the Chinese "character" both literally in writing and metaphorically in her self-definition: at their first meeting, Jiaorui proudly presents to Zhenbao her own Chinese name, but Zhenbao "took a look at her handwriting and could not help bursting out laughing: written on that piece of paper were three tilted and distorted Chinese characters 'Wang Jiao Rui' (王 嬌 蕊) that grew larger and larger and finally the last character 'Rui' fell apart and was turned into three characters" (Chang 1991: 68).

On the surface this anecdote seems simply to suggest Jiaorui's cultural ineptitude: she cannot be a good "Chinese" woman if she is unable to reproduce her name. However, the character that Jiaorui breaks apart is in fact a symbolic critique of the shallowness and rigidity of her husband's chauvinistic interpretations of the Chinese writing system: *rui* (the flower bud) is broken into not illegible fragments but three identical hieroglyphical parts—*xin* (hearts). Jiaorui's mishandling of the character hence indicates not so much a mutilation of her name, Jiaorui, "the precious flower bud," a term that suggests vulnerability and spectatorial passivity, but rather itemizes and liberates the "parts" that have been compressed and transfigured by the essentialist discourse of "correct" Chinese culture. Chang's description further animates Jiaorui's writing in a way that resembles the cinematic process of *blow-up,* because her name "grew larger and larger and finally the last character 'Rui' fell apart and was turned into three characters." This visual magnification and explosion reinforce the idea that Jiaorui is literally and metaphorically a transformational figure. Her writing subverts the decorative nature of her appearance as a flowery icon and reinvents the meanings of her "character." This incident shows how Chang humanizes and feminizes her versions of "cultural China." Using the narrator's distance from both Zhenbao and Jiaorui to play the limitations of each character off the other, she installs a poststructuralist scene that enacts the fragmentation of identity as it is encoded in Chinese names and writing.

The following quotation further illustrates a turning point in the relationship. Bound by morality, Zhenbao has decided to stay away from his seductive landlady despite the temptation. But an incidental collision in the hallway late one night undoes his resistance:

> One night he heard the phone ringing for a long time, but no one answered it. As soon as he rushed out of his room, he seemed to hear the door in Jiaorui's room being flung open. He worried that he might bump into her in the dark hallway, so he was ready to get back to his room. But Jiaorui appeared to have trouble finding the phone in a hurry, so he turned on the nearest light for her. Seeing Wang Jiaorui under the light completely stupefied him. He didn't know if she had just taken a bath, but she had on a pajama made out of a kind of sarong often used by overseas Chinese in South Asia. The printed design on the sarong, a massive darkness that could be dragons and snakes or grass and forests, had an intricate, disorderly, but connected pattern within which an orange-green color was burgeoning out of dark gold. The design on the sarong seemed to have deepened the night inside the house. The hallway glistening under the murky yellow light resembled the compartment of a train traveling from one foreign place to another. Although the woman on the train was a chance encounter, she nevertheless appeared to be very approachable (Chang 1991: 76).

Told from the perspective of Zhenbao, the encounter is fraught with uncertainty, and words like "seemed," "might," "appeared," "if," "could," "or," and "resembled" accentuate the insecurity of his judgment. His indecisiveness is complemented by the disorienting colors ("orange," "green," "dark gold") and interwoven imageries ("dragons and snakes," "grass and forests"), the visual confluence of which makes the world patterned on the sarong a vibrant, unpredictable, and seductive place. Zhenbao's effort to clarify things, to turn on the light, restores neither his sight nor his sensibility but instead intensifies Jiaorui's inscrutability. Like her sarong, she emits the energy of timeless jungles and the shadows magnify her sensuality. A force of nature, she will not conform to order, reason, or nation.

In the midst of this enigmatic spectacle, the anticipated excitement of a train ride echoes an earlier comparison of Zhenbao to a blank "peach blossom fan" (58), which raises the expectation that he will become a spectacular work of art (Lee 1999: 286; Joyce Liu 2002: 150–151). This train also foreshadows the accidental reunion between Zhenbao and Jiaorui on a tram car nine years later, when they will trade reports on their "reformed" lives. Together the two episodes make the image in the midst of their flirtation all the more suggestive. Moving from "one foreign place to another," the train projects a sense of modern adventure, disorientation, exhilaration, and even disconnection from reality. The engine travels at the speed of modernity, and Zhenbao cannot govern its movements; his limitations are reflected in the emphasis on compartmentalization. It is not difficult to read this passage as a figure for China's struggle to manage the itinerary of a modernizing nation that has attracted many passengers of diverse origins.

Ultimately, Zhenbao's Chinese nationalist discourse is threatened as much by Jiaorui's "primitive" otherness and sophisticated Westernization as by the different form of Chineseness she represents—exotic, feminine, liberal, and independent. Jiaorui personifies a new image of the Chinese other, one whose shadowed life, peripheral as it may seem at first, illuminates the provincialism of Zhenbao's greater-China fantasy. Her decentralizing movements disrupt the boundaries between inside and outside,[7] and her feminine guise makes her an amorphous and translingual figure who resists definitions. Jiaorui is a new breed of the freer global woman on whom Hong Kong directors like Stanley Kwan model their progressive female characters.

The geopolitical and cultural fluidity of Jiaorui (Joan Chen) make her an appropriate icon for Hong Kong cinema in the 1990s. Her bad-girl image gives her the kind of democratic mobility, volubility, and visibility that Hong Kong as a political state in flux and a film industry in transition has hoped to put on stage. From this perspective it is not surprising that Kwan's treatment of Jiaorui features a new trope—the pink rose—that signals her moral and cultural hybridity, caught between the chaste white rose and passionate red rose. Kwan introduces his synthetic approach to the text by changing Chang's title from "Red Rose and White Rose" to "Red Rose/White Rose," a move that emphasizes parataxis by juxtaposing the interchangeable roles of the two opposing symbols. The new title not only effaces the moral distinction between mistress and wife but also points to their transgressive boundary-crossing: Jiaorui becomes a loyal devotee to her doomed affair with Zhenbao, while Yanli is suspected of committing adultery with a local tailor.

Kwan's camera shows Jiaorui as a variable, fluid figure in a constant state of becoming while Zhenbao appears to be mainstream, commonplace, and mundane. Their contrasting looks bring out conflicts between the private, peripheral, and domestic sites associated with women versus those that are central, public and occupied by men. Ultimately, though, Kwan uses camera movement, mise-en-scène, and angled shots to deconstruct the privilege of a male viewing position.

As happened in his Paris excursion, Zhenbao's courtship of Jiaorui begins in an ascending motion: the scene opens with a mechanical noise and the movement of an elevator in an apartment to signal Zhenbao's return

Figure 3.13 Zhenbao, an orderly symbol of modernity, ascends toward Jiaorui in elevator.

Figure 3.14 Zhenbao stands just inside Jiaorui's apartment; the roses in the bouquet are pink, a mélange of red and white.

from work (Figure 3.13). The sight and sound of the lift are identified with the motorized, industrial nature of Zhenbao, who, in his immaculate Western suit, appears to be an orderly citizen of modernity. When he walks into the apartment, a medium-long shot first shows him looking around curiously at the doorway. His image is framed between the colorful and chaotic wall design in the background and a vase of pink roses in the foreground (Figure 3.14). In voiceover Jiaorui's "Mr. Sun, please"—clearly a statement to someone else—greets Zhenbao's entrance with asynchronous irony.

This shot is of great interest because Kwan uses the roses as a signifier to help advance the narrative in such a way that the parallel between Jiaorui and the pink roses is visually and thematically established. If roses are a Western symbol of love, the ebullient pink bouquet in the front room embodies a certain faux-European allure of the hostess: visible, available, pungent, but pretentious.

Kwan's camera captures Jiaorui's state of becoming through a constant search for her presence. The instability of the camera's perspective conveys a sense of reversibility that makes viewing an experience of being viewed at the same time. When Zhenbao first walks into the apartment, the camera slowly pans along with his viewpoint to find the shadow of Jiaorui reflected behind a closed door: the hostess is flirting coyly with an old fling, Timmy Sun, on the phone (Figure 3.15). A shot-reverse-shot then aligns the audience with Jiaorui's viewpoint to capture Zhenbao's passing shadow on the opaque glass door (Figure 3.16). The shift of perspective enables the audience to examine the situation from the opposing standpoints: Zhenbao and Jiaorui are both looking and being looked at. This mode of representation involves a strong female position that breaks out of the old Hollywood model in which, as Laura Mulvey puts it, "the man controls the film fantasy and also emerges as the representative of power in a further sense: as the bearer of the look of the spectator, transferring it behind the screen to neutralize the extra-diegetic tendencies represented by woman as spectacle" (2000: 41). When Jiaorui functions as both spectacle and spectator, she guides the audience's viewpoint in just the same way that Zhenbao is expected to, and the parallel treatment deconstructs the expected visual hierarchy between the characters.

Kwan reinforces the "democratic" appeal of his camera movement with his mise-en-scène. The courtship between Jiaorui and Zhenbao emerges both in their interested gaze and in the atmospheric seduction of materialism. Filled with excess, Jiaorui's apartment defies any logic of order and taste. From the ubiquitous roses to the graceful British china tea set and from the assorted European cookies to unrefined everyday food like toast and peanut

Figure 3.15 Zhenbao sees image of Jiaorui through the glass door as she flirts over the phone with Timmy Sun.

Figure 3.16 Jiaorui sees Zhenbao through the glass door.

butter, Kwan enlarges the details that speak of delicacy and indulgence. The characters' desires reflect their places on the social continuum: Zhenbao prefers the more austere Chinese clear (green) tea (*qing cha*) to British tea served with milk and sugar, while Jiaorui is ready to embrace the vice of peanut butter in spite of her diet restrictions. Zhenbao argues for loyalty to one's own culture and expresses a concern for Jiaorui's wayward consumption: their flirtation culminates in an extreme close-up of a piece of toast, held by Zhenbao, on which our hero is methodically and sensuously spreading layer upon layer of peanut butter (Figure 3.17). Departing from the brevity of Chang's description ("Zhenbao ended up spreading peanut butter on her toast"), Kwan's long take of this particular shot underscores the sensuality of Zhenbao's service and provides a visual connection between the physicality of the toast and the sumptuous figure of the hostess. The metaphor also illustrates the hypocrisy of Zhenbao's pretension: he is just as avid a consumer of forbidden food and sex as the hostess. Jiaorui comments in both the film and the story: "I rather enjoy violating the law. Don't you approve of violating the law?" (Chang 1991: 73).

In fact, Jiaorui often uses the language of the "new woman"—freer, more educated, and more aggressive (Brown 1993)—to challenge Zhenbao's narrative authority. Her fondness for peanut butter and toast shows an indiscriminate taste that breaks down the delicacy of class boundaries, and

Figure 3.17 Zhenbao spreading peanut butter on toast for Jiaorui.

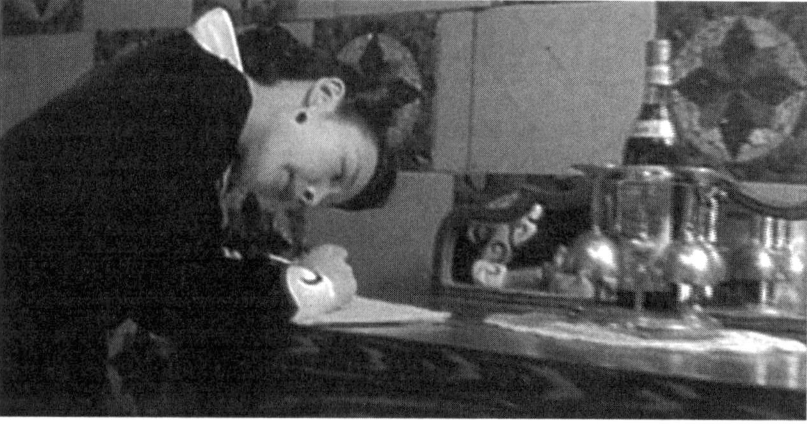

Figure 3.18 Kwan shoots Jiaorui off center to emphasize her power of dislocation.

taken altogether her indiscretions defy stereotyping. Kwan's camera intensifies her power of dislocation with a playful use of off-centered shots, such as those putting characters at odd angles or at the edge of the frame to suggest their marginalization (Figure 3.18).

The revolving camera movement informs the audience of the character's transforming vision of the world: Jiaorui is deliberately paired with the pink roses to foreground her shift from a morally ambiguous adulteress into a loyal mistress. The irony is that this "purification" discolors and tarnishes Jiaorui's "modern girl" image and makes her an imperfect imitation of Zhenbao's ideal of a good Chinese woman. The failure is captured in a sobering scene in which Jiaorui wakes in the night to find Zhenbao by the bedroom window agonizing over the long-term prospects for their relationship. In this dark night full of shadows of the past and the thunder of the future, Jiaorui and the vase of pink roses next to the windows are simultaneously illuminated (Figure 3.19). Jiaorui anxiously professes: "Don't worry. I will be good from now on" (88), but her promise only cements Zhenbao's determination to break up with her. To deviate from the role of seductress is to disrupt the boundaries between wife and mistress and become an undesirable moral burden.

Chang's fourth fictional woman is Yanli, whose grounded nature distinguishes her from the deracination of the previous examples. The fact that she is native Chinese is nevertheless a double-edged sword, for there are both burdens and virtues associated with being *homegrown*. On the one hand, it can be considered as a geopolitical and cultural guarantee that from

Figure 3.19 Jiaorui, again associated with the vase of pink roses, promises to be good, which confirms Zhenbao's determination to leave her.

the seed, so to speak, she has the correct national character, "an equivalent of *minzu xing*"—"a totality of homogeneous ideas, mood, will, and emotion conditioned by social norms and by national history and economy" (Lydia Liu 1995: 64). On the other, this naturalized heritage can easily generate cultural prejudices and foster an environment that breeds what Lu Xun once criticized as an "ignorant and weak" national character (1999: 467). Yanli embodies such a contradiction and can be seen as a female "translation" of Zhenbao's paradoxical Chinese self, one whose embedded localness is both desirable and contemptible.

But the story of Yanli tells more than a dualistic opposition between the Chinese self and the global other. More significant are the ways her regionalism puts her at odds with Zhenbao's own nationalist rhetoric. For both Chang and Kwan, regionalism is an especially acute issue: Chang had extensive firsthand experience with Shanghainese language and culture and Kwan with Cantonese. Their emphasis on Yanli's vernacular nature makes her a voice for the repressed desire of "othered" locals. Their portrayal of her laborious effort at learning Mandarin, for instance, further exposes the constructedness of a unified Chinese vision of the world.

Stylistically, Chang and Kwan employ different narrative strategies that challenge the monological view of China-as-One idealism. Chang focuses on painting Yanli with the varying shades of "white" to mimic her virginal and pliable nature. Associating Yanli with "home," Chang exposes the discrepancy between the inside and the outside of the house to illustrate her Janus-faced existence. Kwan, on the other hand, follows the melodramatic conventions of romanticizing Yanli's affair with the tailor. He uses camera angles to contrast Yanli's interactions with her husband and lover and to tease out the multiplicity of ways the local culture is repressed.

To capture the paradox of Chang's Yanli, one could call her *uniquely indistinct*. In contrast to the ethnic threat of Rose's impurity and the cultural jeopardy of Jiaorui's otherness, Yanli's strength rests on homespun blankness—an ambivalent form of promising void that seems to await inscription. Chang explores the multivalence of the color "white" with which Yanli is blended to suggest, albeit ironically, her pure traditionalism and intellectual ignorance. At the first meeting of Yanli and Zhanbao, the narrator comments that although Yanli "wore a grayish silk blouse imprinted with orange stripes, the first impression she gave people was a sense of generalized whiteness.... Her face was beautiful and delicate, but it gave people a singular feeling of whiteness...Her whiteness separated her from anything bad in her surroundings in a way that made her resemble a white screen in the hospital" (Chang 1991: 92). Instead of attesting to purity, this generalized whiteness draws attention to Yanli's pale, lackluster performance as a student, wife, and citizen of modern society. Receptive and malleable, whiteness in Yanli also becomes a tint of resistance and isolation, eventually conveying a clinical vision of disinfection—"a white screen in the hospital"—as well as a languid kind of disengagement.

In addition Chang's narration characterizes Yanli as an uninspired but assiduous student whose provinciality screens her from the world of learning by "a layer of white membrane" (92). Yanli personifies the stereotypical impressions of an old China that valorizes the intellectual incompetence of women, as in the popular saying, "Having no talent is a woman's virtue." Chang's white rose is born out of this blanched and dated Chinese male fantasy, which prevents women from being either cultivated or "sullied" (darkened) by modern ideas. Of course, this fantasy also reinstates the hierarchy between femininity and masculinity and thus plays into the West's imagining of the "backwardness" of a feminized Orient—precisely the emasculating generalization that, as we have seen, Zhenbao seeks to dispute in his pilgrimage to the West.

This review of Chang's cinematophilic, interlocking visual metaphors and social critique would not be complete without an architectural example. The following passage illustrates the hypocrisy and contradictions of Zhenbao's divided world by comparing his Western-style house to an Orientalized Garden of Eden:

> His house was a small, Western-style building on an alley, with a wall surrounding it. The houses in a row facing the street all looked the same—light gray cement walls, smooth and shiny rectangles like coffin boards, and blooming oleander showing over the tops of the walls. Although the courtyard inside was small, it could be taken for a garden. His house had everything that it should have. White clouds were floating in the blue sky above. On the street, a hawker played one of the flutes he was selling—its sounds a sharp, undulating Oriental song, undulating like embroidery, like the dreamy illusions in illustrations from a novel, like a thread of white mist rising from a bed-curtain, widening as it rises, and with it various dreamlands within, a dream uncoiling like a listless snake, until, finally, both dreamer and dream end in deep sleep. (61)[8]

The house's "light-gray cement wall" evokes the image of Yanli's initial appearance in "grayish silk blouse." Descriptions of a similar off-white color on both "locations" visually identify the house with the wife: they share a bond that adds meanings to Yanli's domestic role as a "housewife." Ontologically it implies that building the house is comparable to the "construction" of the wife: the former is for the habitation of the body and the latter, the accommodation of the sinochauvinistic mind. Both pieces of "hardware" are mechanical reproductions of a generic and scripted image. "The houses in a row facing the street all looked the same."

Symbolically these "edifices" make interchangeable two seemingly opposing sites—the tomb and the womb—which are at once the burial and birthing ground of Zhenbao's dissonant vision of a viable cultural identity. If the Western-style house ("smooth and shiny rectangles like coffin boards") is built to entomb the old China, there nonetheless emerges from the void an "undulating Oriental song," singing to revive the alluring memory of a dreamy, freer, and sensual past.

Still more suggestive is Chang's implicit comparison of Zhenbao's residence to an imitation Garden of Eden in which Yanli plays the innocent and ignorant Eve. Though protected from the outside world by high-rising walls, the Chinese Eve is ultimately seduced by captivating music that uncoils "like a listless snake"—sexual imagery referring to the affair Zhenbao suspects that his wife is having with the tailor. Chang's use of such elusive metaphors as "clouds," "mist," "illusions," and "dream" serves two overall narrative functions: they pay tribute to the classical Chinese references to sexual pleasure and hence overtly liberate Yanli from her frigidly virginal image; they also mimic Zhenbao's intangible idealization of Yanli's submissive femininity as a sanctuary but ultimately illusionary space for the preservation of Chinese cultural integrity.

In contrast to the generically decent appearance of the rest of the house, Yanli's living space is stuffed with metaphors of oppressiveness, degeneration, and ineptitude. Chang characterizes Yanli as an unlikable and incompetent housewife. From the homeliness of her prematurely aged tailor lover ("who wore several ringworm scars on his head," 102) to her incorrigible constipation, the world inside the walls is soiled by "a kind of filth," a wetness "bearing intense human stench" (104). These repulsive sights and smells attack Zhenbao's sense of well-being in such a way that he appears as diseased and trapped in the fortified home as he was years ago in the cheap Paris hotel. In her own way Yanli is as indomitable and threatening as the prostitute. An affair with an ugly tailor is more than enough to demolish Zhenbao's ideal of a homegrown sanctuary.

Kwan's description of Yanli focuses less on her "soiled" relation with the environment than on the return of her repressed localism. While Chang's narrative speaks primarily from the perspective of Zhenbao to satirize his egocentrism, Kwan interweaves perspectives to analyze what romance means to the Chinese locals. Making Chineseness depend upon a complex other-local dialectic, Kwan diverges from Chang's brief description of Yanli's suspected adultery and instead makes the affair aesthetic, even rational. His portrayal of the courtship between Yanli and her tailor questions the representation of Yanli as simply the local vehicle for a modern man's self-expression. Instead, Kwan shows her speaking a native tongue (Shanghainese) so fluently that her articulateness undermines the narrative authority of the official language (Mandarin), which is mediated by Zhenbao and the institution of marriage.

This turf battle between the national and local cultures begins when Zhenbao's younger brother Dubao visits the Tongs. Dubao brings news about

Figure 3.20 Yanli, looking submissive in Zhenbao's presence.

Figure 3.21 The tailor kneels, measuring Yanli, whose arms are open expansively.

Jiaorui, who seems to have moved on after the ill-fated affair with Zhenbao. Feeling his loss of control over the lives of others, Zhenbao is eager to claim territorial ownership at home. He rushes to Yanli's side to demonstrate to her the "proper" way of wrapping up a pair of candlesticks with newspaper (Figure 3.20). "Everything is difficult for a stupid person," he mumbles. Kwan illustrates their unequal power dynamic by staging Zhenbao in the foreground, and Yanli standing next to him in the center of the frame. With only his upper body and parts of his face visible, the master of the house appears to be a formidable and menacing presence that truncates Yanli's self-expression. He resembles the figure of Master Chen in Zhang Yimou's film, whose half-concealed presence intensifies the patriarchal threat.

In contrast to Yanli's subservient silence with Zhenbao is her fluid communication with the tailor. She walks away from Zhenbao's oppressive scornfulness to step into the tailor's web of gentle affection. The viewer first sees the tailor measuring Yanli's body for a garment in the family room (Figure 3.21). A low-angle shot of the two elevates Yanli into the commanding position: standing in the center of the screen, she stretches her arms out wide to mimic a flying bird and to illustrate her delight at these transgressive moments of sexual freedom. The tailor's soft-spoken Shanghainese localizes the encounter as indigenous, intimate, and familiar. Their matching checkered dress and vest further evidences their shared aesthetic and cultural values. The soft yellow lighting gives the scene an aura of romantic nostalgia, fading in time and space.

This old-fashioned courtship mocks the international, impersonal profile of Zhenbao's romance, for he treats Yanli as a vessel, a blank canvas on which he, as her husband, transcribes the rhetoric of his self-importance. Figure 3.22 shows Zhenbao giving a speech to the students at a vocational school. Prominently on display is a partial view of a progressive Chinese idiomatic expression in the 1920s: "Make Chinese learning a part of one's cultural foundation; apply Western learning to improve one's everyday life" (*Zhong xue wei ti, xi xue wei yong*). Dressed in a traditional gray Chinese robe—the proper attire for old-fashioned Chinese scholars—Zhenbao appears to integrate himself physically and intellectually with the characters on the imposing blackboard behind him, for he is at once writing and being written into a system that institutionalizes rules of proper behaviors. However, the omission of the last two characters "*wei yong*" (to improve one's everyday life) makes Zhenbao's high-flown rhetoric symbolically incomplete.

Compared with Zhenbao's notable cultural achievements, the domestic nature of the tailor's dressmaking seems trivial and "feminine" and yet sensually reassuring of Yanli's local identity. As a result, Yanli's *homegrowness* is as much a polarizing force as the threat of other women's *foreignness.*

In the end Kwan collapses the boundaries of opposing imageries by concluding the scene with a mirroring sequence. Zhenbao voluntarily faces himself in the looking glass to practice a mock reunion with Jiaorui: "Long time, no see! How have you been? Have you been living in Shanghai all this time?" (Figure 3.23). His rehearsal is reminiscent of his Parisian experience in which the looking glass revealed his performance anxiety. The difference between the two scenes, however, is that Zhenbao has now learned to use

Figure 3.22 Zhenbao giving a lecture to emphasize the importance of adapting to modern changes.

Figure 3.23 Zhenbao practicing a speech in a mirror for an imagined encounter with Jiaorui.

the mirror as a mask. This is especially visible in Kwan's control of lighting to illuminate only half of Zhenbao's face in the mirror. This shaded view creates a strong sense of dividedness and even disfigurement of an identity that has been mutilated by the polarizing demands of what was to be his redemptive nationalist mission.

Zhenbao's "incomplete" picture contrasts with the other mirroring view of the scene: standing at the doorway, Yanli in a full-body shot stumbles upon Zhenbao's rehearsal and is herself caught between two symbolic frames of mind: the red roses in the hallway and the white roses in the living room (Figure 3.24). It is no accident, I believe, that we see here for the first time the juxtaposition of these two colors in the same frame to suggest their paradoxical coexistence. Like Zhenbao, Yanli is conflicted by her roles as virtuous wife and passionate adulteress. All these looking-glass images ultimately point to the multiplicity of local desire, which mirrors the heterogeneity of the nation.

The story "Red Rose and White Rose" sets up a narrative structure in which the main male protagonist remains inflexible throughout the story, and where his dogmatism reflects a set of Chinese attitudes that suppress the dialogical exchange between China and other cultures. Problematizing and complicating this self-limiting mentality, Chang rotates a set of women around Zhenbao to construct a feminine space that renegotiates Chinese gender and race relations.

My analyses suggest that Kwan is an ideal interpreter of Chang's story. Both artists question the masculinist association of vision with power and make studied use of visual metaphors such as lights, roses, mirrors, and architectural space to explore the discrepancy between physical appearance and emotional reality. As their styles destabilize the authority of the Chinese male perspective, they affirm a more nuanced approach to cultural hybridity. And yet while Kwan fully understands the feminine strengths of Chang's original story, he noticeably condenses some of her more provocative race issues. As we have seen, he rebrands the symbolic figure of Rose as an "overseas Chinese," which erases the miscegenated origin that Chang so carefully constructs for her. And Kwan cannot be said to give Jiaorui's questionable Chinese Singaporean ethnic identity Chang's level of scrutiny. Such revisions tend to streamline his cinematic representation and prioritize gender over race.

One explanation for the differences is political. For Chang, the raging wars in the 1940s brought a strong imperative to treat race and sex as equally urgent issues. Her literary analysis of China's sinochauvinism reveals a nation whose relations with others, and with its own diverse population, often falls

Figure 3.24 Yanli standing between the red and the white roses.

into complex and paradoxical traps of antagonism and self-representation. In particular, her expositions of the crises of the Chinese male subject invite her readers to rethink widespread, codified definitions of Chineseness. Kwan's overwhelming concern in 1994 was Hong Kong's imminent return to China in 1997. He skillfully borrows from Chang the gendered allegory of interactions between masculine "fatherland" and feminine "mistresses," using the sexual hierarchy to present and critique—sometimes openly, sometimes not—key political issues between Hong Kong and China. Many, of course, are still being negotiated: democracy, individual freedom, cultural diversity, and social mobility. Taken together, Chang's mixed-media fiction and Kwan's literary adaptation propose a more diverse and symbiotic future for Chinese culture. Their open-minded, feminist, and globalist vision will surely play a part in continuing debates over Chinese cultural politics.

CHAPTER 4

Liu Yichang and Wong Kar-wai

The Class Trap in *In the Mood for Love*

A key representative of the Hong Kong Second Wave,[1] Wong Kar-wai (Wang Jiawei, b. 1956) stands out as one of the hippest and most critically acclaimed directors in the world. He experiments with different genres, makes complex and beautiful movies, and can generally be taken as a pure example of why Hong Kong cinema has become popular in the West. From *As Tears Go By* (1988) to *My Blueberry Nights* (2007), he has innovated in genres as diverse as gangster and martial arts films, melodrama and road films. Combining fast editing, superimposed slow motion, parallel narrative structures, expansion of off-screen space, and angled shots, his virtuoso styles and fluid narratives have generated a loyal following around the world. One excellent illustration of his restless, composite vision is his adaptation in 2000 of Liu Yichang's 1972 novella *Intersection* into *In the Mood for Love*.[2] Liu's story is hailed as representative of Chinese modernist writings—in part because it captures the impressionistic movement of character consciousness—while Wong's film is usually considered a romantic melodrama (Stephen Teo 2001c).[3]

This chapter is an example unlike any other in the book, for the novel and the film tell completely different stories. In fact, the point must be put more firmly: the film has very little plot, and the novel almost none at all. Thus, instead of inviting the usual set of questions about how the plot and narrative perspectives change in adaptation, Wong's movie raises new ones about the commensurability of things like structure, form, mood, and ideology. In particular, he privileges two broadly nonnarrative ways that cinema can intersect with literature: formalism and historicism. His formal experiments include invoking multiple parallels between text and film (on the level of image, character, and motif, among others), while his historical emphasis lies on the contrasts between Hong Kong's burgeoning capitalist culture and fading traditional Chinese values.

These few remarks are already enough to suggest why Wong has been hailed as a director's director. Ackbar Abbas uses postcolonial theory to argue that Wong has rendered visible an ephemeral Hong Kong, one that is becoming "a space of the *déjà disparu,* of disappearance" (1997: 48); from a more formalist perspective, David Bordwell salutes him for brilliantly balancing aesthetic experimentalism and popular entertainment (2000: 281); Peter Brunette celebrates his use of sound and visuals in his "'mysterization' of everyday life" (2005: xvi). Few critics, however, have made much of Wong's attachment to literature. In fact, Brunette argues explicitly that Wong's art cannot be reduced to the literary techniques of "narration, dialogue, and conventional drama" per se (2005: xvi). For many ordinary viewers also, Wong's genius lies precisely in his ability to construct spellbinding and seductive cinematic moods while muting or dispensing with traditional narrative-based film practices. *Ashes of Time, In the Mood for Love,* and *2046* are three well-known examples in which Wong creates alternative styles of storytelling that exploit phenomena such as ambiance, beat, and the look of moving images. His unflagging desire for innovation helps explain why he prefers to rely on improvisation rather than finished scripts on the set, and a practical result of this technique is that key scenes in his films often convey an edgy, open-ended narrative feel, a sense that anything could happen (Stephen Teo 2001c; Bordwell 2000; Brunette 2005). A related theoretical result is that his narratives are made to depend upon categories far beyond the "plot, character, and diction" bestowed upon us by Aristotle's *Poetics.*

These are all good reasons to think of Wong as a postliterary director, an auteur who thrives in the audiovisual medium of cinema. And yet I argue that we must also interpret Wong as a preeminently *literary* director, one whose films cannot be understood outside their relationship to Hong Kong's broader cultural milieu and literary contexts. Like Stephen Teo—one of the few critics to emphasize Wong's literary sensibility—I see written fiction as the source not only of Wong's plots but also of many of his stylistic and structural choices, and I think his interest in adaptation is especially crucial (Stephen Teo 2005b: 3). It is no accident that all three of the films mentioned above as examples of a postliterary imagination are actually adaptations of novels by two famous Hong Kong writers: legendary martial arts author Louis Cha (also known as Jin Yong) and acclaimed modernist writer Liu Yichang (b. 1918).

In fact, my broader argument is that Wong's films establish a powerful new relationship between cinema and literature, one that is much more associative and conceptual than mimetic or generic. I see two possible ways to substantiate such an assertive and speculative thesis. The first is to study the way Wong absorbs and ultimately distinguishes himself from previous artists in the traditions in which he works. Such a project would entail a thoroughgoing analysis of literary and cinematic traditions in which Wong operates. The second is to analyze in great detail the best example of the new relationship, so as to make my claims as explicit as possible and offer them as contributions to the ongoing critical conversation. Since it is impossible to pursue both options within the confines of this chapter, my solution is to indicate the broad lines of influence and then follow with a detailed comparative textual analysis.

How can one hope to trace the patterns of influence on Wong and narrate the origins and evolution of his unique cine-literary aesthetic? Teo suggests that Wong's understanding of the relationship between film and fiction derives mainly from "literary" directors like Alain Resnais, who transformed literature "into images of pure cinema through composition, lighting and camera movements" (Teo 2005b: 3). If Wong's dialogues are "highly literate and poetic," argues Teo, it is because they are directly influenced by writers from across the world: Latin America's Manuel Puig and Julio Cortázar, Japan's Haruki Murakami, and Hong Kong's own Jin Yong and Liu Yichang. The questions are why Wong was attracted to those figures, whether they share attributes that contribute to his aesthetic philosophy, and how and why he chose to adapt aspects of their writing. If Brunette is right to see Wong as part of a global postmodern movement now shaping the future of cinema, then we would like to know the basic features of that movement and how, specifically, he fits in.[4]

The first thing to note is that Resnais, Wong, and the writers mentioned all tend to consider fiction, film, and even photography as interdependent representational and narrative media. Resnais—an iconic French director associated with both the French New Wave and the Left Bank—worked with the texts of Vietnam-born French writer Marguerite Duras and the Argentinian novelist Adolfo Bioy Casares. He uses an experimental cinema to interpret Duras's postmodern writing in a way that creates revolutionary interpretations of memories in flashbacks. By the same token, Julio Cortázar's short story *Las Babas del Diablo* (1959) about an amateur photographer who loses himself in his images famously inspired Michelangelo Antonioni's 1966 classic *Blowup,* while Manuel Puig's *Kiss of the Spider Woman* (1976) was adapted into both a 1983 stage play by the author himself and a 1985 film with the same title directed by Hector Babenco.

These directors and writers also share a thematic focus on the individual and collective psychology of memory. What interests Resnais about the human mind is that we not only have to remember what has already happened, we also "have to imagine what is going to happen in our heads" (Wilson 2006). In different ways Resnais, Duras, Cortázar, Puig, and Antonioni represent and analyze the interplay between remembrance and anticipation and often link these processes to much wider historical movements such as the diasporic experience of boundary-crossing modern citizens.[5] Along with all of this, Wong shares two other crucial intellectual investments with these predecessors: he represents his characters' localized historical consciousness, and he directly mixes literature and cinema so as to make them speak to each other.

With this brief, broad genealogy in mind, I turn now to Wong's adaptation of Liu's *Intersection* into *In the Mood for Love.* Not only was this adaptation a blockbuster hit—it won thirty-one awards in major film-festival competitions—but it is also the single best example for understanding how Wong has altered the relationship between Chinese film and literature. Instead of reconstructing the literary text, Wong creates a new story line, thereby challenging the assumption shared by many adaptation scholars that "narrative" is the property that makes the two media commensurable.[6] Liberating filmic adaptation from almost every question of fidelity, Wong's style pushes us to recognize what I call "abstract adaptation," a style that demotes the Aristotelian elements but creates a new theoretical dialogue about how film and literature can intersect to reproduce the aesthetic resonances and social preoccupations of specific historical contexts.

For Liu and Wong the context at issue is 1960s Hong Kong, a setting that both artists have personal and philosophical reasons to explore. They are both Shanghainese immigrants: Wong moved to Hong Kong in 1963, when he was five, and Liu Yichang in 1948, when he was thirty. Although they entered into the expatriate community—a stronghold of diasporic mainland culture—at different ages, they share anxiety over the ways a rapidly evolving capitalist economy in Hong Kong has redefined gender and class relations and disintegrated other familial values. For Liu, in particular, Hong Kong's capitalist economy erodes humanity in a way that escalates the individual's insatiable desire for self-indulgence in materialistic comfort. For Wong, a capitalist economy prioritizes work over family and changes the traditional structure of a marriage. Working married women become newly able to earn their financial independence and raise the standard of living, but at the same time they get trapped between what Janet Salaff calls the demands of "the centripetal family" (1995: 44) and a modern woman's personal desire for self-fulfillment.

Often seen as an unofficial sequel to *The Days of Being Wild* (1991) and a prequel to *2046* (2004), Wong's *In the Mood for Love,* takes place from 1962–1966 and features, by way of a quasi plot, a flirtation between two married people, Mrs. Chan (Maggie Cheung) and Mr. Chow (Tony Leung), whose spouses are having an affair with each other. They are first thrown together when a coincidental hunt for an apartment in Hong Kong leads them to become neighbors in a community full of the watchful eyes of Shanghainese expatriates. They flirt, confabulate, and commiserate. The passage of time is marked by the change of Mrs. Chan's cheongsams (*qipao*), a slow, circular process that mimics the stagnancy of their relationship. They finally part ways: Mrs. Chan returns to her husband and Mr. Chow moves by himself to Singapore. They almost cross paths again in their old neighborhood, but the film concludes without a happy ending.

Liu's novella follows the life and dreams of two unacquainted protagonists: an old Shanghainese immigrant Chun Yubai and a young Hong Kong girl Yaxing. While the old man reminiscences about his extravagant Shanghai past and laments the grim reality of his Hong Kong present, the teenaged girl indulges herself in get-rich-quick reveries of becoming a singer or a movie star. Liu uses literary cross-cutting to align their daylong meanderings, which climax, not coincidentally, in an encounter between the two at the movie theater. Although they exchange no words, their interior monologues show they mutually distrust each other. Liu's ending has the two going separate ways after the show and continuing their dreams about the past and future.

While Liu's first experimental novel—*The Drunkard,* published in 1963—served as the inspiration for Wong Kar-wai's *2046, Intersection* especially intrigued Wong with its stylistic commitment to exploring the parallel movements of different minds. Liu mentions in several interviews that the original inspiration for the story happened in 1972 when he bought a pair of stamps from a London auction: "'*dui dao*' [intersection] is a philatelic term which translates the French "*tête-bêche,*" meaning twin stamps positioned upside down to each other" (Liu 2005: 21). Figure 4.1, which shows the cover of *Dui dao,* illustrates such a juxtaposition. In a 2005 interview, Liu noted that for him "the parallel narrative structure creates the best contrasting effects in storytelling" (21).

In *tête-bêche,* Wong finds not just an interesting arrangement of two images but the makings of an aesthetic philosophy. Far beyond the "terminology of stamp collection" or the "methodology of novel-writing," he notes, it has the potential to be "a language of cinema," to express "the intersection of lights and colors, sounds and images." In fact, the concept of

Figure 4.1 The book cover of Liu Yichang's Intersection.

tête-bêche "can even be seen as the intersection of times," as when "a novel published in 1972 and a movie screened in 2000 are interwoven into a story of the 1960s" (Wong 2005: 335).[7]

Wong's ideas about *tête-bêche* are important to consider because his method of adaptation is radical. No other director—not even Stanley Kwan or Ann Hui—challenges as aggressively as he does the conventional aesthetics of the narratological approach to adaptation. In fact I am tempted to nominate this film as the purest example of what Dudley Andrew considers an "organic" and "aesthetic" respect for the source text, that is, when the "uniqueness of the original text is preserved to such an extent that it is intentionally left unassimilated in adaptation" (1984: 99). In my view what matters most is that Wong takes both the formalist and historicist halves of his *tête-bêche* theory equally seriously. First, as we will see, he "images" Liu's novel directly on the screen by condensing his text into stills: three separate quotations in—one could also say *as*—the movie. An opening shot, an intertitle, and a concluding still represent his specific literary and cinematic con-

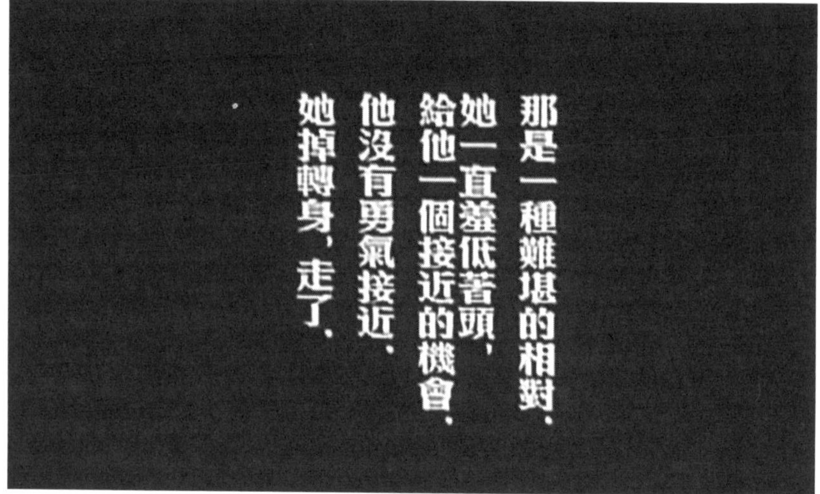

Figure 4.2 Text as image in the opening of *In the Mood for Love*.

tacts—words as images—and transform the viewer, however momentarily, into a reader of Liu's novel. Next, Wong intersects Liu's text by representing the historical consciousness unique to 1960s Hong Kong. Wong, following Liu, shows characters interacting with the materialistic environment and mingling private memories with the social history of the city.

Wong opens the movie with an intersection, a quote from Liu's text (Figure 4.2). Translated, it reads: "That was a very uncomfortable encounter./She kept her head lower out of shyness./To give him an opportunity to come closer./He had no courage to approach her./She turned around and was gone." Here we have what Wong calls "the language of cinema": the prose has been poeticized in its layout, cadence, and imagery. In fact, this cinematic quote calls for a kind of literary analysis that foreshadows the parallelism of visual constructs in the movie. It speaks of an encounter (*xiangdui*), an original *tête-bêche* that evolves into a paralyzing face-off. It mimics a kind of inverted twinship that suggests at once similarities—shared inertia in *xiu di zhe tou* (she kept her head lower out of shyness) and *mei you yong qi jie ji* (he could not approach her for lack of courage) and differences (she finally turns around and is gone). This fifth line, which stands all by itself, abruptly ends the narrative stasis: the girl takes control and walks away. Thus, despite the interpersonal contract or potential for it implied by this quotation, it seems to have its own organic existence. It is a self-contained narrative-as-image, one intersecting only tangentially, or emblematically, with the narrative framework of each person's story, perhaps the way a stamp on an envelope provides an ephemeral but necessary contact between a sender and a recipient.

The form (inverted parallelism) and narrative (romantic paralysis) of the quotation anticipate several critical moments in the film. One is the human-as-object critique of the overall capitalist entrapment in Hong Kong in the 1960s. Accessories such as women's handbags and men's ties appear in the film as symbolic gendered commodities whose value decreases as their numbers multiply. As they become deromanticized, these objects reflect and even personify the two protagonists. Wong brilliantly structures several different but equally effective dialogic scenes in which the back and forth shot-reverse-shot mimics the inverted stamps that inspire both Liu Yichang and Wong.

Viewers first encounter this kind of formalized, commodified construction of humanity in the film's only scene of dialogue between Mrs. Chan and her husband. Mr. Chan is packing, getting ready for a business trip to Japan, and Mrs. Chan is getting dressed. Wong's camera shows briefly the mid to lower sections of the characters' bodies, which are literally truncated by the overpowering presence of the briefcase in the foreground (Figure 4.3).

Although Wong explains in interviews that these midsection shots attempt to mimic the viewing range of a child—an autobiographical standpoint that reconstructs Wong's own recollection of how he as a five-year-old

Figure 4.3 Preparing for a business trip, truncated bodies, with briefcase dominating the foreground.

Figure 4.4 Image of Mrs. Chan in the mirror, straightening her stockings.

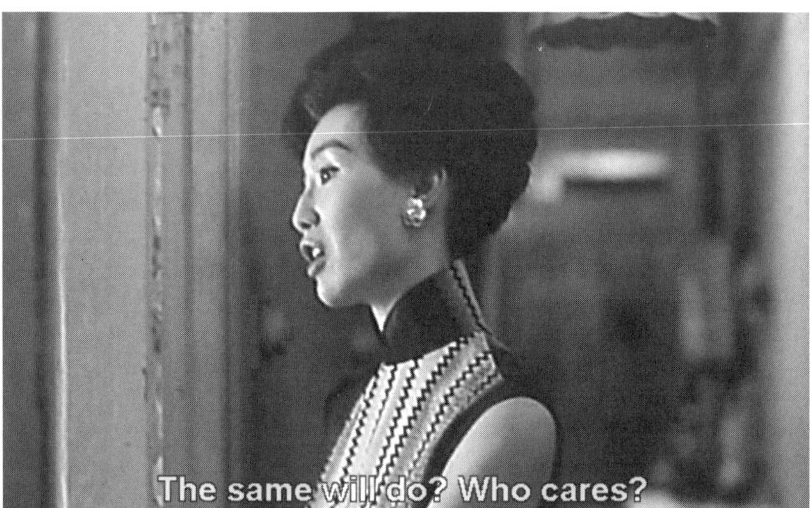

Figure 4.5 Mrs. Chan laconically asks Mr. Chan to bring back identical handbags for her boss's wife and mistress.

saw the adults interact with each other when they first moved to Hong Kong in 1963,[8] they are also quite consistent with the general moral tenet of the film that prioritizes work over family. In particular, Wong's camera foregrounds the briefcase in a way that essentializes its symbolic meaning as an agent of transactions. It literally and metaphorically blocks the intimacy of the couple's private communication. Like Stanley Kwan, Wong also effectively uses reflections in mirrors to probe into the psychology of his characters. In Figure 4.4, Mr. Chan moves to one side and exposes the multiplied and yet fragmented image of Mrs. Chan in a mirror. Fully engaged in the act of dressing for work, she is smoothing out her stocking and speaking distractedly to her husband, visibly torn by multiple pressures. Even their personal space is dominated by professional worries so it is not surprising that their parting words are workmanlike.

In the same scene Wong also accentuates the capitalist commodification of human value by making Mrs. Chan play the role of a gift-bearing broker for her boss. Before leaving for work, Mrs. Chan smartly asks Mr. Chan to bring back from Japan two identical women's handbags, one for the wife of Mrs. Chan's boss and the other for his mistress (Figure 4.5). There is no need to buy the bags in different colors, Mrs. Chan explains, because these two women are never expected to see each other: they live in parallel universes, intersecting only symbolically through the handbags and sexually through a shared partner. That Mrs. Chan colludes with her boss in shielding his adultery from his wife makes it all the more ironic when she later becomes a victim of her own trick: her husband gives her and his mistress identical handbags that he has brought back from an overseas trip.

Wong announces this accidental discovery in a critical scene in which Mr. Chow sees Mrs. Chan carrying the same handbag that his wife has. On the basis of this discovery, he initiates a meeting with Mrs. Chan, a rendez-

Figure 4.6 Mr. Chow sees Mrs. Chan carrying the same handbag as his wife.

vous that leads to their mutual confessions about their spouses' infidelities. In Figure 4.6, the viewer sees Mrs. Chan returning from a movie alone and being startled by Mr. Chow emerging from her apartment house. This is an unmistakable human-as-object moment during which Mrs. Chan is of interest to Mr. Chow only, it seems, because of her handbag, which appears to resemble that of his wife. Ironically, if the handbag is expected to perform as a gesture of romantic goodwill, its value is obviated by its being one of the many identical items. A similar logic applies to Mr. Chow's tie (Figure 4.7). During their coffee date, Mrs. Chan inquires about Mr. Chow's tie, because her husband has the exact same one. It becomes clear to the viewer that Mrs. Chow gave the two-of-a-kind accessory to both her husband and lover. Noticeably, Wong refuses to use close-ups to isolate the objects in these two shots; instead, he chooses to let the purse and tie appear in a larger, more natural context in which they are seen carried, worn, and integrated into the everyday life of the characters. Their naturalized appearances thus strengthen an existential link between owners and their possessions: you are what you have.

Wong objectifies human value in a way that echoes Liu's critique of the middle-class obsession with money, image, sex, and materialism. But there are important differences. Wong's figures are productive workers, while Liu's are leisured consumers. Wong largely confines his characters to indoor crammed spaces—offices, apartments, and restaurants—but Liu takes his readers out onto the streets of Hong Kong. These distinct approaches cre-

Figure 4.7 Mr. Chow wearing the same tie as Mr. Chan.

ate complementary perspectives that sketch out the diverse facets of Hong Kong's city life in the 1960s.

If Wong uses the contrasting and yet comparable perspectives of Mrs. Chan and Mr. Chow as an exemplary construct of *tête-bêche,* Liu juxtaposes the diverging viewpoints of an old male immigrant and a young local girl to scrutinize Hong Kong's populated commercial region of Mongkok. Documenting the cityscape with the prosaic impressions of his characters, Liu provides cinematic "panning" shots of a city view that Wong is unable to reproduce.[9] The following two passages show the ways the figures interact differently with the same street scene. First, Chu Yubai tours a familiar place:

> This was Mongkok. He didn't remember how many times he had walked on the same street before. There were simply too many pedestrians and too many cars here. Mongkok had always been crowded. Everyone seemed to have important matters to tend to and those people working up a sweat were not necessarily rushing to buy gold. The Japanese dolls in the department stores were wearing a cute smile. The female singer in the opera house had undergone cosmetic surgery to create double-fold eyelids. The rotating restaurant. Acceptance of prepayment for next year's mooncakes is now available. This edition is all 30 percent off. Offer of giant crabs from Foreign Clear Lake will be available at 3 PM tomorrow. Steamed shrimp dumplings and spring rolls and taro cakes and bean noodles and barbecue buns.... (Liu 2005: 75)

Yubai's gaze unites three basic human desires: money (fluctuations in gold prices and the stock market), sex (beautiful stars remaking themselves with cosmetic surgery), and food (sumptuous advertisements of dumplings, giant crabs, and so forth). But there is also an important tension in this passage, reflected in the way Yubai is both disdainful and respectful, a critic of Hong Kong's commercial excess and an avid consumer of its capitalist goods. This bind creates a sense of contradiction, for the crowds are both comforting and problematic, bringing energy and diversity but also chaos and greed: doing anything to get rich moves the city forward.

My translation of this passage switches tenses from past to present in the last part to reflect a key change in Yubai's relations with the environment. By the end of the section he stops being a social critic deriding the city's overdeveloped sensual imagery and instead becomes an active participant in savoring it. The present tense marks a shift in psychological state from discontent to excitement.

No longer calmly looking, he is now actively reading signs and searching for a place to eat; the array of choices only heightens his expectations.

True to the form and structure of *tête-bêche,* Liu juxtaposes Yubai's critical scrutiny with Yaxing's mundane survey of the same street scene. This offers the reader another outlook on this place and era of social change:

> Next to the photo shop was a toy store. Next to the toy store sat an optometrist's. Next to the optometrist's was a gold shop. Next to the gold shop was a restaurant. Next to the restaurant was a grocery store. Next to the grocery store was a trendy fashion store. Yaxing walked into the trendy clothes store and saw a few strange-looking trendy shirts: one was printed with a gigantic mouth; another had two hearts; one showed dozens of footprints. There was also one with many prints of "I LOVE YOUs." Yaxing was most interested in the one with prints of "I LOVE YOU." "Mama doesn't know English," she thought to herself, "if I buy this and bring it home, mama won't fly into a rage.... If I wear this shirt, perhaps I can attract new men to come talk to me." (79)

Gone are Yubai's self-conscious musings in intricate syntax. Yaxing uses simple, repetitive, and nonreflective language, mechanically listing and itemizing stores in a way that registers her indifference to most of them. Living in a world overloaded with stimuli, Yaxing is drawn only to people, places, and objects that appeal directly to her senses and desires. Not surprisingly, the monotony of her gaze is temporarily suspended by in-your-face crude symbolism: common English phrases in shouting capitals. Unabashedly superficial, she belongs to a postwar generation too desensitized to decode nuanced emotional expressions. That Yaxing chooses a phrase over pictures further reminds us of the film's opening quote in which Wong uses "words-as-images" to break the boundary between literature and cinema. For Yaxing's generation, the fashionable English phrase, repeated Warhol-style on the shirt, has a more immediate appeal.

On the whole, despite their different experiences and expectations, both Yubai and Yaxing share an appreciation for what Hong Kong has to offer as a unique commercial port. As Liu explains in a 2001 symposium of his work, the virtually plot-free *Intersection* presents the vibrant "local color" (*ben tu se cai*) of Hong Kong (2005: 241). Both characters experience street scenes in ways that emphasize "consumer values, media symbols, public goods like housing, and education," and both passages illustrate the general diversity and freedom of a capitalist city that is on par with Tokyo, Paris, and New

Figure 4.8 The labor-saving rice cooker Mr. Chan gives Mrs. Chan.

York (Salaff 1995: xxix).[10] As a result we are tempted to see Yubai and Yaxing as modern flaneurs who recognize what Jonathan Raban calls "the plastic" (1998: 9) nature of cities, which allows the residents to remake themselves by "possessions and appearances" (Harvey 1990: 3). Yaxing confirms this with her naïve hope that shirts emblazoned with "I LOVE YOUs" will enhance her sexual attraction.

Like Liu, Wong points out a kind of naïveté (or perhaps optimism) about the correlation between commodities and quality of life. He illustrates the ways that materialistic desires have economic and cultural consequences in the inauguration of Mrs. Chan's electric rice cooker (Figure 4.8).

Purchased by Mr. Chan on a business trip to Japan, the new cooking device impresses the whole community. It is automatic, with a self-regulating mechanism that requires little human intervention and saves female labor.[11] Mrs. Chan's landlady, Mrs. Suen, has told Mr. Chow that he should buy one of the devices for his wife because she often works late, the implication being, of course, that this will allow the couple to enjoy a more relaxed family meal, because their dining ritual has been eroded by their dual professional demands. At the same time, however, a decrease in domestic labor is also expected to increase women's industrial productivity: now she will have more time to work harder on the job.

In addition, the rice cooker promises to give women more leisure time, as we see in Figure 4.9, which shows Mrs. Chan sitting apart from the commotion and reading a newspaper. She has an above-the-fray smugness

Figure 4.9 The rice cooker frees Mrs. Chan to read the newspaper.

about her new freedom to cultivate personal interests such as reading serialized martial arts stories, going to the movies late at night, and having coffee or dining out with friends.

Mrs. Chan's pursuit of bourgeois individualism distinguishes her from the women we have seen in other chapters: Jen in *Crouching Tiger,* Lotus in *Raise the Red Lantern,* and Yanli in *Red Rose/White Rose.* She is a married, working, middle-class woman who regularly is in the company of men other than her husband. Still, Wong is very careful to show how her modern freedoms conflict with the traditional expectations of being homebound, submissive, and faithful. The tensions sometimes paralyze her, as in her first coffee date with Mr. Chow, when both characters are endeavoring, without letting the other know, to find out why their spouses are having an affair with each other. Wong constructs the scene as a horizontal, dialogic version of *tête-bêche* in which shot-reverse-shots suggest that the one character is only ever the other's half. This technique structures a kind of visual tug-of-war, a thesis-antithesis that never produces a synthesis, as Wong's shot composition again reenacts the symmetrical aesthetic from the film's opening quotation.

Wong starts the scene with an abstract establishing shot that reveals an undistinguished decor of an indistinct location. He then stages a medium-long look of the couple partially concealed behind the tall booth (Figure 4.10). The solid impenetrable wall is emblematic of the defense mechanisms of Mrs. Chan and Mr. Chow, who seek to outmaneuver each other rhetorically. Similar to an earlier dialogic scene between Mr. Chan and Mrs. Chan, this distant view

Figurer 4.10 Mrs. Chan and Mr. Chow partially obscured by the restaurant booth where they are sitting.

calls attention to the obstructive staging, which reinforces a sense of restraints and barriers. But Wong's camera moves quickly to set up more conventional shot-reverse-shots, giving the viewer access to the intense exchange between the main characters. At the same time, he meticulously ensures that every shot reveals as well as obscures the emotional turmoil of each character. He uses profile shots, which add a third dimension to the two-dimensional image of *tête-bêche* and deflect us from seeing the characters' internal struggles with lying and truth-telling straight on. Even more strikingly, his camera insistently frames only the lower halves of the characters' faces and thereby draws attention to their body language. We see this in the following two shots (Figures 4.11 and 4.12) where Wang creates mirroring images of Mrs. Chan and Mr. Chow in a stylized, *tableau-vivant*-style composition.

Very few directors would be as bold as Wong to half-decapitate his actors on the screen. But in the spirit of less is more, and, as we saw earlier in his meaningful truncation of his characters' bodies, Wong succeeds in conveying a sense of the incompleteness, fractalization, and mutilation of these characters' emotions. Their *xiangdui* (face-to-face) shows a shared anguish about their diminished egos: they are the less desirable partners in their marriages, unlike their spouses (*ling yi ban*),[12] who document their sexual escapades by purchasing mass-produced, intentionally expensive but easily replaceable souvenirs.

In fact, the attractiveness of these accessories entraps both Mrs. Chan and Mr. Chow, because despite their suspicions and even knowledge of their

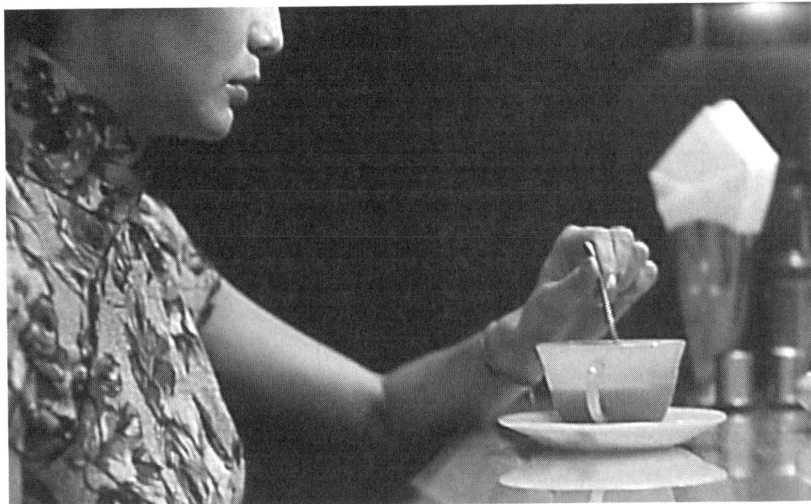

Figure 4.11 Mrs. Chan in cut profile.

Figure 4.12 Mr. Chow facing Mrs. Chan in cut profile.

spouses' infidelity, they are unable to simply forgo either the objects or their marriages. Boxed into a middle-class posture, appearance, and morality, they each wear constricting formal clothes (a tight *qipao* with a high neckline; a relentlessly confining tie) as they sit civilly opposite each other, stirring and sipping half-full cups of a Western beverage. Their coffee date leads to a desire to get into the minds of their "other halves" and to imagine how,

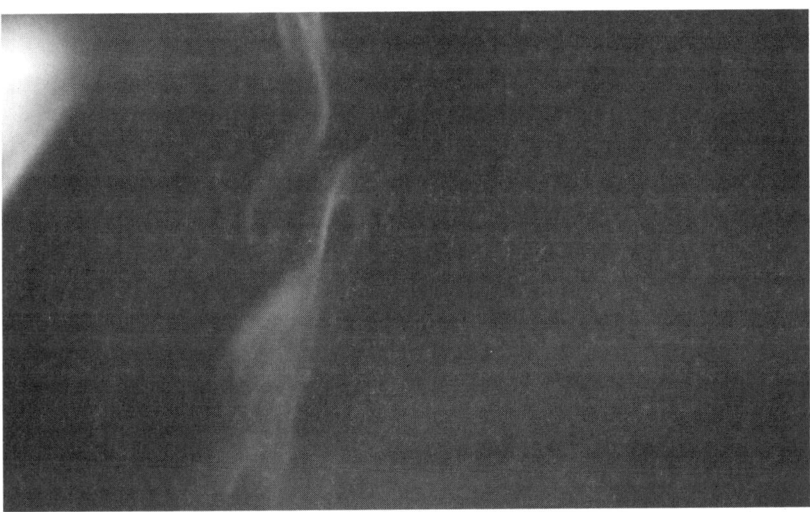

Figure 4.13 Kwan's smoke screen provides a pause for reflection.

right under their noses, the affair began. Like Resnais, Duras, Antonioni, and others, Wong is keen to explore the psychological torments of modern citizens. Here he accomplishes this by using vacant space to give free rein to speculations, suspicions, and other mind games. In the last shot of the scene (Figure 4.13), Wong literally uses a smoke screen to provide the characters and the viewers with a reflective pause on why their marriages go astray. Once again Wong has boldly distinguished himself from other Chinese directors (especially Zhang Yimou and Stanley Kwan) by enigmatically leaving a screen empty of interpretable and tangible symbols.[13] Instead, he allows the audience to conjure up various scenarios. Who is to be blamed for the extramarital affairs? Is Mr. Chow so oblivious a spouse that he lets his wife run wild, as Mrs. Chan insinuates? Or is Mrs. Chan herself too tolerant of her husband's rampant sexual adventures? Wong ends their first outing with a shot of their backs as they walk side by side along an empty street (Figure 4.14). Their synchronized steps accompany their retrospective thinking: rather than moving forward to find a solution to their current marital crisis, they both look backward, playing detective to reconstruct the origin of the ongoing extramarital affair.[14] Mrs. Chan's query—"I wonder how it began?"—triggers a series of hypothetical scenarios in which the two walk in the shoes of their respective spouses trying to trace their (mis)steps.[15] These acts of looking back show that both characters are pacing in circles, both stuck in the moralistic dictum "we are not like them," as they each declare on separate occasions. Implicitly both assert they are better.

Figure 4.14 Mr. Chow and Mrs. Chan, seen from the rear leaving the restaurant, wondering how their spouses began their affair.

Maybe they are, and maybe not. What is sure is that they are experiencing life in several Hong Kongs all at once: old and new, stagnant and progressive, local and global. All are colliding in the 1960s and 1970s, a time when wars, revolutions, and socialist and nationalist movements were raging around the world and echoing in Hong Kong.[16] Such sweeping ideological and social ferment contrasts with the placidity and political emptiness of these characters' self-indulgent psyches. And yet the larger forces inscribe themselves in the formal parallelisms that abound in Wong's film. One example is the dizzying international choreography: Mrs. Chan works for a travel agency and her husband frequently travels at home and abroad; Mr. Chow goes to Singapore and Cambodia before returning to Hong Kong; Mrs. Chow also travels to Japan and other places; the landlords of both families immigrate, one to the United States and one to the Philippines. All this mobility reflects the growth of an educated middle class that connects Hong Kong to the rest of the world. But the paradox that interests Wong, and which he represents with varying degrees of irony, is that all of these characters also remain bound by a centripetal Confucian familial structure "characterized by the drawing inward of the family resources and creation of long-term interpersonal links" (Salaff 1995: 44). This is especially visible in Mrs. Chan's unconditional compliance with the moral standards of the expatriate Shanghainese community, in which her landlady, Mrs. Suen, serves as the surrogate matriarch of the extended family.[17] The inertia and hypocrisy of this old structure become palpable as Mrs. Suen and her friends remove themselves from the productive force of Hong Kong society to engage in time-killing games of mahjong or, in the case of Mr. Koo, in drinking themselves to oblivion. This sense of paralytic claustrophobia, perfectly crystallized in the figure of Mrs. Chan, captures the unique local conditions in Hong Kong as a colonized city uncertain about its own national identity and democratic future.

Liu uses interior monologues to expose his characters' similar anxieties about a fragmenting modern world. In the most important scene of the novel, the male immigrant Yubai and the female local Yaxing happen to sit next to each other at a movie theater. Yaxing finds Yubai too old, while Yubai thinks that Yaxing is only average-looking but has large, attractive breasts. Liu describes in some detail the ways they think of each other without their actually exchanging a word: Yaxing is offended by Yubai's unrelenting interest in her breasts, while Yubai speculates on whether the teenager is wearing a bra or has surgically enhanced her breasts.

Silently trading gazes and barbs, the two are temporarily distracted by the preview of a pornographic film. Yubai is morally outraged by it:

> "Banning the public screening of a corrupt movie is as important as sending the criminals to jail. Why can't the Hong Kong government ban such corrupt movies? Considering how terrible Hong Kong's social order has been, can we still call it 'the Window of Democracy'? If democracy amounts to this, what's so good about democracy?"
>
> Right at this moment, the lights went off in the theater. The feature started. This was a romance and the filmmaker constructed a compelling plot to draw the audience into the story. The female protagonist was very beautiful; she had the look of a young Helen Hayes; the male lead was very handsome.
>
> Yaxing thought: "I like this male lead. It is best to marry someone like him. In the future, I would be so happy if my husband is as good-looking as he is."
>
> Chun Yubai thought: "This protagonist looks exactly like Helen Hayes forty years ago. Forty years ago, I used to put Helen Hayes's picture up on the wall next to my bed." (Liu 2005: 138–139)

This scene juxtaposes the voices of three figures—Yubai, the narrator, and Yaxing—and exposes the hypocrisy of a conservative political ideology. Yubai's speech is that of a free individual, but his call for interventionist social policies reveals his disingenuousness. Behaving like a pedophile himself (he believes that Yaxing is a fourteen- or fifteen-year-old), Yubai feels exposed by the pornographic preview that screens his own dirty secrets. Solipsistically, he attempts to cover up his own oversexualization of Hong Kong life by attributing it to a deteriorating social order and to pornography. Democracy itself, it seems, is to be blamed for fostering a liberal culture that breeds such vice.[18] The narrator's comment on the movie further provides a compelling contrast between the show being screened in the novel and the novel itself; the narrator lists three of the movie's attractive characteristics that are ostensibly absent in the novel: romance, plot, and iconic protagonists. Liu's own story features neither romance nor plot, and Yubai and Yaxing do not have iconic star power. It is almost as if the narrator were seeking to ensure that the reader see the differences between Liu's story and a conventional Hollywood narrative drama.

Liu is more concerned to *present* than to *integrate* the multiplicity of temporal and spatial viewpoints in a fragmented modern society. Yaxing's stream of consciousness, for example, reveals thoughts about marriage and a superficial association of good looks with a good life. Yubai's reminiscences, on the other hand, take a nostalgic plunge into the past: the actress who looks like Helen Hayes reminds him of his youthful dreams. Despite the fact they are simultaneously watching the same picture on the screen, Yubai and Yaxing embrace the hopes and fantasies of very different eras.

Figure 4.15 Kwan's object-centered interests begin scene with long panning shot of a radio.

The way Liu uses the movie theater to screen the characters' different thoughts recalls Wong's earlier experiment with quotes to foreshadow the actors' divergent paths. When their "friendship" finally reaches a breaking point, Mrs. Chan and Mr. Chow are forced to decide whether they should stop seeing each other or move forward to consummate their relationship. Consistent with the film's object-centered obsessions, the scene begins with a long panning shot of a radio (Figure 4.15). In a close-up, Wong's camera then caresses the surface of the radio slowly and horizontally as the radio announces Mr. Chan's happy-birthday wishes to Mrs. Chan from abroad. He requests a song for her: Zhou Xuan's "In Full Bloom," or "Huang Yang Nian Hua," which was the original Chinese title of the movie. The radio—a larger-than-life symbol in this shot—materializes the emotional message that Mr. Chan hopes will bind Mrs. Chan to their marriage. Zhou's song shows Mrs. Chan's nostalgic musical taste. A popular Chinese actress and singer in the 1930s and 1940s, Zhou's "golden voice" represents a bygone era in Shanghai—the besieged "orphan island"—whose ambivalent national identity as a colonized city mimics the ambiguous political status of Hong Kong.[19] Believing in the familiar tunes of old Shanghai, Mrs. Chan shares with Chun Yubai an out-of-date vision of life and a sense of disjointing confusion. In this modern era of busy air travel and radio transmission, she is too behind the times to challenge the moral constraints that suppress her personal desire.

Throughout the film Wong employs different styles of dialogic scenes and variations of shot-reverse-shots to reveal the characters' emotional depths, adapting with special sensitivity Liu's technique of contrasting parallelism: he juxtaposes Mrs. Chan's old-fashioned visions with Mr. Chow's future-oriented mind; he shows how the people around Mrs. Chan (a travel agent who seldom travels) travel and eventually move away, but how she, more than four years later, moves back to the same apartment where she first met Mr. Chow; Wong emphasizes the contrast between her circular motion and the purposeful forward movement of other characters. Finally, while Liu has his characters try to escape the confusion of modern life in a movie theater, Wong shows them attempting to create an alternative universe in escapist literature: Mr. Chow writes martial arts fiction, and Mrs. Chan, an avid reader of the genre, at times works as Mr. Chow's unpaid editor. For the viewer these and other formal/structural examples create a psychological atmosphere, or world, permeated with the asymmetries of paradox, hypocrisy, and duplicity.

One last example will show how meticulously Wong has adopted and expanded Liu's aesthetic vision of *tête-bêche* into filmmaking. Wong exploits the plastic nature of intersection by experimenting with what seems like

Figure 4.16 Kwan's visualization of *tête-bêche*; Mrs. Chan caught between two men on one side of a wall

Figure 4.17 Kwan's visualization of *tête-bêche*; Mr. Chow sitting on the other side of the wall, holding the unused rice cooker in his lap.

a structural parody of it: he has the two protagonists sit motionlessly on either side of the same wall, the mise-en-scène projecting an active reflection on their static predicament. Mrs. Chan is listening to Zhou's song in a subdued, contemplative posture (Figure 4.16). Holding a glass of tea, she sits alone between two walls. Wong's mise-en-scène illustrates her psychological dilemma in the crammed space: she is sandwiched between two men and remains in a state of paralysis because of her indecision. While Zhou Xuan's song about a "happy family" makes an ironic comment on Mrs. Chan's situation, it also solidifies her sense of duty to her marriage. It is not an accident that Wong places Mrs. Chan in the kitchen, a symbolic site of the familial hearth that houses the core values of a marriage.

Slowly Wong's camera moves to the left and reveals a pensive Chow holding a rice cooker on his lap (Figure 4.17). Sitting in a similar position on the opposite side of the wall, Mr. Chow not only mirrors Mrs. Chan's position but also seems to share her quandary. Consciously caressing the massiveness of the wall, Wong's camera reminds the viewer of how insurmountable the barrier between the two is. In fact, Wong stages the symmetrical movement as an aestheticized form of shot-reverse-shot with the characters, looking away from each other, engaged in a kind of telepathic dialogue. Mr. Chow is holding an unused rice cooker, the emptiness of which exacerbates the bareness of a deserted kitchen in the background. In Chow's stale and listless life there is no hearth, only a dissolving marriage in which both people are drifting into affairs, and the rice cooker ironically reminds him and the viewer how once its newfangled industrial appeal promised to improve Mr. Chow's marriage. But now, while Mrs. Chan listens to the radio and looks to the past for answers about her marital future, Mr. Chow has already made plans to move forward. He has asked for a transfer to the news bureau in Singapore.

Figure 4.18 Mrs. Chan's contemplation gives way to dejection.

When the camera moves gradually back to Mrs. Chan, we see her leaning dejectedly against the wall, which has grown in size on the screen (Figure 4.18). Wong's slow panning shot of the wall evokes the earlier screening of the radio and suggests that Mrs. Chan has resigned herself to the fact that she needs to save her marriage and stay with her husband. Still, her body language speaks of languor and defeat, a giving in to the wall that creates an indomitable barricade. Despite her professional success, Mrs. Chan's compliance and passivity make her seem like a dated figure. Thus the scene culminates in a temporal *tête-bêche.*

Unlike the directors and writers in the first three chapters, Wong does not construct progressive figures or develop a feminist consciousness within the film to critique or redefine gender relations. Instead his film presents the complexity of human emotions from outside, in ways that expose the moral and social predicaments of working married women in the 1960s in Hong Kong. The audience sees the main characters in their circumscribed environments: crammed apartments, narrow walkways, deserted streets, forgettable restaurants, and dehumanized office spaces. Mimicking these imprisonments, Wong uses material metaphors—men's ties, women's handbags and cheongsams, an electric rice cooker—to show the constraints on the characters' minds and behaviors and to provide reasons for why they never achieve consciousness of their shared predicament. The commodities organize the protagonists' desires in Hong Kong's burgeoning capitalist market, and the fact that cultural and individual identity equate so easily to the possession and display of merchandise makes the viewer all the more aware of how ideology emerges from, or is reinforced by, material surroundings. Ultimately, both Liu and Wong expose Hong Kong's ideological ambivalences about its colonial democracy, capitalist market, and fading Confucian familial values. Wong's film adaptation, extending the formalism of *tête-bêche* into a sociohistorical critique, strikingly visualizes Liu's analysis of the human-as-object paradigm and the psychological discontents of modern citizens.

CHAPTER 5

Dai Sijie

Locating the Third Culture in *Balzac and the Little Chinese Seamstress*

Unlike the writers and directors examined in the other chapters, Dai Sijie is a relatively unknown artist in the Sinophone world. Because China has banned both the film and novel versions of *Balzac and the Little Chinese Seamstress* (novel 2000; film 2002), his most popular work worldwide, curious readers cannot even find his name in the China Film and Television Bureau's 2006 publication *One Hundred Years of Chinese Cinema* (*Zhong guo dian ying bai nian*). This inclusive anthology has allowed more than seventy directors from China, Taiwan, and Hong Kong, many without Dai's global presence, to introduce themselves in their own voice. Nor have Dai's works inspired as many scholarly essays and monographs as have other Chinese directors and writers. This disjunction of being famous abroad but obscure at home is further complicated by the double role that Dai plays in contemporary Chinese cinema: he has adapted his own literary writings into film. And his "doubleness" extends even further, for he uses his second language, French, to write about his homeland, China, and typically works with French producers and crew to make Chinese films. His interdisciplinary and cross-cultural experiences have made him an intermediary figure, uniquely qualified for an exploration of the idea of a hybridized, or "third," culture derived from both national and international perspectives.

Dai's versatility and multiculturalism are compounded by the fact that his texts are richly intertextual: the French novelists Honoré de Balzac, Gustave Flaubert, Alexandre Dumas, and Romain Rolland are just a few of the sources he draws upon. This explains why, despite his Chinese upbringing, Dai's European connection has been the focal point for scholars (Hsieh 2002; Bloom 2005; McCall 2006). Yet Chinese culture has also shaped his art: in his writing, we find Shen Congwen's lyricism and Scar Literature's testimonial realism; in his films, the work of the Fifth and Sixth Generation directors. Thus in Dai's adaptations we can glimpse a third culture artist reworking the binaries into which he has been thrown by politics and history. Typically, his third perspective is indigenous and unofficial, existing outside the dichotomy of a liberating West and an oppressive China. Creating alternative cultural representations to mock dogmatism and moral binarisms,[1] Dai develops perspectives on cultural resistance to Maoist approaches.[2] In so doing he visualizes literature and poeticizes film in ways that are unique among contemporary Chinese authors and directors.

Born in 1954 in Fujian province, Dai Sijie grew up in Chengdu, the capital of Sichuan province in western China. Like many Fifth and Sixth Generation directors,[3] Dai was labeled a "young intellectual" and sent to the countryside for "re-education" during the Cultural Revolution (1966–1976). From 1971 to 1974 he was stationed in a remote mountainous region, Yaan, in Sichuan. After the Cultural Revolution, he entered Sichuan University in 1977 and graduated with a degree in history. In 1982 he earned a government-sponsored fellowship to study in France. This opportunity motivated Dai to study Western civilization and cultural history, art history, and French language for eighteen months before he left for France at the end of 1983. He entered the Université de Paris I and majored in art history. A year later he transferred to the most prestigious film school in France, *L'école nationale supérieure des métiers de l'image et du son* (or Fémis), where he studied for three years.[4]

After graduation Dai Sijie wrote and directed three Chinese films in France: *China, My Sorrow* (*Niu peng* in Chinese; *Chine, ma douleur* in French; 1989), *The Moon Eater* (*Tun yue liang de ren* in Chinese; *Le Mangeur de lune* in French; 1994), and *The Eleventh Child* (*Di shi yi ge zi* in Chinese; *Tang le onzième* in French; 1998). Although *China, My Sorrow* won a special mention and was nominated for the Golden Leopard at the Locarno International Film Festival in Switzerland in 1989, Dai's directing career fizzled. It was not until he wrote his first novel, *Balzac and the Little Chinese Seamstress* (*Xiao cai feng* in Chinese; *Balzac et la petite tailleuse chinoise* in French; 2000) and adapted it into film with the same title in 2002 that Dai secured both commercial and critical success around the globe.

Balzac et la petite tailleuse chinoise won five prestigious literary prizes (Hsieh 2002: 93) and has now been translated into more than thirty languages. After its initial publication in 2000, it instantly sold more than half a million copies in France and in 2003 its paperback translation was listed on the *New York Times* best-sellers list for ten consecutive weeks. Equally popular and influential is the film version, which premiered at the 2002 Cannes Film Festival and was nominated for the best foreign film at the Golden Globe awards in 2003. Dai's second novel, *The Traveling Couch of Mr. Muo* (*Di de qing jie* in Chinese; *Le complexe de Di* in French won a prestigious French Prix Femina in 2003, and his latest film *The Chinese Botanist's Daughters* (*Zhiwu xuejia de nüer* in Chinese; *Les filles du botaniste* in French; 2006) won the People's Choice Award and was nominated for Grand Prix des Amériques at Montréal World Film Festival in 2006. This brief summary confirms that, as Alan Riding noted in the *New York Times,* Dai originally wrote fiction because "his movie career was faltering," but the success of *Balzac* "put his movie career back on track" (2005). What is the appeal of *Balzac,* as literature and as film?

The plot is a familiar one from the period of the Chinese Cultural Revolution. It is a semiautobiographical account of two urban youths from Chengdu who are sent to a remote region, Phoenix Mountain, in Sichuan to be "re-educated by the poor peasants" who are opium farmers-turned-Communists (Dai 2002a: 6). The teenagers' lives are transformed not by the work they perform but by a passion to "civilize" a gorgeous illiterate seamstress and to broaden her perspective of life through a trunk full of stolen Western literature. The story ends on a mixed note: new knowledge leads to both hope and disillusionment.

Despite its blockbuster debut, the critical reception of his story in China, Europe, and the United States was ultimately mixed. Some American critics complain that Dai tends to cater to the French sense of cultural superiority, and that is one of the reasons that the book sold so well there. Yu Zhong, the Chinese translator of *Balzac,* also notes that although the seamstress in the story "represents native Chinese culture," what seduces her in the end is "Balzac and the French culture he embodies," and this plot "panders to the French reader's sense of pride and value judgment."[5] Ironically, some French readers have the opposite criticism: as Dai himself notes in an interview, they like to point out that after the little seamstress comes into contact with Balzac's novel, she becomes more and more shallow, corrupted by superficial Western materialism. Many even accuse Dai of using the French language to mock French culture (Dai 2003b).

Not all critics deride Dai's French connection, however; many commend the ways he uses European culture as an oppositional discourse to challenge Communist totalitarianism. Ian McCall appreciates the way intertextual references to French film and literature provide his protagonists with "an alternative paradigm of love, sexuality and desire, voicing feelings and emotions that are not discussed or deemed desirable" in Chinese culture (2006: 162). Michelle Bloom salutes "Occidentalist" panculturalism for privileging French literature over classical Chinese texts: Dai's *Balzac* is ultimately "much more accessible" than Chinese writers "because more universal" (2005: 314).

Positive or negative, these Eurocentric interpretations tend to see Dai as a dualistic figure who embraces French culture as a means of challenging or rejecting his own. This approach sometimes obscures the fact that Dai sees himself more as a composite than a divisive artist. European and American readers are drawn to the story, he suggests, not for the political reason that they think he is siding with the West but for a more aesthetic one: he uses French culture to tell a serious Chinese story in a winningly humorous way. For general readers this unthreatening hybridization demystifies the loaded, even forbidden, political subject of the Cultural Revolution. "Although there may have been many humorous Chinese stories in the past," Dai explains,

> their sense of humor was often lost in translation. Therefore, a lot of readers think that Chinese novels are very heavy. Now if we take a look at Chinese cinema, each film seems more depressing than the previous one. Since I wrote [*Balzac*] directly in French, my colorful sense of humor is not as compromised (Dai 2003b; my translation).

Dai's argument raises questions about cross-cultural criticism because he and his critics take different positions.[6] While detractors and advocates both tend to center their attention on Dai's Franco-centered perspectives, Dai argues that his work should be read and evaluated in the context of (translated) Chinese literature, because it speaks from a Chinese viewpoint about a local cultural experience. His popularity in the West, Dai contends, is indebted not so much to Francophilia but to his more universally appealing ability to communicate a self-deprecating, comedic diagnosis of a tragic historical period. The ability to provide a French translation of Chinese humor—*that,* says Dai, is what makes him compelling and accessible in the West.

What is the "Chinese humor" that Dai conveys? He explains that the best kind is "self-deprecating mockery" (*zi wo chao feng*),[7] and his novel opens with an example of it. It is 1971, and the two boys, Ma Jianling and Luo Ming, have just arrived at a remote mountain village in Sichuan, western China. Their professionally accomplished parents have been labeled as "enemies of the people" and "reactionar[ies]" and the teenagers, like millions of other city youths before and after them, are exiled for re-education (Dai

2000a: 8–9). Examining the contents of their belongings, the headman—the Communist leader of the village—discovers several forbidden objects. The following conversation shows an important exchange among Luo, Ma, and the headman. The headman wants to burn Ma's violin because he perceives it to be a bourgeois toy, but Luo intervenes and convinces him to let Ma play a Mozart sonata.

> "What's a sonata?" the headman asked warily.
> "I don't know," I faltered. "It's Western."
> "Is it a song?"
> "More or less," I replied evasively.
> At that instant the glint of the vigilant Communist reappeared in the headman's eyes, and his voice turned hostile.
> "What's the name of this song of yours?"
> "Well, it's like a song, but actually it's a sonata."
> "I'm asking you what it's called!" he snapped, fixing me with his gaze.
> Again I was alarmed by the three spots of blood in his left eye.
> "Mozart..." I muttered.
> "Mozart what?"
> "Mozart Is Thinking of Chairman Mao," Luo broke in.
> The audacity! But it worked: as if he had heard something miraculous, the headman's menacing look softened. He crinkled up his eyes in a wide, beatific smile.
> "Mozart thinks of Mao all the time," he said.
> "Indeed, all the time," agreed Luo.
> As soon as I had tightened my bow there was a burst of applause, but I was still nervous. However, as I ran my swollen fingers over the strings, Mozart's phrases came flooding back to me like so many faithful friends. The peasants' faces, so grim a moment before, softened under the influence of Mozart's limpid music like parched earth under a shower, and then, in the dancing light of the oil lamp, they blurred into one.
> I played for some time. Luo lit a cigarette and smoked quietly, like a man. This was our first taste of re-education. Luo was eighteen years old, I was seventeen. (Dai 2002a: 5–6)

In an era of anti-intellectualism, it is natural for the teenagers' re-education to begin with politicization. Mozart must be introduced as a Mao loyalist to mollify the machinery of public scrutiny, and the sonata domesticated and incorporated into the familiar code of the propaganda song to produce acceptable meanings for the rural community. Told from Ma's adolescent viewpoint, the story reveals the teenager's anxiety about a new life of foreseeable physical and psychological toils. Throughout the exchange the narrator remains hesitant: he "faltered," "replied evasively," or "muttered" responses too equivocal to be credible. Such self-doubt contrasts with the headman's assertiveness, which is magnified by Dai's descriptive close-ups: "the glint of the vigilant Communist"; "fixing me with his gaze"; "three spots of blood in his left eye"; "menacing look"; "his eyes in a wide, beatific smile." Associating vision with authority derisively, these close-ups exaggerate the grotesqueness of the inspector and mock the way a tongue-in-cheek improvisation—Mozart thinking of Chairman Mao!—can pacify a Communist loyalist whose political faith seems based on illusion rather than reality. Despite the intensity of his look and looking, the duped headman wills himself to see nothing but plausibility.

The political tensions facilitate Dai's "Chinese humor" by staging dramatic irony: the reader is keenly aware of the incongruity created by Luo's deliberate cross-cultural mistranslation.[8] Especially cinematic is Dai's counterpoint strategy of matching the headman's intimidating look with the narrator's timorous voice, since the comic dissonances contrast with Dai's romantic description of the way Mozart's sonata breaks the spell with harmony. Bathed in difference-dissolving music, the social traumas of China's class antagonism momentarily begin to heal.

The story's transition from being critical and comical to lyrical and even sentimental also marks the shift in the narrative from the personal to the communal. Helping him overcome his earlier stutter, "Mozart's phrases" are for Ma an eloquent universal language that sings without words and travels without borders. The sonata softens the peasants' grim expression and edifies their spirit like the shower on the "parched earth," an image that naturalizes Mozart's heavenly agency. The sudden change of Dai's narrative tone from sacrilegious to reverent also moves the story from tight, humorous dialogues and rapid cinematic "shot-reverse-shot" scenes to clichéd similes, such as the descriptions of Mozart's phrases "like so many faithful friends," the faces of peasants like earth receiving rain, and the suddenly matured Luo smoking "like a man." The characters may be stock figures, but the stylistic shifts are so distinctive that readers cannot help but wonder about their cultural precursors. Despite his sporadic invocations of it in interviews, however, Dai's complex indebtedness to earlier Chinese literary movements represents a cultural bond that has been almost unanimously overlooked in the criticism.[9]

The two literary movements that most directly impact Dai's writing are the "critical lyricism" of the 1930s and the Scar Literature of the 1970s. Dai studied with one of the greatest modern Chinese writers of all time, Shen Congwen (1902–1988), who pioneered what David Wang characterizes as a form of pastoral, rhythmic writing (1992: 203).[10] Dai met Shen because of a family connection: the sister of Shen's wife, Zhang Zhaohe, married the teacher of Dai's mother. When Dai was in Sichuan University, he started corresponding with Shen and sending him his short stories. Over a period of two years, Shen responded with comments and critiques that helped Dai improve his narrative technique. When Dai was studying art in Beijing's Central Art Academy (before leaving for France), he visited Shen several times.[11] Dai's literary connection to Shen partially explains several characteristics in his fiction (and film—a point I will explain later).

First, using an observant style that is never didactic or moralizing, Shen often separates the narrator and the story[12] and cultivates an impersonalized narrative voice analogous to the one adopted by James Joyce in *A Portrait of the Artist as a Young Man*.[13] For example, in Shen's autobiography, which is composed of many episodic narratives, he tells a story based on his own experience about how a beautiful female bandit named Yaomei was executed because she had an affair with a warlord, one of Shen's friends. The gruesome scene of her beheading—smeared with dried blood, ashes, and burned paper money—contrasts with an earlier account of her delicate features and lively beauty. Shen's friend mourns her death for seven days and then declares: "Brother, I am really an unlucky person, and my misfortune caused the death of Yaomei. I cried for seven days, and now I am all better." Shen's autobiographical narrator sees this as "both laughable and pitiful" and, saying nothing, squeezes his friend's hand and smiles (Shen 1971: 101). The narration of the scene is typical of Shen: in tragic circumstances, he often adopts a bird's-eye camera viewpoint and a considered, humorous emotional response. While it may seem absurd to measure the worth of love by counting the days of mourning, Shen's technique respects the idea that there may not be any more practical way of dealing with loss. The narrator's little smile acknowledges the irony: his friend does not realize that his actions impugn his sincerity.

Dai uses ironic distancing like Shen's to move beyond the incongruities of Chinese political icons and Western musical geniuses. In a postproduction interview he explains that once his "own story" has been transformed into a text and a film, he looks at it "from a distance, like it was someone else's story, which is a strange feeling" (Dai 2002 DVD, postproduction interview).[14] *Balzac* is a good example of how depersonalization transforms autobiography into "everybody's story." The text quietly builds a third perspective, one reinforced by the second major idea that Shen gave to Dai: the technique of mixing realism and lyricism. Shen, as David Wang puts it, combines "pastoral motifs with horror and pain" and sanctions love "through scenes of death and violence" (1992: 205).

Shen mixes love and violence in "Three Men and One Woman," a story about how a bean-curd shop proprietor and two soldiers, a crippled bugler, and a squad leader, all fall for the daughter of a wealthy family. The first-person narrator calls her "a beautiful flower, an angel on earth" and "a divine creature" to underscore her ethereal beauty, and these descriptions make the final violence against her corpse all the more visceral: the proprietor steals and rapes her corpse in the hope of resuscitating her (Shen 1981: 256). Shen reveals pastoral culture as both simple and enigmatic, innocent and vile. In Dai's novel, Shen's influence can be felt in the characterization of the little seamstress: she is the focal point of Chinese rural ignorance and innocence on the one hand and the teenagers' translated knowledge of the West on the other. But rather than identifying the seamstress with the silent victim in Shen's story, Dai's character ultimately embodies a third perspective, one that coalesces different forces of conversion and leads her to an independent path.

One major element of Dai Sijie's fiction cannot be traced to Shen: his faith in the power of emotion to communicate. In fact, Dai is a romantic at heart, and one, he acknowledges, who can "be faulted for exaggerating the effects of emotion, for caring too much about feelings and for being unrealistic" (Dai 2003a). The romantic sustains life, he explains, because his belief in emotion "ultimately commands the power of communication." This is precisely the faith that originates the abrupt shift, in the long headman-meets-violin passage quoted above, from a dialogic style to descriptive sentimentality. Dai learned this method from the testimonial realism of Scar Literature (*shanghen wenxue*), a post-Mao literary genre that emerged in the 1970s with Liu Xinwu's 1977 story "Class Teacher" and Lu Xinhua's 1978 story "The Scar" being the two founding tales (C. Berry 2004: 88). Thematically, Scar Literature often exposes the wrongful persecution of intellectuals during the Cultural Revolution and speaks of an individual desire for catharsis and restitution.[15] These characteristics are manifest in *Balzac* in the way the first-person narrator simultaneously assumes the role of a cultural critic and mimics the author's own firsthand experience of being victimized by the corrupt revolutionary machine. Dai negotiates victimhood by transforming Ma from a stuttering youth to a sophisticated storyteller and role-player over the course of the novel.

But Dai departs from the spirit of Scar Literature by writing a novel that remains ambivalent about the dichotomy of good and evil. Leo Ou-fan Lee characterizes Scar Literature as "a return both to a Soviet style of revolutionary romanticism that privileges the individualism of the wronged party cadre and to a mode of critical realism focusing once again on the ills of socialist society" (1993: 374). Lee notes the didacticism embedded in the ideological "mission" of the genre: to right wrongs. Dai does not define his heroes as the embodiment of a collective social conscience but portrays them as individuals. If they question the hierarchy of power, it is not because they are interested in the grand project of social justice but because they are on a personal quest for the meanings of life.

While Dai's novel incorporates Shen Congwen's critical lyricism and Scar Literature's reflectionism, his film transitions between the rural epic dramas of the Fifth Generation and the urban docudramas of the Sixth Generation. Dai's connection to these two influential Chinese movements is both historical and ideological. Just the year after Dai Sijie left for France, one of the first Fifth Generation films, Chen Kaige's *Yellow Earth* (1984), drew unprecedented attention to the emergence of a new Chinese cinema. Notably, Dai shares with Chen and his cohort the life experience and intellectual concerns that define the style and tenets of all their work. They can be summarized as follows: all Fifth Generation filmmakers were sent to the countryside for re-education during the Cultural Revolution, and this experience made them reevaluate the relations between peasants and urbanites; they were all cynical about the moral didacticism of their political environment and sought to destabilize the power hierarchy between center and periphery (Ni Zhen 2006).

Beyond this, and even more than any of his peers in the movement, Dai was interested from the start in exploring relations between China and the West, especially the influence of materialism and capitalism on a changing Chinese society. To this extent his ideological concern about China in a global context connects him to the works of the Sixth Generation. In a postproduction interview, the lead actress in *Balzac* (Zhou Xun) explains that Dai probably chose her to play the little seamstress because he saw her in Lou Ye's *Suzhou River* (2000), one of the most influential works of the Sixth Generation directors.[16] Dai later confirms his appreciation of the new movement by praising the realist style of Jia Zhangke—a seminal Sixth Generation figure—whose works, Dai comments, are "profoundly sincere."[17]

Here, a brief summary of the differences between Fifth and Sixth Generation filmmakers will help clarify Dai's intermediary role as a director of a new generation and provide background for Dai's adaptations of his own fiction. Critics often distinguish the Fifth and Sixth Generation by the subjects they treat. The Fifth Generation filmmakers tend to focus more on the "the classical form of larger-than-life heroes" (Lau 2003: 17) while the Sixth Generation directors have shown more interest in "the truly ordinary" (17). This distinction is especially pronounced in the works of Zhang Yimou and Jia Zhangke, who are the pivotal figures of the respective movements. From *Red Sorghum* (1987) to *Hero* (2002), Zhang Yimou epitomizes the Fifth Generation directorial vision of patriotism and heroism. Jia Zhangke, however, introduces to the audience the peripheral world of petty criminals and migrant workers with his works *The Pickpocket* (*Xiao wu,* 1997), *The World* (*Shi jie,* 2004) and *Still Life* (*San xia hao ren,* 2006).

These different subjects are closely related to a second critical distinction: different filming politics and poetics. Fifth Generation directors started by working with provincial studios (Guangxi, for example, was one of the most famous) and applied for shooting permits from the China Film and Television Bureau (whose precursor was the China Film Bureau until 1989) (Lau 2003: 16), but Sixth Generation directors often abandoned seeking political approval through official channels from the Culture Ministry. Instead, they developed an "underground" aesthetic of shooting on location, a democratizing filmic technique characterized by Zhang Zhen as a means of producing "a dynamic feel of *xianchang* [on location] and contemporaneity, implicating both the filmmaker and viewer as a direct or indirect 'witness'" to China's social changes (2002: 117). The goal of such experiments is to find a spontaneous cinematic language that showcases "the vitality of lived speeches and experiences while also demonstrating the multiplicity and complexity of Chinese society" (117).

We are now in a position to see how Dai's *Balzac* shares the critical concerns and practices of both movements. Thematically, it is a story about city meeting country, an encounter that underlines Dai's Fifth Generation focus on "the grand theme of reflecting on cultural roots or socialist tradition" (Lau 2003: 19). This vision is especially manifest in the final scene of the film in which the narrator, Ma Jianling, embarks on a nostalgic return to the Sichuan region to search for a past being demolished by China's Three Gorges Dam project. While the official dismantling of his memories of "re-education" might convey a kind of lyrical nostalgia for the loss of youthful idealism, Dai's documentary camera also, more coldly, captures his generation's "'ruin' consciousness." This is a crucial Sixth Generation filmmaking style, a technique used to record "scenes of demolition and relocation" caused by "the most recent wave of modernization in China" (Zhang Zhen 2002: 115). I would summarize these points by arguing that Dai's presentation of the encounters between urbanites and peasants, past and present, China and the West, combines Fifth Generation humanism with the hyperrealism of the Sixth Generation and addresses the goal shared by both movements of making film a medium of both elitist and plebian expression.

Achieving this goal is not easy. If Dai's filmic adaptation of his own novel reveals his professional roots in Chinese filmmaking, it also reflects responses to his native milieu not so freely of his own making. Dai admits that he found shooting a film to be "a thousand times more difficult than writing a novel" (Dai 2002 DVD, postproduction interview), because his freedom in charting his literary path was compromised when filming in China. His novel secured the support of the French publisher Gallimard but his movie had to undergo several revisions to pass the China Film and Television Bureau's censorship.[18] Not only did he change the shooting locations due to technical issues, but he also modified his portrayal of peasants and revised the list of the stolen books to please the Chinese censors.[19] These practical and political concerns were coupled with the marketing demands of creating an attractive picture of China that would appeal to a global audience.

To understand this example of compromising self-adaptation, it is worth looking at some of the key changes Dai made in the film.

The novel's first-person narrator is replaced in the movie by a combination of subjective and objective cameras in order to make room for an alternative viewpoint that acknowledges, at least in part, the independent agency of the peasant community. Second, in the novel Dai constructs an antagonistic relation between the protagonists and nature (the man-eating coal mine, the terrifying cliffs, the depressing rain, among other scenes) to signal a metaphorical connection between the hostile political climate and the oppressive landscape. However, in the film Dai draws attention to the ways that the beauty of the motherland is able to mitigate, rather than exaggerate, human conflicts. Finally, Dai reconceptualizes the edifying effects of indigenous lyricism: in the novel, Dai emphasizes the Bakhtinian subversiveness of the local ditties, which both confront the hypocrisy of the official propaganda and expose the pretensions of idolizing Western literature.[20] In the film Dai visualizes the indigenous narrative of sex and passion in a way that parodies the characters' romantic awakening by the foreign novels.

Many of these differences come together in the very first encounter between the peasants and the urban teenagers. Dai's camera uses reaction shots to diversify the viewing perspectives in the scene and draw attention to the heterogeneity of the community. Rather than focusing exclusively on the alienating offense of the violin, as the novel does, Dai organizes the scene around the discovery of three bourgeois objects: an alarm clock, a cookbook, and a violin. It starts with various close-ups that intensify the contentious nature of their meeting. We first see the village headman rummaging through Luo Ming's luggage to look for contraband and pulling out an alarm clock that will industrialize the rhythm of the village life (Figure 5.1). A close-up contrasts the darkness of the headman's weather-beaten hands with the delicate white surface of the new timekeeper and registers the opposition between nature (the peasants' earthy hands) and culture/technology (the modern clock). Crucially, the device generates not alarm but excitement in the crowd. The clock is perceived as an impersonal but beneficent device that objectifies time and will help the peasants control their lives.

If the alarm charms the villagers with its assumed scientific efficiency, Dai uses reaction shots to humanize the community. When the headman,

Figure 5.1 Headman's weathered hands holding the alarm clock.

Figure 5.2 Faces of peasants to the left examining the alarm clock.

Figure 5.3 Faces of peasants to the right examining the alarm clock.

Figure 5.4 Luo shown as disdainful loner, above the fray.

still bending over the luggage, begins his interrogation, the camera pans to the left (Figure 5.2) and then to the right (Figure 5.3) to capture the intense interest that the village spectators have in the newly arrived visitors. Unlike Ma's vague general impression of the villagers' indistinguishable oneness in the novel, Dai's medium shots individualize the orderly crowd. The camera's focus on the interaction between the interrogation and the diegetic spectators gives the community a sense of agency: like the urban visitors, they are inquisitive, malleable, and ready to engage in cultural exchange.

When the camera cuts to Luo, he is framed in a lower-angled shot, monotonously reciting his dentist father's "crime" of treating Chiang Kai-shek's (Jiang Zhongzheng's) teeth (Figure 5.4). Luo's distinctiveness as a disdainful loner, slightly above the eye level of the audience, is manifest in his martyrlike, white-shirted image and above-the-fray gaze into the distance.

While Luo's appearance and attitude set him apart from the onlookers, the headman's discovery of the second object of interest—a cookbook—further testifies to Luo's ownership of "bad" knowledge (Figure 5.5). In a rare medium long shot, Dai's objective camera positions the two youths near the window, the only source of light in the shack. The loosely formed crowd creates a pyramid structure that looks "up" to the sent-down teenagers, who are literally closer to the light and hence metaphorically associated with enlightenment: they are the only literate people in the community. When Luo mocks the headman for holding the book upside down, the headmen defiantly responds by asking Luo to read a recipe from the book to prove the guilt of his literacy (Figure 5.6). In a clever maneuver Dai juxtaposes Luo's truncated body with the book to chastise, with some irony, his "corrupt" bourgeois upbringing. Coupled with the evidence of his culpability, Luo's faceless image marks him as a scapegoat of the political witch hunt emerging

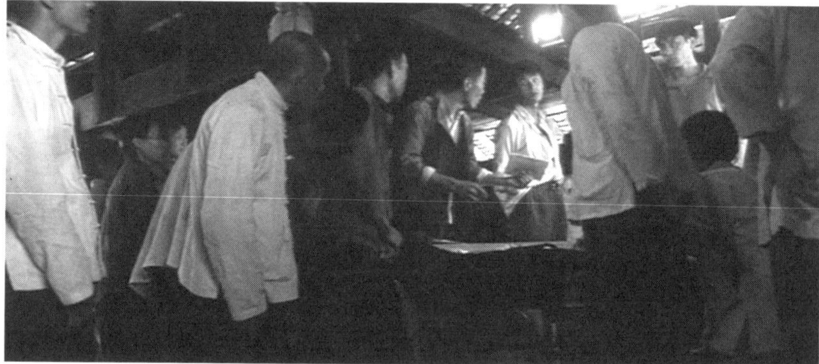

Figure 5.5 Luo and Ma in the light of literacy and enlightenment.

Figure 5.6 Luo ordered to read a recipe.

from class antagonism. But in the reaction shots that follow, Dai again gives the community a sense of intellectual autonomy that seems to survive and even challenge the totalitarian vision of conformism (Figures 5.7 and 5.8). These close-ups emphasize the spectators' animated interest in the forbidden chicken recipe that Luo is reading. The camera's democratic attention to the people, whose voices and faces attest to the significance of a third narrative viewpoint—that of the people—show them engaged in shaping the unfolding conflict between the urban youths and the village headman.

Dai continues to use close-ups to escalate the dramatic tension of political distrust and cultural misunderstanding. When the headman lectures the teenagers on the merits of physical labor, Dai's camera reflects the intensity of the exchange between the two parties through a series of rapid but unevenly framed shot-reverse-shots (Figures 5.9 and 5.10). Dai juxtaposes a medium close-up of the boys (Figure 5.9) with an extreme close-up of

Figure 5.7 Peasants' curiosity about recipe contradicts notions of totalitarian conformism.

Figure 5.8 Peasants show intelligent interest in recipe.

Figure 5.9 Medium close-up of boys learning about the merits of physical labor.

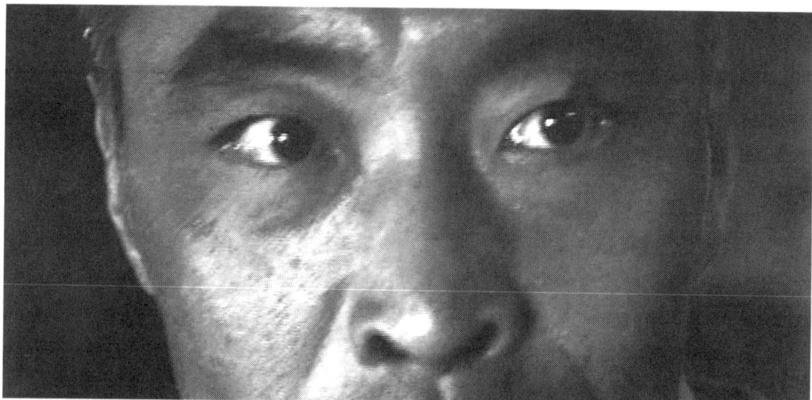

Figure 5.10 Extreme close-up of the village headman lecturing the boys.

the headman (Figure 5.10) to underscore the hierarchy of powers. The boys appear decentered and marginalized by shady lighting and angled shots on the screen, but the features of the chief, which take up more than half of the frame, highlight his obvious authority. This confrontation exacerbates the claustrophobic oppression of this interior scene in which the physical proximity among the characters reflects the lack of personal space.

When Ma Jianling begins to play the violin, however, the camera shifts from static framing to a gentle turning around him, a move that romanticizes the music's power of persuasion (Figure 5.11). It soothes the spirits of the weary travelers and appeases the rustic listeners.

In the film the unifying power of Mozart's music creates an important transition from culture to nature. Leaving behind the urban visitors in their claustrophobic dwelling, Dai's camera slowly moves outside and pulls back

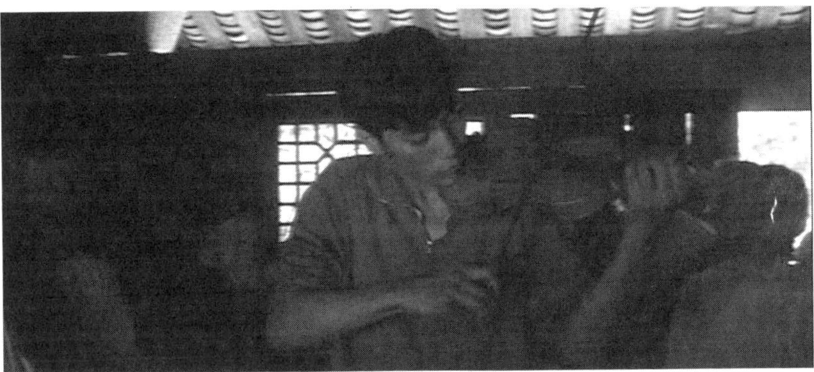

Figure 5.11 Ma's violin playing soothes all.

Figure 5.12 The camera reveals the shack in a breathtaking natural scene.

to situate the makeshift shack in a breathtaking landscape next to a lake in the mountains (Figure 5.12). Distancing the camera from the human world widens the viewer's vision, and as the long shot proceeds, the insignificant interpersonal conflicts recede. The camera gradually brings into full view the breadth, beauty, and tolerance of the landscape, and this ultimately reflects the broadening of the characters' minds. As Mozart's sonata fuses with the music of a Chinese orchestra, which both harmonize with the idyllic space, the extradiegesis quietly hints at a dialogue between East and West.

Dai's cinematic optimism of "opening up" reverses his literary pessimism of "closing down." In the film Dai moves from dramatic close-ups to long shots to introduce the landscape to the viewer in a way that provides a hopeful transition from oppressive culture to peaceful nature. In the novel Dai takes precisely the opposite approach, moving from "long shots" of objective description to "close-up" narrations of unpleasant personal experience with a nature that entraps rather than liberates. In other words Dai's novel, with its touch of Scar Literature's sentimentality, consistently paints the landscape as a backdrop for human angst and nature in general as conspiring with a political system that subjects the teenagers to discriminatory treatment. A good example is the description of the boys' living conditions:

> It rained often on Phoenix mountains. It rained almost two days out of three. Storms or torrential downpours were rare; instead there was a steady, insidious drizzle that seem to go on forever and the peaks and cliffs surrounding our house on stilts were constantly veiled in a thick, sinister mist. The unearthly panorama depressed us. What with the perpetual humidity inside the hut and ever more oppressive damp in the walls, it was worse than living in a cellar. (Dai 2002a:16)

The rain is "insidious," the mist is "thick" and "sinister," the "unearthly panorama" is depressing, and the damp is "oppressive." Many menacing natural features cumulatively threaten the teenagers' psychological wellbeing. Dai's images intensify our sense of the narrator's claustrophobia, for the viewpoint moves from the exterior (mountains, peaks, and cliffs) to the interior (humidity and damp walls in the hut) in a way that creates an anxiety about the world closing in and bearing down. The arc of this carefully sequenced imagery produces a cellar-like atmosphere appropriate to the misery of being buried underground.

It may not be obvious at first glance, but Dai Sijie's very different interpretations of nature in his novel and in the film reflect his complex relations with China. His writing brings to light an anxiety about life under the Communist regime, while his film illustrates an alternative way of seeing possible changes in an oppressive world. These differences complicate his presentation of the relations between China and the world. In addition, it is also important to note that Dai's notion of "China" is heterogeneous and multivocal throughout the whole process of adaptation. In his criticism of the Communist politics of conformism, Dai has recourse not only to Mozart, Balzac, and the rest of Occidental culture as a platform for individualism but also to suppressed regional culture, especially the folk songs of the miller as paradigms for self-expression.

In fact, Dai (2003b) uses the character of the miller to organize a crucial theory of regional lyricism that negotiates the fraught relations between Chinese politics and Western culture by transcending them. In an interview

Dai notes that his "only regret" about the film "is the old miller. In my mind, he is the best Chinese of them all. Very few people understood this completely, but in the novel I put a great deal of emotion into building this character." Although the Chinese censors mistakenly thought that the miller represented poverty and limitation, and therefore insisted that Dai reduce the number of his scenes in the film and their importance, the character of the miller overcomes these circumstances; he is the "best" Chinese because, Dai explains, even though he lives in

> impoverished circumstances, he is completely transcendental. People like him do not worry about flattering anybody, because he is self-sufficient and self-contented. I consider such a state of mind one of human's highest achievements. In other words the old miller has accomplished the goal of being himself. Although he may seem laughable at times, he has arrived at a sphere that I personally had once hoped to reach but ultimately failed. When I was shooting the movie, my biggest regret was that I wasn't able to recreate such a character. (2003b)

This is Dai's most forceful explanation of how politics suppress his creative vision. Even with the miller's limited presence in the film, however, I would argue that the character is organically integrated into the narrative: he represents an uncompromised, uncompromising model of rusticity whose life and art shape Dai's third-culture perspective.

The encounter between peripheral rural life, embodied in the miller, and the life of political exile that has been forced upon the boys, takes place in Thousand Meter Cliff, a remote village so deep in the mountains that it seems independent of socialist ideology and Communist propaganda. In the novel, just as the boys re-enact North Korean films and European novels for the villagers, Ma plays the role of a Communist officer and Luo his interpreter when they come to the miller's home to collect "authentic, robustly primitive words of ancient ditties" (Dai 2002a: 69). They plan to trade the old miller's local songs for the forbidden Western novels of their friend Four-Eyes, whereas Four-Eyes intends to transform the ancient ditties by giving them revolutionary lyrics. To convince the miller of the seriousness of their mission, Ma dresses up as a Communist officer and pretends that he speaks only Mandarin—China's official language.

> I greeted him, not in the Szechuan dialect of our province, but in Mandarin, as if I were an actor in a film.

> "What language is he speaking?" the old man asked Luo, puzzled.
>
> "The official language," replied Luo. "The language of Beijing. Don't you speak Mandarin?"
>
> "Where's Beijing?"
>
> We were taken aback by his question, but when we realized he was speaking in earnest we couldn't help laughing. For a moment I almost envied him his complete ignorance of the outside world. (Dai 2002a: 67)

At first the two teenagers mask their intention of purloining the miller's ancient songs by pretending to be government officers. While Ma's Mandarin seeks to assert the assumed power hierarchy between center and periphery, the miller's ignorance about the location of the center (Beijing) gives him a kind of intellectual autonomy and self-sustainability. His sincerity, visceral and naïve, contrasts with the calculated lies of the urban visitors who, like their political oppressors, are adept at exploiting others.

This exchange juxtaposes the official with the nonofficial, Mandarin with the vernacular, seriousness with comedy in a way that further mocks the posturing of both the officiating Chinese discourse and the affectedness, in this context, of Western culture.

> "So you want to hear some old songs?" [the miller] offered.
>
> "Indeed we do. It's for an important official journal," Luo said in a confidential tone. "We're counting on you, old man. What we need are sincere, authentic songs, with a touch of romantic realism."
>
> "What d'you mean by romantic?"
>
> Luo pondered the question, then placed his hand on his chest, as though bearing witness before a heavenly power: "Emotion and love." (Dai 2002a: 73)

This is the first time that Ma and Luo seek to conflate local lyricism with Western literature by construing both as the expressions of "emotion and love." But Luo's request speaks of contradictions. He uses such adjectives as "sincere" and "authentic" to characterize his expectations about the miller's *indigenous* music. At the same time he demands "a touch of romantic realism" that exoticizes his request. The miller's question about the definition of "romantic" (*lang man*) highlights the word's transliterated origin in Chinese: it is an imported Western concept that finds no corresponding Chinese expression and hence results in a coined interpretation—*lang man*—that literally means "wave" and "vast." Together they suggest an unrestrained indulgence in personal fantasies about sexual love. When Luo theatrically explains that being romantic is to testify to the power of emotion and love, Dai seems to deride the characters' reductive reading of art as a manifestation of individual passion.

But the miller's ancient ditties never pretend to be authentically romantic. Like the blind beggar's ditty that haunts the last pages of one of Dai's favorite novels, Flaubert's *Madame Bovary,* they are jovial parodies of transgressive sexual fantasies, and they carry larger cultural truths. As soon as the miller starts singing, his performance puts the boys in stitches:

> Tell me:
> An old louse,
> What does it fear?
> It fears boiling water,
> Boiling bubbling water.
> And the young nun,
> Tell me,
> What does she fear?
> She fears the old monk
> No more and no less
> Just the old monk
>
> We held our sides laughing. We tried to control ourselves, of course, but the giggles inside us mounted and mounted until we exploded. The old miller smiled, too, and went on singing while the skin eddied across his stomach. Luo and I rolled over the ground in a paroxysm of hilarity. (Dai 2002a: 74)

Mimicking the politics of fear during the Cultural Revolution, the song starts with a common assumption about parasites and proceeds to insinuate the sexual anxiety of sworn celibates. This narrative seems to compare the paralyzing terror of an insectlike existence to that of a monastic life. As a result the miller's lewd lyrics articulate a kind of blasphemy that destabilizes both social and moral orders and exemplifies the subversive function of laughter that Bakhtin identified. Laughter, Bakhtin argues, is "the social consciousness of all the people," an eruptive phenomenon that defeats fear and suspends class boundaries. "This is why festive folk laughter presents an element of victory not only over supernatural awe, over the sacred, over death; it also means the defeat of power, of earthly kings, of the earthly upper classes, of all that oppresses and restricts" (1984: 92). Bakhtin's description of laughter's equalizing and liberating power is instructive to our understanding of how Dai uses the miller's song to validate a vernacular viewpoint, one that is neither suppressed by the centralizing Communist discourse nor contained within defamiliarizing Western narratives. In fact, it is not coincidental that this is the only moment in the novel in which the characters can laugh freely and openly about the cultural miscues that make the association of bawdy songs with a narrative desire for serious romantic literature seem amusingly incongruous. I would even suggest that the miller's song deconstructs the opposition between "official" Communist discourse and "anti-official" Western narratives. The song asserts itself as the *non*official, collective voice of an underclass that challenges the political and moralistic dichotomies that dominate at the time of the Cultural Revolution.

While Dai's novel consciously uses a distinct third culture to create an alternative vision of self-definition, his film uses the miller's scene to project a utopian picture of cultural blending. In the film Ma is drawn to the miller because he is looking for self-improvement in the form of inspirational tunes to advance his compositional skills. In contrast to the scene in the novel, in the film Ma visits the miller without Luo as "interpreter." On screen it is evident that despite using different languages—Ma Mandarin and the miller Sichuanese—the two communicate quite well.

This dramatically alters the novel. If the miller understands Mandarin, then he is suddenly part of the official culture. Rather than being a remnant of an earlier civilization uncontaminated by twentieth-century history and politics—"Where's Beijing?"—he represents the powerful spread of Mandarin. Instead of generating a subversive but transcendental, satirical

Figure 5.13 The miller's hut.

yet community-building laughter, his riddle—now sung in a Chinese rap style—seems responsible for "romantically" igniting the on-screen passion between Luo and the little seamstress. Dai's camera cuts between the miller's dimly lit shack and Luo and the seamstress in the Garden of Eden–like "heavenly pond" to sharpen the contrast between the two locations and associate the song with romantic fantasy and sexual pleasure.

The scene begins with an idyllic view of the miller's dwelling, nestled deep in the mountains (Figure 5.13). The shot of the miller doing his daily work emphasizes an intrinsic correlation between physical labor and earthy talent. The local musician embodies an organic union of life and art, one that evolves naturally through experiential practice, not through a hyperbolic exaltation of love and emotion. Sitting in the dimly lit shack, the miller wants to share with Ma the "little pleasures" of the mountain people. Dai uses

Figure 5.14 Close-up of miller in conversation with Ma.

Figure 5.15 Close-up of Ma in conversation with the miller.

a series of shot-reverse-shots to illustrate the "enlightening" conversation between the two (Figures 5.14 and 5.15). Wearing a vest made of animal skin, the miller naturalizes a look of unprocessed simplicity. He identifies himself as one of the locals and proposes to sing a riddle passed only "from father to son." His enclosed worldview sustains an indigenous identity that is different from Ma's ambitious plan of making himself into a more sophisticated cultural official. In his blue Maoist suit, Ma appears contemplative and disengaged. As soon as the miller starts to sing, however, Dai cuts to an outdoor scene that visualizes almost verbatim the sexual fantasies in the miller's lyrics about "pond of the sky." Changing from the interior shot of the miller's shabby dwelling to a medium long shot of an outdoor scene, Dai stages a Garden of Eden–like paradise (complete with symbolic snake) in which Luo and the little seamstress frolic in a secluded pond (Figure 5.16). Continuing to play in the scene is the miller's bawdy rap about the bird and the brown grass. His music suggests a parallel action, one that juxtaposes Ma's and Luo's separate activities in different locations. A quick intercut from the outdoor to the miller's shed again contrasts the two scenes (Figures 5.17 and 5.18). In the dim light of a boarded dwelling, the viewer sees the performing miller singing with gusto at the top of his lungs. Sitting next to him is the studious Ma holding a pen and a notebook in his hands. Quickly, Dai's camera cuts back to the lovemaking of Luo and the seamstress in the pond (Figure 5.18). The cross-cutting visually suggests that it is the miller's song that evokes the only romantic interlude in the film and hence tacitly confirms that the ancient ditty is indeed "authentic" and "romantic": not only is the song performed in a local dialect about an esoteric riddle, but it also inspires a picture in which Chinese music narrates a cadenced tale of love, innocence, and sexual

Figure 5.16 The Garden of Eden for Luo and the seamstress.

Figure 5.17 The miller singing the ancient song.

Figure 5.18 Luo and the seamstress making love in the Garden of Eden.

desire. This cultural and visual blending reminds the viewer of an earlier, more transcendental scene in which the fusion of Mozart's sonata and orchestral Chinese music projects the possibility of a grand cultural integration.

Departing from the parodic structure in the novel, the film does not cultivate the kind of Bahktinian laughter that privileges the disruptive power of a vernacular perspective. Instead, Dai shows that the miller's third culture is a force of reconciliation that symbolically interweaves a local narrative with utopian romanticism. Unlike other dominant but elusive personalities in the story, such as Mao Zedong, Mozart, and Balzac, the miller is just as real, present, and human as he is folkloric. His lyrics naturalize sexual desire and express a universally attractive spectacle of love and pleasure.

All in all, Dai's self-adaptation shows that his marketing and political concerns limit the freedom of his filmmaking. His novel is humorously self-deprecating: it seems both to endorse and to ridicule the teenagers' reductive, elitist vision of searching for a solution to China's intellectual crisis *outside* the bounds of the nation. This literary logic creates a sense of dissonance among different cultural discourses and sets nature in opposition in a way that caricatures the encompassing hostility of political authoritarianism. Dai's film, however, constructs a more sober and one-dimensional political mood, especially in its self-conscious, documentarian efforts to be inclusive and to individualize and affirm "other" perspectives, such as the "real" peasants, the headman, the miller, and the newly ascendant Chinese urban middle class. As a result, the film places less emphasis on the subjective privilege of the narrator's personal experience, and, ultimately the final impression is nostalgic on the level of history rather than the self. We understand that the underwater dream sequence that ends the film is but one of myriad episodes from the time of the Cultural Revolution and that this film is but one example of widespread attempts at reconstructing and reinterpreting the past. Such attempts may be humorous and beautiful, but they are governed by an unrealizable idealism: one cannot return to one's native soil, for it has been irretrievably flooded over by history, politics, time, and water.

Dai Sijie's progress from little-known filmmaker to popular novelist to renowned director represents a good example of how self-adaptation is a transforming process. Writing in French, working with a French crew, and filming in China, Dai testifies to the political complexity and marketing viability of translating a novel into a "world" film. His Occidentalism has dominated his critical reception, but we have seen that his production is best understood as an attempt to create a third culture, that is, a both-and and neither-nor, East-West mixture that draws on the narratologies introduced by Balzac, Dumas, Flaubert, and the others, and on Shen Congwen's critical lyricism, the post-Cultural Revolution Scar Literature, and Chinese Fifth and Sixth Generation film movements. His "China complex," of which much still remains to be understood, echoes Chang's and Kwan's critiques of sinocentrism and shares with Hou Xiaoxian, to whom we now turn, a keen eye for the possibilities and paradoxes involved in representing a multicultural political identity.

CHAPTER 6

Hou Xiaoxian and Zhu Tianwen

Politics and Poetics in *A Time to Live, A Time to Die*

So far in this book we have seen novelists who are aficionados of cinema and filmmakers who are literary buffs. We have seen interactions, borrowings, and transformations between literature and film on topics ranging from politics to aesthetics to historical representation. And yet, despite robust cross-fertilization, Chinese adaptation has almost always been a one-way street: film directors read and remake literature, not the other way around. Thus Zhu Tianwen (b. 1956) and Hou Xiaoxian (b. 1947) represent an important exception: working together in both directions since 1983, they have produced extraordinary cine-literary results. In this chapter we will look carefully at Zhu's 1986 fictional adaptation of a movie for which she herself served as a screenwriter: Hou's 1985 autobiographical classic *A Time to Live, A Time to Die* (*Tong nian wang shi*). The movie is about the life of an immigrant family in southern Taiwan in the 1950s and 1960s. More than any other story in this book, Zhu's 1986 version breaks new ground by incorporating Hou's filmic techniques to construct a new identity politics, one that sketches a composite, multilingual and multiethnic personality.

If Zhang Yimou is the most renowned Chinese director today, Hou Xiaoxian is the most acclaimed Taiwanese one. David Bordwell is one of many to laud Hou's expansion of the stylistic possibilities of cinema, commending him for the way his expressive use of staging and lighting has reintroduced "pictorial intricacy to Asian filmmaking" (2005: 237). In 1995 Japanese film critic Hasumi Shigehiko declared his thanks to Hou Xiaoxian "for re-inventing the cinema after it was invented for so many years" (1995: 87). Many more applaud him for intertwining personal and national memories and for revitalizing a neorealist aesthetic: he uses nonprofessional actors, shoots on location, experiments with long takes and still camera shots, and explores mundane and quotidian subjects (Neri 2003; Yeh and Davis 2005). Critics in *Cahiers du cinema* and the *Village Voice* have also praised Hou as one of the best directors of our time, recognizing him for helping define Taiwan New Cinema and for influencing other prominent directors in Asia, Europe, and North America (Assayas 1999; Jones 1999).

Despite many studies about Hou in general, few have examined Hou's literary poetics, the origins of which can be traced to his appreciation for Shen Congwen, Eileen Chang, Chen Yingzhen, Wang Zhenhe, Wang Wenxing, and Huang Chunming. Even more important is his longtime screenplay collaboration with Zhu Tianwen, one of the most prominent contemporary Taiwanese women writers. Between 1983 and 2005 Hou and Zhu collaborated on adaptations from fiction to film and from screenplay to fiction, ultimately producing thirteen films, many of which won international acclaim. Although *Growing Up* (*Xiao bi de gu shi,* 1983) was a Zhu story directed by Chen Kunhou, most of her short stories emerge from the screenplays she has created in collaboration with Hou. Key examples include *The Boys from Fengkuei* (*Feng gui lai de ren,* 1983), *A Summer at Grandpa's* (*Dong dong de jiaqi,* 1984), *A Time to Live, A Time to Die* (*Tong nian wang shi,* 1985), and *The Daughter of the Nile* (*Ni luo he de nüer,* 1987). Of all of their works, I think *A Time to Live, A Time to Die* best exemplifies the way Hou and Zhu negotiate the aesthetic interdependence and ideological relations between film and fiction.

In order to appreciate the way these two artists develop their signature art of two-way adaptation, it helps to review their careers. In the case of Hou, we can speak of three major phases, each of which features a different kind of literary influence: for his commercial past (1975–1982), there is his popular female fiction; for the New Cinema period (1983–1988), there is nativist literature (1970s–1980s); and for the international auteur (1989 to the present), there is urban fiction (1990s to present).[1] The second phase is of particular significance to our study because during that time Hou was fostering awareness of Taiwan's democratic potential and drawing attention to the island's social and economic reality.[2] He often uses auto/biographical modes to conflate personal memory with Taiwan's social history.[3]

Hou first met Zhu when he was working as a screenwriter for Chen Kunhou, who was adapting her semiautobiographical "The Story of Little Bi" (1991a; first published in 1982) into *Growing Up* (1983).[4] His own debut as a New Cinema director began with his adaptation of the nativist writer Huang Chunming's tale "His Son's Big Doll" into *The Sandwich Man* (1983).[5] Between 1983 and 1986 Hou made two autobiographical films—*The Boys from Fenggui* (1983) and *A Time to Live, A Time to Die* (1985)—as well as two biographical ones: *A Summer at Grandpa's* (1984), based on Zhu Tianwen's childhood memoir, and *Dust in the Wind* (1986), based on Wu Nianzhen's story of his first love. These four movies mark the beginning of his productive years working with Zhu Tianwen.

Zhu is one of the most versatile and influential of contemporary Taiwanese novelists (Sung-sheng Chang 2001; Yeh and Davis 2005). Born into a family of writers, she is well versed in Western, Japanese, and classical and modern Chinese literatures.[6] Like Hou's filmmaking, Zhu's writing can be divided into three stages. She began her literary career in what is called the "Three-Three" phase (1970s to early 1980s), during which she and her literary cohorts held on to a kind of "China complex" and advocated a romantic vision of Chinese nationalism. These early nostalgic works are often compared to those of Eileen Chang and Hu Lancheng.[7] She then shifted to a nativist phase from the early 1980s to the late 1980s, when she embraced the New Cinema's "Taiwan complex" and produced auto/biographical short stories that are considered a part of "realistic neo-nativist" movement (Sung-sheng Chang 2001: 84). In her third phase, "new urban fiction" (from 1990 onwards), she began experimenting with a form of pastiche narrative, producing such edgy postmodern short stories and novels as *Fin-de-siècle Splendor* (*Shi ji mo de hua li,* 1997), *Notes of a Desolate Man* (*Huang ren shou ji,* 1999), and *Remembering the Flower's Previous Life* (*Huang yi qian shen,* 2006). Critics like David Wang, Zhan Hongzhi, and Sung-sheng Yvonne Chang consider her writing during this period to be "decadent," by which they mean that it is stylistically postrepresentational and thematically concerned with the desire, despair, and debauchery of city dwellers (Sung-sheng Chang 2001: 107–108).

If we look closely at the collaboration between Zhu and Hou in *A Time,* we can see how the impact of the New Cinema philosophy shifted her attention to Taiwan's social reality. It also opened up the stylistic possibilities she used to develop what she herself has called the "cinematic novel" (Zhu 1991c), a blended form that matures even more in her new urban fiction.[8]

This chapter begins by exploring Hou's literary connection to Shen Congwen, an important link that helps explain the self-distancing narrative style that both Zhu and Hou share. I then turn to the way Zhu adapts Hou's discontinuity editing into her storytelling, producing experiments with spatial and temporal disjunction that mimic the flow of narrative consciousness. Next I analyze the way social visions are generated by their literary and filmic "establishing shots," a technique used by both artists that reflects a Taiwan-centered democratizing aesthetic that prizes egalitarianism and cultural hybridity. And finally I present a key difference made visible by the adaptation: compared with Hou, Zhu provides a nuanced feminist outlook on women's emerging autonomy.

A Time starts with a male adult's (Hou's) voiceover recounting the changes in his family since they moved to Taiwan from Mei county in Canton, China, in 1948. The everyday routine of this family of eight seems to be interrupted only by deaths and school entrance exams. Aha (He Xiaoyan, played by You Anshun), the narrator, mentions four memorable deaths. First, his cousin, a pilot in the Nationalist (Kuomintang, KMT) army, dies as a war hero while Aha is in elementary school. Then when he is entering middle school, his father, a stern intellectual, dies of tuberculosis. Later when Aha is in high school, his mother dies of throat cancer and his grandmother of old age. These deaths are interspersed with memories of several career-changing exams in the family. When the narrator passes the entrance exam to Fengshan middle school, his sister passes the one to the best girl's high school in Taipei; she cannot attend, however, because family resources are too limited. The story ends when Aha fails the college entrance exam and is about to begin his mandatory two-year military service.

An autobiographical film, *A Time* epitomizes Hou's Taiwan New Cinema phase, one that "begins with a cycle of self-exploration and self-disclosure" and tells "the story of the fathers, including the ambiguous origins of Taiwan itself" (Yeh and Davis 2005: 147). Similarly, when Zhu adapts the film into a biographical story, it illustrates her own ideological transition from a romantic Nationalist ideologue in the Three-Three phase to a more Taiwan-oriented realist who is attentive to the cultural conflicts between the first-generation Chinese immigrants and their Taiwan-born-and-bred children.[9] Critical to their successes as a filmmaker and novelist, this ideological flexibility allows them to experiment with the aesthetics of mixed media and explore the complex evolution of Taiwan's identity politics.

As a screenwriter, one of Zhu's first contributions to Hou's filmmaking was to consolidate his interest in literature. While shooting *A Time,* Hou faced the predicament of balancing intimacy and objectivity in autobiographical storytelling. Zhu recommended that he read Shen Congwen's autobiography, believing that its narrative style of self-distancing could serve as an inspiration. Like Dai Sijie, Hou benefited from this exposure to Shen's work. In many interviews he has credited Shen's writing with helping him find a "clear perspective and formulation" in autobiographical film (quoted in Michael Berry 2005: 247). Shen provided key components of Hou's literary cinematics, some of which were later translated, revised, and incorporated once more by Zhu into her own writing.

In Chapter 5 we saw how Shen's "critical lyricism" influenced Dai's narrative style; this and other features of Shen's texts are also critical to Hou. Hou finds Shen's "bird's eye view" and objective approach to autobiography especially appealing: "Everything that [Shen] was describing was about his own life and experience growing up, yet he took a very cold, distanced approach" (quoted in Michael Berry 2005: 247). Two effects of depersonalization in Shen's hands are that it conflates individual memory with national history, and it naturalizes a cyclical view of life and death. Hou explains that Shen often represents death simply as a death under the sun, which evokes not sorrow but a form of desolation. This self-distancing philosophy helps explain such technical decisions as Hou's use of the objective camera, establishing shots, discontinuity editing, and deep focus. It also allows us to trace Shen's philosophical influence on Hou to *A Time* where, despite a narrative flow that is punctuated by the tragic deaths of his cousin, father, mother, and grandmother, he is able to "objectify" these sad circumstances by exploring the larger political and cultural implications of private memory.

Shen's influence on *A Time* is manifest in the opening scene in which Hou juxtaposes still shots of an empty house with the narrative voiceover of Hou himself. Following a sequence of discontinuity editing, the narrator explains that his father decided to move the whole family from Mei county in Canton, China, to Taiwan in 1948 in order to enjoy the island's more modern living standard: Taiwan has tap water. The complex story involves a brief comparison of the living standards of China and Taiwan, the mobility and ambition of an educated father, the chaos of war, and the unpredictable consequences of an incidental encounter.

The first seven shots of the film reflect what I call Hou's cinematic language of disjunction, a stylistic practice that incorporates obstructions of viewpoint and multiple framing to explore the possibilities and constraints of representation. The first is an out-of-focus background shot with a sign that reads "Kaohsiung County Government's Staff Dormitory" (Figure 6.1). This is the actual locale where Hou's remembered happy family life and his abrupt transition from childhood into adulthood occurred. And yet, quite noticeably, the documentary authenticity does not recreate a space of incontestable reality. Not only does Hou highlight the haziness of remembrance, as the blurred background attests, he also methodically renders the shots incongruous with the narration.

Here we can see Hou mixing some of the DNA of film and literature: the image carries, liberates, but also deforms the narrative imagination, combining the power of the autobiographical story to move the reader with the antinarrative power of images to freeze time in units from seconds to years.

Figure 6.1 Sign reading "Kaohsiung County Government's Staff Dormitory" against an indistinct background.

Figure 6.2 Eyelike windows of the empty house.

The viewer's sense is that the literary language of narratives and the filmic language of images are both essential to human memory, and this sense grows stronger as the narrator's account of his father's unexpected Taiwan connection is juxtaposed with a view of an empty kitchen and deserted backyard (Figure 6.2). Hou's still camera traps the natural sunlight within the open window and door frame in a way that makes the two parallel but uneven rectangles resemble the eyes of the vacant house looking out from inside. This spatial and temporal hindsight simulates the interiority of the

Figure 6.3 The empty chair on screen as the father's story is narrated.

memory standing still to contrast with the moving imagery of the narrator's story that travels through unseen time (the year 1947) and space (Mei county and Guangzhou). Hou's use of a still, empty house to stand for the turbulence of war creates a strong sense of discord: his quiet and dispassionate camera makes the narrator's account, lively as it is, seem like a memory far removed.

The disjunction between the screen images and images projected by the narration persists in the following shot (Figure 6.3) in which the empty chair sits impassively in the center of the screen to receive the narrator's story about his father's active professional transition between times and between places. Again, Hou literalizes Shen's philosophy of detachment. Slightly blocked by the screen door on the left, the camera preserves a critical distance between the viewer and the vacant seat, the narrator and the absent father. It hints at the standoffishness of a patriarchal authority whose symbolic position in the family remains irreplaceable after his death.

Hou also uses discontinuity editing to render the act of recollection more incidental and less dramatically complete or coherent. Again during the opening sequence, a medium shot of the father (Tian Fung) reading at the desk (Figure 6.4) is followed by an establishing shot of a domestic routine in which two boys are playing in the center of the screen, while the mother is working in the kitchen (Figure 6.5). Altogether, the many different camera positions, depths, and viewing options produce a remarkably multiperspectival—I would also say democratizing—aesthetic for an autobiographical context. The relatively shallow background and close view of the father in Figure 6.4 does not generate a sense of intimacy, for he makes no attempt to interact with the camera or the viewer, but instead remains aloof throughout. He is contained within his world, and the camera, looking outside from within the house, underscores the disconnection. By contrast, the still camera outside the house in Figure 6.5 reveals a quotidian past in which the carefree frolicking of the brothers and the hardworking mother convey normalcy and everydayness. The depth of the shot visually enlivens the scene with layered movements, but its descriptive nature propels no narrative.

Figure 6.4 Medium shot of father sitting apart, reading quietly.

Figure 6.5 Long shot of everyday domestic activity.

According to Zhu Tianwen, Hou considers straight chronological narration too artificial for the incidental unfolding of real events, so it is not surprising to see him create a story that is more lyrical than linear (Zhu Tianwen and Wu Nianzhen 1989: 30).[10] His films often use an episodic narrative structure and discursive, even obstructive techniques of discontinuity editing to force the audience to fill in gaps of time and space. Typical examples include multilayered framings—walls, windows, and doorways—that invite but obstruct viewing. Other scenes manipulate divided spaces to expose barriers to communication among the characters on such sensitive topics as gender exploitation and sexual suppression. In *A Time* we are introduced to the sister (Xiao Ai) when she is working in the backyard (Figure 6.6). Confined within the fenced-in wall and sandwiched between the cooking stoves on the left and large containers on the right, she runs back and forth in the narrow alley to help her mother prepare for dinner. The oppressiveness of the different barriers and containing devices limit her movement to the crammed space; as the only girl with four male siblings, she is expected to give up an opportunity to attend the best girl's high school to tend to her family's other pressing needs. The compressed space allegorizes her self-sacrifice.

Hou further illustrates the theme of gender exploitation in the subsequent shot (Figure 6.7), where the faceless images of mother (Mei Fang) and daughter, working silently side by side and mirroring each other's past and future, are framed by and plastered against the window panels: their lives

Figure 6.6 Sister confined by walls and family obligations.

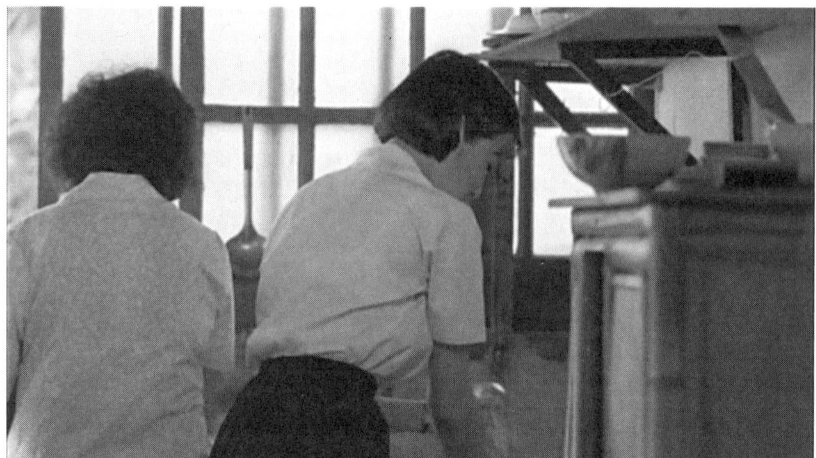

Figure 6.7 Mother and daughter faceless in their existential bondage.

are compartmentalized by the divided squares, the multiplication of which symbolizes the endless demands for their self-effacing service. Throughout, the women are exiled to enclosed spaces of existential bondage: the back of the house, the kitchen, and the backyard.

Hou's treatment of gender issues reflects the influence of Zhu, whom he credits with helping him "understand the perspective of a woman's world view" and with sharing "invaluable insights into their social positions" (quoted in Burdeau 1999: 106). More generally, the montage sequence shows that this is an era of political repression. The empty house quietly translates the silence imposed upon the island by the ruling KMT during the Martial Law period (1948–1987), and the irreplaceable but diseased fatherly authority still dictates the hierarchical relations among family members.

While Hou draws extensively on the literary techniques he finds in authors such as Shen and Zhu, Zhu borrows just as much from the language of cinema, especially the way Hou speaks it. Once again, some background helps to explain the elective philosophical and aesthetic affinities between the two.

In a 2005 interview with Michael Berry, Zhu gives an important, detailed statement on the "attitude toward creation" involved in adaptation:

> When it comes to cinematic adaptations of literature, it is ridiculous to even attempt to "be loyal to the original." Once you become familiar with the medium of film, you realize that these

> are two completely different worlds. It is a fundamentally different approach when you tell a story through language as compared with telling a story through images. There is an entire thought process and system of logic that go hand in hand with the written word. In the language of images, on the other hand, there is a completely different vocabulary for expressing your story. They are completely separate. Once you understand this, you come to realize that when a director wants to adapt a certain work of fiction, it may very well be only a certain portion of the work that moves him. It may even be simply a certain feeling that he wants to capture, or perhaps only a certain sentence. Your job as a screenwriter is to take this feeling, take this sentence, and think through it in images. Images have to guide your thoughts, your language, and your entire adaptation." (Berry 2005: 246)

Zhu distinguishes so sharply between the "language of images" in cinema and the "the language of words" in literature that her theory assigns a great deal of autonomy to the adapter: a director may try to capture "a certain feeling" or even "a certain sentence" of a literary work. This provocatively suggests that cinematic adaptation can be shaped by emotive and intuitive response as well as by interpretative or intellectual positioning. And Zhu's observations work the other way, too: a novelist can adapt a movie (script) along the same lines. To try to describe and interpret such an open process, it is best to begin pragmatically with an example of how Zhu translates and revises Hou's cinema.

When Zhu adapts Hou's *A Time* she not surprisingly eliminates the first-person narrator and transforms the genre from autobiography to biography. As a result she abolishes the paradoxical mixture of intimacy and distance that Hou carefully constructed—which itself was created on the basis, we have seen, of Shen Congwen's literary technique. At the same time, the opening passage reveals one of Hou's signature influences on her writing: his use of discontinuity editing. Bordwell and Thompson define discontinuity editing in film as "any alternative system of joining shots together using techniques unacceptable within continuity editing principles." They name such possibilities as "mismatching of temporal and spatial relations, violations of the *axis of action,* and concentration on graphic relations" (2005: 502; Bordwell and Thompson's italics). For Zhu, Hou's techniques open up narrative options for mismatching temporal and spatial relations; among other things these disjunctions register the disintegration of people's lives during an epoch of war.

In her retelling, Zhu defines the characters' relationships in the categories of past, present, and future so as to register the hopes and fears of the different generations. Grandma, for instance, lives simultaneously in the memory of her past life on mainland China and in her vision of a better future, while her grandson Aha (or Ah Ha Gu, a nickname used only by his grandmother) exists simply in a present time unconnected to other privileged temporal categories. Zhu skillfully interweaves these contrasting rhythms by juxtaposing Grandma's otherworldly aspirations with Aha's mundane exploits. Right at the beginning of the story, the third-person narrator explains:

> Grandma called him Ah Ha Gu. She believed that he would become an important government official in the future, so she was especially nice to him. Grandma treasured a common saying: "For those who didn't accrue merits in their previous life, their sons will become daughter-in-laws in their next life." She invariably evoked this bitter adage whenever she saw him doing the dishes as punishment. (Zhu 1991b: 135)[11]

Grandma's life exemplifies Zhu's point about the discontinuity of time and space: she is a divided character who lives in two times, past and future, and two places, China and the underworld. Her faith in the old saying is deeply rooted in her anxiety about the consequences of an unmeritorious past. Her current Taiwan experience is made empty by her effort to return to her past in China and to prepare for her future in the underworld. It is a terrible dialectic: even as she constantly searches for a magic road home back to the golden landscape of her exuberant youth, she makes paper silver dollars all day long for her journey in the afterlife.

If Grandma removes herself from her own present life and simultaneously inhabits past and future, then the resolutely present-tense Aha is an outsized, romanticized metaphor for a new hybrid Taiwanese-Chinese-Hakka generation. He is fully at home in all three cultures:

> Every evening, the eighty-year-old grandmother would be out on the street calling Aha home for dinner. At that moment Aha would have been gambling away with others in a narrow alley next to the Chenghuang Temple. Ignoring the shouting of "Ah Ha Gu" that sounded at times close and at times far, he focused solely on winning or losing the money.... Father paid great respect to Grandma and would never start dinner without having her seated first. That is the moment Aha sneaked home. He first dug up a hole near the

> papaya tree and then buried the two pocketfuls of glass balls and several coins he had won into the ground. (136)

Throughout Zhu's text, Aha is associated with fragments of time intensely experienced while the grandmother's life is circular and repetitive. Every evening, continually calling Ah Ha Gu up and down the street, she performs ritualistic wastes of time as she tries, to no avail, to regularize her grandson's time. Meanwhile, his father's time is one of constant deferral: he sets no limit to the process of waiting for his mother as she futilely searches for her grandson in hiding.

By punctuating the descriptions of Aha's clandestine activities—gambling, stealing, hiding, or fighting—with denominators such as "at that time" and "at this time," Zhu creates a cumulative effect of ongoing instantaneity, as if each "present" were filled with more than one event. These temporal "nows" are stylistically associated with so much excitement that they generate a palpable narrative energy and transform transient images into a whir of motion. Many of the verbs associated with Aha's operations—"sneaked," "dug up," and "buried"—also create suspense and the fear of potentially being exposed. Aha's secrecy and instability make him live on the brink of disaster.

The key here is that Zhu does not narrate Aha as operating in the void but localizes his desires and grounds his movements in the community: from gambling in the alley next to the Chenghuang Temple to hiding money near the papaya tree at home, he is "here and now"—one of the local boys. Zhu's localization of Aha suggests her second major adoption of Hou's stylistic practice: the use of an establishing shot, a shot "involving a distant framing, that shows the spatial relations among the important figures, objects, and setting in a scene" (Bordwell and Thompson 2005: 502).

As we saw in Figure 6.5, Hou uses an establishing shot to introduce the different domestic relations of the characters with the house and with each other. Departing from the active editing of most Chinese directors, Hou's noninterventionist objective camera sits quietly at a distance and lets the picture speak for itself; he refuses to dramatize or interpret the action for the viewer. This same logic allows Zhu to give a more detailed and natural description of Aha's interaction with his environment in a way that contextualizes his cultural relations with the local community. In other words Zhu adopts Hou's nonjudgmental "establishing shot" to represent a realistic everyday picture of Taiwan's rural life. This Taiwan-centered vision is later expanded in both artists' shared philosophical concerns about creating an egalitarian representation of Taiwan's race and class relations. They develop in both film and fiction a *democratizing aesthetic* that tells stories about "the people,"[12] a philosophy Hou characterizes in a 1999 interview:

> [Zhu Tianwen] has brought me, or we have brought each other, what I would call an attitude toward creation: that is, the manners with which we treat people and subjects. Living in a very mundane world, I have always been interested in people and have never felt that I am superior to anybody, because each life has its own value. I am like everyone else; we are all equal. This is my attitude toward creation. I believe in egalitarianism in diversity. When I film people, I always try to stay on the same footing with them, but I will continue to change the angles of filming to capture their different backgrounds. Zhu Tianwen sees things in a similar way, but she has an even deeper understanding of such a position. Because intellectuals often stand out among ordinary people, she has had to learn to make herself fit in. (quoted in Burdeau 2000: 106; my translation from Chinese into English)

Hou's comments are very important, not only because he rarely formulates explicit theoretical remarks on his filmmaking, but also because they reveal how committed he and Zhu are to egalitarian modes of representation. This underlies much of the decision-making in their back-and-forth adaptations and helps explain their use of quotidian subject matter, common people, and a democratizing treatment of class and race issues. Hou's *The Sandwich Man,* for example, humanizes the ghastly looking temporary worker who wanders up and down the street in a clown costume, advertising for upcoming features at the local movie theater. In *Growing Up* (*Xiao bi de gushi,* 1983), *The Boys from Fengkuei* (*Feng gui lai de ren,* 1983), and *Dust in the Wind* (*Lian lian feng chen,* 1986), Hou and Zhu describe the lives of a country doctor and his local community, factory workers, students, and miners—diverse characters who illustrate Taiwan's economic transformation from an agricultural society into an industrialized nation in the 1980s.

In the case of both Hou and Zhu, personal experience undergirds the egalitarian search for diversity and cultural hybridity in Taiwan's changing social and racial body. Both are second-generation Chinese in Taiwan: Hou's parents are Hakkas from Mei county in Canton; Zhu's father is from Shandong and her mother is Hakka born in Miaoli, Taiwan. It is therefore not surprising that their movies routinely use three of Taiwan's most commonly spoken languages (Mandarin, Taiwanese, and Hakka) to reflect the island's multiculturalism and ethnic complexity. The public square in *A Time*

Figure 6.8 Everyone in the community gathers under the banyan tree.

Figure 6.9 Children spinning a top.

is a key example of a democratizing space of congregation. One of Hou's favorite shooting locations, a local temple in Fengshan attracts villagers of all origins, ages, classes, and sexes; they gather under the banyan tree to kill time (Figure 6.8). The horizontal composition of the establishing shot lays out the natural pulse of a location that accommodates and commingles the young and the old, men and women, parents and grandparents, peasants, workers, and shopkeepers.

Hou further explores the ideal of equal footing through the long take of a plebian game: a group of kids in almost identical white T-shirts and khaki shorts (their school uniforms) are spinning a top in the square (Figure

Figure 6.10 Teenagers create an edgier atmosphere under the banyan tree.

6.9). Hou's camera stays still at a distance to present the scene as a part of everyday reality. Giving no preference to any particular character, Hou naturalizes the egalitarian rhythm of a childhood experience.

But Hou's democratizing aesthetic does not simply construct a utopian vision of a harmonious community. Changing from a child's more limited and less critical view of the world, his camera fades out and moves into the world of the adolescent narrator who, ten years later, has become a divisive, angst-ridden local gang member. Differentiating the past from the present, Hou shifts the camera's position from a distant observer to a medium-positioned onlooker in a way that reflects the teenager's more compressed and anxious viewpoint of his social network (Figure 6.10). Still in a horizontal formation, the square nevertheless looks flattened and hence more crowded and shallow than it did before. The once idyllic view of a peaceful community is now replaced by a more intense and confrontational look, with distracted teenagers hovering around the tree giving off aimless energy: they chase away out-of-towners, goof around with pretty girls, and pick fights with rival gangs. They are the new postwar generation coming of age under the KMT rule of the island that began in 1945. Unlike many first-generation Chinese immigrants in Taiwan, these teenagers neither bear any political burden for consolidating Taiwan's Chinese interest, nor show any nascent concern for the island's political indeterminacy. Under the banyan tree they lead a sheltered life of social disengagement. Putting as much weight on the ways his antiheroic characters kill time as on scenes of death and love, and filming the public space from different angles, eras, and narrative viewpoints,

Hou expresses his democratizing aesthetic both as a film art and as an attitude toward life in general.

In Zhu's adaptation, a similar impulse to democratization yields a comparable construction of the public square: it is a free and equal social space open to people of all ages, professions, and ethnic origins. Again Zhu emulates Hou's use of a placid, encompassing objective camera:

> They all went to the square near the temple to play spinning tops. Sometimes Grandma would come by the street, carrying a cloth handbag. When she would see him, she often called out, "Ah Ha Gu, let's go back to the mainland." He didn't want to. Then Grandma would walk away by herself, swaying with a limp. A playmate would mock him: "Aha, Aha, Big Prick, Aha, Aha, Big Prick." He would jump up to chase that kid and push him to the ground. His alias in Fengshan no doubt came from the kids' mocking Grandma's unique way of calling him. Even twenty-five years later, when he came back here as a director and his friend Zhang Ah had been murdered long ago, Zhang Ah's older brother came to see him and still called him Aha the Big Prick. There was also Monkey, who came by on a bike and told everyone that in the old days Aha did nothing but sing and goof around. (Zhu 1991b: 138)

Not only do Zhu and Hou both invest this square with a sense of plebian everydayness, they imagine it as a graphic record of social memory and a literal and metaphorical "home" for different generations. Like Hou, Zhu juxtaposes the children's popular games with Grandma's back-to-China obsession, using the motion of a spinning top as a visual metaphor for Grandma's circular movement between past and future.

In the brief exchange between Grandma and Aha, Zhu departs, however, from Hou's immobile camera by switching the narrative viewpoint from an omniscient third-person to a first-person entreaty by Grandma—"Ah Ha Gu, let's go back to the mainland"—before returning again to a third-person perspective. The exchange simulates the camera's movement from an objective position to a close-up and creates a contrasting effect between the two characters. Grandma may be displaced and disoriented, but she speaks her desire to return to China clearly and in the first person. By contrast, Aha's third-person response is tepid—"He didn't want to"—and this indifferent candor reveals his commitment to Taiwanese life. On the whole, both Hou and Zhu see the square as the people's place. Hou emphasizes its inclusive, accommodating horizontal layout, while Zhu underscores its humanistic, timeless nature at the heart of a community.

There are, however, differences between the two, the most visible being Zhu's revisions of Hou's gender politics, which we can measure by examining the depth and complexity of Zhu's transformations of one of Hou's key domestic scenes. One day, after Aha's sister has been engaged, she and her mother are sitting together in the living room while the rain comes down outside. Recounting the origins of her jewelry, the mother tells the daughter how hard her life has been, while, as if in counterpoint, her son Aha sings at the top of his lungs in the next room. In what feels like a structural paradox, Hou uses a minimalist aesthetic to represent the complex human psychology involved in these three characters. His simple mise-en-scène seems to translate the characters' ideological outlooks, especially in the representation of ongoing contrasts between Aha's individualism with his sister's collectivism. In a crucial twist, however, Hou constructs Aha's individualism as transethnic and transcultural, while Hou sees the sister's collectivism as domestic and somewhat ethnocentric. Gender seems to determine this choice: as a teenaged male, Aha is linked to the world of free imagination, while his sister plays the triple role of a homebound daughter, sister, and bride-to-be. These gendered boundaries are manifest in the characters' different locations in the house: Aha sits by himself on the window sill, singing to the rain and evoking offscreen love and abandon, while his sister is grounded in the center of the living room, deeply engaged with her mother's stories of the past.

Figure 6.11 Misty rain evokes a pensive mood in the neighborhood.

Figure 6.12 Aha singing a melancholy song in Taiwanese.

Hou opens the scene with an establishing shot to stage a pensive mood in a misty rain that blankets the whole neighborhood (Figure 6.11). The still, darkened view of an empty road speaks of emotional repression: every family seems to be hiding its own dark secrets behind closed doors.

In Figure 6.12, the view shifts to the indoor and shows a half-naked Aha (You Anshun) singing in affected melancholy. The multiplying window frames and the streaming rain imprison Aha's body and sexuality. Performing with adolescent sentimentality, he croons about his unrequited love and intolerable loneliness and his lyrics express the "*meidang*" ("unable" or "can't help it" in Taiwanese) distress of being helpless. But Hou's Aha is more than a forlorn teenager. His Taiwanese song indicates for the first time that the local dialect is used in a household where his Chinese immigrant parents and grandmother (Tang Ruwen) communicate exclusively in Hakka, and his siblings talk to each other in Mandarin. Transgressing the linguistic boundaries, Aha embodies a new composite figure who rises above the divisions of different ethnic cultures.

Aha's egocentric self-expression contrasts with the community-oriented role his sister plays as a chronicler of family history. A collection of group photos prefaces her appearance and prepositions her in different combinations with friends and family. Before she even arrives on camera, she has been constructed as a culture broker among different generations. (Figure 6.13). While these photos showcase Aha's sister as a binding force of the family, they also encapsulate her framed vision of the world. In particular, Hou highlights the constraints and burdens of her life in the following two shots. Figure 6.14 shows an important ritual in which the mother passes on to her daughter vari-

Figure 6.13 Family pictures position the sister as cultural broker for the family.

Figure 6.14 The mother gives family heirloom jewelry to the daughter.

ous family heirlooms and gently explains in Hakka the origin and significance of each item. Along with her jewelry, she uses her language (Hakka) and her spirit (as the survivor of an oppressive marital system) to impart to her oldest daughter a message of exemplary womanhood. Hou employs a rare close-up to highlight the ritual of ring-giving, which symbolizes a pledge, enclosure, and bondage. In Figure 6.15 we see the sister lowering her head as if under the weight of her cultural burden. In the background, there is the vacant bamboo chair, an emblem of her father's reigning intellectual authority embedded in the family consciousness. Aha's sister inherits not only her mother's gendered expectations but also her father's social concerns: in addition to being a good daughter, she is his biographer, while he remains the displaced intellectual for whom personal fulfillment is more important than anything else.

When the camera pulls away from the confessional sobriety of the mother and daughter (Figure 6.16), Aha's sister shouts to Aha in Mandarin: "Stop singing! You are selling copper and iron like a street beggar. That sounds truly awful!" Aha's sister deliberately misinterprets the song's lyrics and translates "*meidang*" (can't help it) into the Taiwanese homophone that means "selling copper." This mistranslation works on two levels. On the

Figure 6.15 The daughter bows her head under the weight of her cultural burden.

Figure 6.16 Aha's sister tells him to stop singing his Taiwanese song.

one hand, she treats Aha's affected self-pity as a kind of emotional panhandling similar to a street vendor walking up and down the local alleys. On the other, her reaction shows not only a critique of Aha's adolescent narcissism but also a response to her brother's self-romanticizing local literacy. Aha has thoroughly integrated into the local community and speaks, acts, thinks, and sings in fluent Taiwanese. His singing, however, feels like an affectation to his sister. It may seem like a cross-cultural achievement for him to express his private feelings on life and love in precisely the modes of the island, but Aha's sister interprets—and rejects—his gesture as self-nativitization.

Hou deepens this problematic with the following scene, a boldly envisioned one consisting of the mother's storytelling that lasts over five minutes. In play is real living time and the rhythm of the mother's reminiscences about past hardships. In Figure 6.17, we see mother and daughter sitting together, facing each other. Again, Hou's use of mise-en-scène is effective and powerful. The two women are associated with two pieces of luggage. The bag on the mother's left is packed as full as her memory: she has reached a destination. The other, next to her daughter, is wide open, with items loosely mixed together: she is at a new stage in an open-ended life.

This moment crystallizes the way the mother channels the past to her daughter. As she transfers her precious stones, she describes the injustices she has endured: despite her education, marriage gave her few options in life. Throughout the scene her speech seems to be guided or disciplined by the

Figure 6.17 Suitcases act as metaphors for the lives of the mother and daughter.

conservative ideology of the patriarch, represented by the empty chair and desk in the upper right-hand corner. Hou's camera is quiet and motionless throughout the long take, and with no directorial interruption the picture carries a sense of Shen's dispassionate lyricism, as if the viewer were being given time and space to connect with the mother's story. As in the opening scene of the film, Hou exploits the contrasting dynamic between the active words (which narrate a turbulent life and tragic events) and still images (which freeze spaces such as domestic interiors) to reinforce the narrative dissonance of life.

In Zhu's fictional adaptation of this scene, we see the combined influences of Shen and Hou: she describes Hou's mise-en-scène—Aha's singing, the domestic space, and mother's gift-giving—with a sequence of disconnected sensual imageries. This creates a reflective mood similar to the way in which Shen Congwen composes "a dreamlike 'associational rhythm'" and "perception of the world that brings the chronological flow of time to a halt" (David Wang 1993: 203).

> He started to like Wu Shumei at sixteen and began looking at himself in the mirror. At times when he felt troubled by love, he would often sit on a window sill and sing "What a Boring Life" to the rain outside, can't can't can't continue to live, please forgive me, what a boring life, can't can't can't continue to live...The Taiwanese pronunciation of "*meidang meidang*" sounded like the street vendors walking up and down the alleys to collect and sell discarded copper and iron. They sang from one street to another, and their streaming voices rained in and out of each household. Sitting in front of the Japanese glass window were mother and sister, whose silhouettes resembled paper puppets cut out of silver paper, floating in the reflection of the misty silver rain. Facing the light, the mother unrolled a piece of cloth and presented objects one by one to his sister. The jade pendant came from the mother's mother, who brought it back from South Asia. The watch was from the mother's father, who bought it in Shanghai as a present for the mother's seventeenth birthday. The sister accepted the jade pendant, but she already had a watch, so she wanted her mother to keep it. The sister tried on the jade pendant and scrutinized her appearance in the vague reflection of the glass window. The reflection of her face was overlapped with the shadows of the lamp and trees outside in the rain. (Zhu 1991b: 151–152)

If Hou's long take resists the cinematic constraint of screen time, Zhu's associational description liberates her story from narrative time. She cultivates a lyrical tempo, accented by nonspecific temporal denominators such as "at times," to coordinate Aha's singing with the local scrap collectors' shouting. Similarly, the way the mother itemizes the origins of her treasures integrates her past with her daughter's present and highlights their overlapping responsibilities to the family.

But Zhu adjusts Hou's gender politics by rewriting his passive image of Aha's sister and making her as thoughtful a character as her brother. This egalitarian, mirroring effect is literalized in the opening sentence (in which Aha looks at himself in the mirror and realizes that he is a sexual being) and is reinforced when his sister scrutinizes her own image in the glass window. What makes this revision compelling rather than simply corrective is that Zhu gives the brother and sister very different voices. Aha's song reveals the angst of going from boyhood to manhood, but his disorientation endows him with great cultural flexibility. The analogy to a collector of scrap metal may seem pejorative, but it suggests his mobility, for he collects local languages and stories to weld his postwar multicultural identity—his three languages are emblematic of Taiwan's mixed cultural origins. And Aha's sister no longer functions as a passive vessel of memory, the way that Hou tends to treat her, but as a reflective subject consciously engaged in self-discovery. Hou emphasizes her still posture, but Zhu creates a narrative rhythm in conversation that connects, in part through shared places, the mother with a daughter who has evolved beyond being a pawn of destiny.

Although Zhu starts transforming Aha's sister by comparing the women to "paper puppets cut out of silver paper," an analogy that emphasizes fragility and manipulability, her narrator soon discredits this as illusory and emphasizes the valuable possessions of jade pendant and watch, durable objects that symbolize the timeless love that circulates among places and generations. The scene ends with Aha's sister turning down the watch and trying on her pendant in front of the glass window; she recognizes, like Aha, her desire in a mirror. Rejecting Hou's placid vision of women as vessels of history and memory, Zhu sees them shaping an egalitarian society.

In the end, one can point to many good reasons why Hou's film inspired Zhu's literary adaptation. Not only is he a "literary" director who is influenced by many types of writers, but Zhu, as a screenwriter and novelist, was well positioned to understand his auteurial decisions and write cinematic fiction. Sharing an appreciation for Shen Congwen's aesthetic philosophy and regionalist tendencies, they each undertake *A Time* at a crucial point in their careers—exactly when both are transitioning from a romantic phase to a neorealist one in which they will investigate Taiwan's cultural identity politics. Hou's realism depends upon insights about women's social position and cultural representation that he learns from Zhu, and Zhu's depends on Hou's innovative use of discontinuity editing, establishing shots, mise-en-scène, still camera, long takes, and episodic narrative. Both artists use these quintessentially "adaptive" techniques to create a measured pace for dispassionate storytelling, a style that helps them articulate the emotional, political, and gender repressions of a bygone era at which they look with both regret and reminiscence.

CHAPTER 7

Chen Yuhui and Chen Guofu

Envisioning Democracy in *The Personals*

In the overall context of the book, my final two artists Chen Yuhui (b. 1957) and Chen Guofu (b. 1958) stand out for the ways they reconfigure autobiography, democratization, and gender politics. They investigate the fragmented subjectivity of postmodern professional women and mix such narrative genres as documentary, drama, anthropological field study, diary, fiction, and poetry. Their deconstructive confessions quietly criticize the utopian collectivism envisioned in the neorealist nativist tales of Hou and Zhu.

Unlike the more established artists discussed in this book, the two Chens are not as well known either inside or outside of Taiwan. In fact, few anticipated that the literary and cinematic versions of *The Personals* would become two of the most popular narratives in the island's domestic market in the past decade.[1] In 1992 Chen Yuhui composed *The Personals: Forty-two Men and I* as an autobiographical novel about a thirty-something woman's ambivalent search for a husband through a marriage ad. She based her story on personal ads that she herself had placed in Taiwanese newspapers between 1989 and 1990 and the subsequent conversations she had with 42 men (out of 108 contacts) from all walks of life in Taipei. From a physician and a musician to a factory worker and a pimp, from newspaper ad to essay to fiction, Chen included a wide range of viewpoints and narrative genres on the changing meanings of relationships and marriage in Taiwan's pluralistic society. Chen's antiestablishment, self-conflicting spirit proved attractive to Chen Guofu, perhaps because he had been sensitive to the autocratic rule of fear during Taiwan's Martial Law period. He, too, was looking for artistic ways to articulate the equitable coexistence of multiple subjects in a democratic society, and in 1998 he adapted her novel into a box-office cinematic hit. To understand the complex, uniquely Taiwanese mixtures of class, gender, and ethnicity involved in this example of adaptation, it is necessary to begin with an overview of cultural politics in Taiwan at the turn of the twenty-first century.

Visitors to Taipei are often impressed by the city's clean, sleek, and comfortable metro system (Municipal Rapid Transit or MRT), whose major arteries connect different corners of the sprawling metropolis. In addition to being efficient and convenient, the MRT is also unique in that it openly communicates Taiwan's democratic cultural politics: each destination is broadcast in four languages: Mandarin, Taiwanese, Hakka, and English. The constellation of these different tongues in a postmodern civic setting proclaims a commitment to the diversity and internationalization of a city-state that tends to equate the kind of monolingual rule it has twice endured—once during the Japanese colonial period (1895–1945) and again during the Martial Law period of the Kuomintang (KMT) (1948–1987)—with political oppression and cultural exploitation.

Taiwan's vision of multilingual inclusiveness reflects its search for a democratic equilibrium. In its continual struggle with China on issues of reunification and independence since the end of the civil war in 1949, Taiwan has steadily embraced different political voices and transformed itself from a one-party monopoly into a state with four major parties.[2] On its way to democratization, however, the island has also improvised with controversial policies. Residents wonder, for example, how much textbooks should reflect the shift of political, historical, cultural, and geographical emphases from China to Taiwan under the rule of different political parties. Should state-owned companies like the postal service or the oil companies substitute "Taiwan" for "China" to highlight the Democratic Progressive Party's political stewardship? How should Taiwan reconfigure the political evaluation of Chiang Kai-shek in the post-KMT era?[3] These and other unresolved disputes have sparked arguments and energized the political theatrics in the last two Legislative Yuans and on the streets.[4]

Thus Taiwan's ubiquitous manifestations of *democraticity* reveal both its diversification and its fractured self-visions. On the one hand, the polyglot MRT can be understood to reflect a globalist, centrifugal image that validates the coexistence of different cultures, but on the other, such public multilingualism can be seen as paying only lip service to "diversity" as a common ground for building a nationalist, centripetal island identity.[5]

Reading Taiwan as a democratic state that wants to be a nation helps us understand the island's ambition to ensure a balance of powers through the simultaneous validation of different cultures. Many recent fictional and cinematic accounts have attempted to represent, diagnose, or even shape the debate on Taiwan's political psychology and social reality. From major filmmakers such as Cai Mingliang (Tsai Ming-liang), Hou Xiaoxian (Hou Hsiao-hsien), and Edward Yang (Yang Te-chang) to cultural critics like Long Yingtai and Yang Zhao (Yang Chao) to such leading novelists as Huang Fan, Zhang Dacun (Chang Ta-chun), and Li Ang, there have been rich, honest, and satirical representations of the island's performative politics that dramatize the notion of democratization on both personal and national levels.

Gaining less critical attention but more popular interest is a new kind of intimate, self-deprecating, and self-conscious account of urban experience, one that I call "deconstructive confession": it is a composite narrative commingling of the genres of fiction with auto/biography and a challenge to the narrative boundary between fact and fantasy. Working from unpretentious demotic angles, these stories expose the ideological pretensions and follies of educated elites and reveal the contradictions that arise when social discourses too reductively identify multiculturalism and multilingualism as egalitarian forms of power-sharing. Among contemporary artists questioning the performance of democratization, the two Chens deserve special attention.

A reporter, actress, stage director, essayist, and novelist, Chen Yuhui is an artist with many professional identities. Her versatility in different art forms has led her to consider postmodern art as a kind of cannibalistic pastiche composed of stylistic mimicries and heterogeneous narrative perspectives. Although she is best known for writing essays, her fiction often combines poetic diction, dramatic tension, and antinarrative lyricism. Her writing, she says, hides "clues" like "rhythm, picture, sentiment, and story" to elicit the reader's dialogic imagination (Chen Yuhui 2006: 16).[6]

Complementing Chen's boundary-crossing aesthetic is her Taiwan-centered global vision of the island's relations with the world: she has lived abroad, mainly in France, the United States, and Germany, for more than two decades and has worked as a foreign correspondent for major Taiwanese papers. She sees a unique function in her role as a reporter: she wants to remedy the Taiwanese media's exclusive reliance on foreign news organizations, a practice that invariably casts Taiwan aside as the "Other." Her goal is to introduce to the local residents "a distinct Taiwanese individual's observations of international affairs" (23).

To a significant degree Chen Yuhui's genre-mixing artistry and subject-building political reporting match Chen Guofu's innovative spirit and ambivalent sense of nationhood. A critic-turned-director, Chen Guofu was one of Taiwan's most influential film commentators in the 1970s and 1980s, a time when he helped shape the critical discourse of Taiwan New Cinema

(1982–1989). (For more on this movement, see Chapter 6.) He is now a key representative of Taiwan's Second New Wave, a cinematic movement that began with his directorial debut, *High School Girls* (*Guozhong nüsheng*) in 1989.[7]

Chen Guofu's prolific output includes editing the popular film magazines *Yingxiang* (Influence) and *Dian ying xin shang* (Film appreciation), writing a collection of film commentaries entitled *Pian mian zhi yan* (Partial reflections, 1985), and completing a translation of *Dian ying li lun* (Film theory, 1983). He also edited *Buliesong* (Bresson, 1982) and *Xiqukaoke yanjiu* (Studies of Hitchcock, 1983). An avant-garde artist, he validates "skepticism and antitraditionalism" (Chen Guofu 1985: 3) in filmmaking. Both a theorist and a pragmatist, he sees film as intertextual and relational and therefore encourages dialogues not only between the Taiwan New Cinema and its predecessors (16) but also between different cinematic markets around the world (57).

Both Chens seek to challenge the power of the mainstream culture over marginalized subcultures and to procure for those marginalized groups a sense of social justice and aesthetic autonomy. In interviews Chen Yuhui points out how dualistic and deeply rooted this cultural hierarchy is in Taiwanese society: "If you are not mainstream, you are peripheral.... Taiwan pays attention to the mainstream culture only. Whatever is associated with a marginalized position is discriminated against. There is no space for marginal culture" (Chen Yuhui 2002: ii). Chen Yuhui recognizes this circumstance as a threat both to the egalitarian structure of Taiwan's democratic society and to its claim to a unique, nonperipheral identity. For his part, speaking from a postcolonial perspective, Chen Guofu considers Taiwan's mainstream culture, like that of many Third World nations, to be inextricably linked to Hollywood's imperialistic dominance. As a result, the Taiwanese audience's subjection to capitalist Americana often leads to the domestic suppression of local, organic art and to the creation of a passive audience "who are the perpetual consumers, never participants or creators" (Chen Guofu 1985: 58).[8]

Despite their philosophical commitment to recalibrating the cultural equilibrium in Taiwanese society, the two Chens are keenly aware of the ways that they can be trapped into solidifying the kind of binary between center and periphery they oppose. Chen Guofu, in particular, is uneasy about his own ambivalent role as a film critic who is paid by the very mainstream market that he criticizes.[9] He confesses that his own "critique of commodification has been consumed as a kind of commodity" (79). By the same token, Chen Yuhui is conscious of her own duplicity as an artist working in and against the system that harnesses her talent: publishers advertise her as a major mainstream writer, invoking precisely the hierarchical systems to which she objects in her work.

Nonetheless, because of the compelling way it gives voice to the marginalized figures, Chen Yuhui's novel *The Personals* remains one of the most important postmodern representations of Taiwan's performance of democracy to date. The narrative structure is so decentralized, paratactic, and egalitarian that it all but vacates perspectives of narrative authority. From the first-person narrator to the "the 1st Man" to "the 42nd Man," Chen gives names to none of the respondents to her ad, thereby effectively leveling the participants' many self-perceived distinctions.

We see Chen's signature mixing of genres and subjects right away in the personal ad that starts the novel:

> No regrets in life; no fear for death; no need of financial stability; won't be frustrated by breakup or separation. Be willing to be friends first before getting married. Not a matchmaking facility; don't try without sincerity. 7XX–06X9. (Chen Yuhui 2002: 18)[10]

Is this an ad or a poem? A command or a personal philosophy? An imaginative product or an autobiographical reminiscence? Is it "you" or "I" that is expected to possess the ascribed attributes? The narrator leaves all possibilities open and makes the ad ambiguously informational and lyrical, demanding and descriptive. The interchangeability between the first- and second-person pronouns, in particular, suggests that narrative authority can belong to anyone.

The mood of the ad is contradictory, for it comprises a series of negations seeking to exorcize distressing emotions. From "regrets" and "fear" to "need" and "frustration," it points out the psychological burdens that hinder one's ability to embrace "here" and "now" and to pursue free expression. Only when one is able to abandon the past (regrets) and ignore the future (death), the ad insinuates, can one live for the moment and pursue happiness. But this idealism implies an impending doom for love-seekers, for it all but predicts a failure. As is suggested by the multiplication of negatives—"No," "no," "no," "don't"—ultimately the narrator's optimistic logic of being "anti-unhappy" is in fact rather pessimistic.

The final statement—"don't try without sincerity"—epitomizes the irony of the narrator's rhetorical strategy: the narrator is herself insincere. She has assumed a fake identity (Ms. Wu) to conduct pseudointerviews, which are carefully analyzed more as a sociological experiment for a book than as an honest quest for a marriage partner. In fact, as the story unfolds, it is also in the insincerity of the interviewees that the emotional foundation for the book's calculated appeal lies: emerging from a kaleidoscope of lies, deceptions, and other moral failures is a nuanced vision of the ways these contradictions turn out to be surprisingly honest expressions of complex human emotions.

Chen Guofu's film adaptation of *The Personals* began as an entry into the 1997 Competition for Outstanding Movie Scripts, sponsored by Taiwan's Government Information Office. The screenplay, co-written with Chen Shijie, won one of the ten prizes awarded that year. In the preface to the publication of his script (1997), Chen was apologetic about how different his narrative was from Chen Yuhui's original story and vowed to follow her text more faithfully in the movie, but the completed movie nevertheless differs from the novel in several important aspects. Instead of making Du Jiazhen (René Liu) into a writer, as Chen Yuhui does in the novel, and hence reaffirming the story's auto/biographical nature, Chen Guofu transforms the protagonist into an ophthalmologist, an eye doctor who questions the veracity of seeing. These different professions reflect the Chens' preferences for distinct metaphors—language in the novel and vision in the movie—as conceptual tools to analyze Taiwan's complex identity politics. Another crucial difference is Chen Guofu's insertion into the film of an absent lover. His protagonist's involvement with a married man discloses her moral hypocrisy, a psychological duplicity that draws attention to the ways in which different narrative perspectives manufacture various forms of truth-telling experiences.

Despite these thematic differences, the two Chens share many important stylistic features. Chen Yuhui considers her writing to be influenced by the traditions of European art cinema and her literary style to combine "stream of consciousness with the editorial control of montage.... I try different organizational principles to construct paragraphs," she explains. "I interweave parts and fragments to piece together a work of collage. In other words, I coalesce and edit clips and snippets in ways that make a narrative" (Chen Yuhui 2006: 19). Chen's collage is most visible in the way the narrative vignettes of *The Personals* mix the language of personals ads, essays, reportage, fiction, and autobiography. Her rapid switch among different viewpoints (you, I, he, and other collective pronouns) further structures the narrative as a montage sequence of different faces.

Chen Guofu's adaptation works with the appeal of the novel's auto/biographical veracity by giving each interview a quasidocumentary feel. At the start of each blind date, Chen Guofu adds to the image the name, profession, and birth year of the respondent. In Figure 7.1, for instance, there is the ex-con (Chen Zhaorong), the only interviewee who manages

Figure 7.1 Quasidocumentary message, but it provides fictional information.

to capture Du Jiazhen's amorous interest. The print on the screen (Chen Wuxiong / Furniture maker / [born in] 1968) gives him an identity label, a formal-looking typescript that categorizes his existence. The irony is that, despite its "authentic" appearance, the information is fictional. Not only is this data not in the book, but many local viewers are also aware that Chen Zhaorong—one of the most prominent actors in Taiwan cinema—is playing the ex-con. As a result, Chen Guofu screens the disjunction between fiction and reality in ways that cast doubt upon the "truth-telling" assumption of the narrative. This should not be seen as a revisionist approach to Chen Yuhui's book, however, for the "autobiographical novel" also blends facts with fiction and reality with fantasy.

Further mimicking Chen Yuhui's style of discrediting the narrator and decentering the narrative authority, Chen Guofu highlights the blind spots of the camera eye to show the limitations of seeing. He stages various kinds of screens—the pupil of the eye, a TV, a mirror, and a movie—to identify the illusion of seeing a reflection within reflection.

Establishing the atmosphere, meaning, and objective of the movie, Chen Guofu uses an extreme close-up of an eye (Figure 7.2) to foreground his critique of mono-visional tyranny. The eye looks like a supernova: this collapsing, self-referential view of the camera, the subject "I/Eye," and the film as a visual art call attention to the ways that seeing can become paralyzed. The eye may look like an exploding sun, but it sees nothing through the lens except for its own reflection and registers no new or practical information.

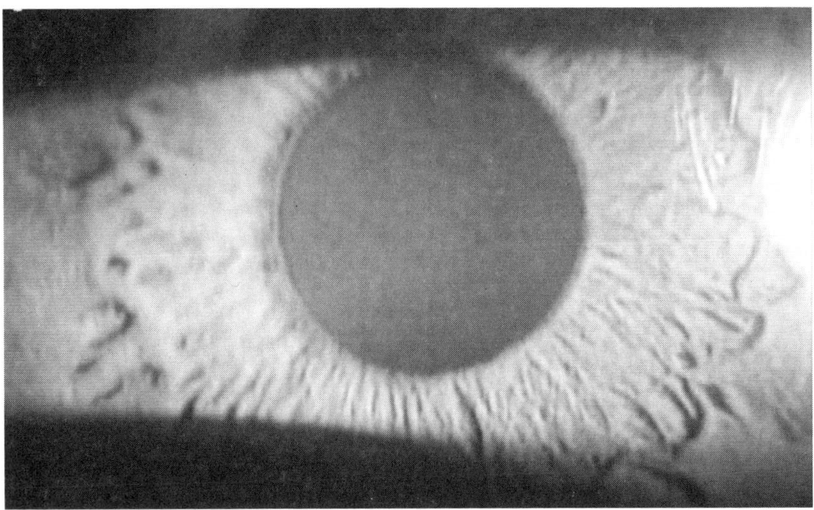

Figure 7.2 The supernova eyeball.

Even more suggestively, Chen stages the visual scrutiny in the office of an ophthalmologist and works throughout with the metaphor of disease to examine various impediments to healthy "vision" in contemporary Taiwanese society.

One of these impediments is the fact that urban dwellers are self-confined narcissists; they live, work, think, and see inside the box/mirror, a framed vision of the world that accepts and reinforces the supremacy of image and the mainstream culture. This iconic captivity is especially pronounced at the turning point of Jiazhen's life when she stumbles upon a TV show hosted by the celebrated political commentator Chen Wenqian. There is an important but untraditional shot-reverse-shot screening of the face-off of two women contained in different "boxes." We first see Jiazhen looking spellbound inside the layers of door frames that exemplify the depth of her social, moral, and gender constrictions (Figure 7.3). The blue lighting in the back almost makes her darkened face into a ghostly figure who has been aroused from a progressive postmodern dream—being a successful, independent, and desirable woman who needs no man's support—to confront the paralysis of her own boxed-in image: she has been waiting in vain for her lover's return and now decides to take control of her own destiny. An eye doctor, she sees a potential cure for her lovesickness by embracing the image of an iconic figure—Chen Wenqian—who epitomizes intelligence and autonomy in Taiwanese media (Figure 7.4). When the camera cuts to Jiazhen's point-of-view shot of the TV screen, Wenqian's flattened image (as opposed to the depth of Jiazhen's

Figure 7.3 Jiazhen's image, deeply boxed in and constrained.

Figure 7.4 Chen Wenqian's TV image, apparent enlightenment but actually capitalist construction.

constraints) is sitting next to a lamp—a literal provider of illumination and a metaphor for enlightenment—and appears to be free and detached. Glowing in the spotlight, she seems to offer visionary advice to women seeking guidance. But by not referring to the content of the program, Chen Guofu validates Chen Wenqian's appearance more than her intelligence. Her star power is constructed by the media's iconic packaging (makeup, costume,

Figure 7.5 Camera fails to penetrate below the surface.

lighting, stage set, and so forth), a capitalist production that sells not wisdom but illusion. Chen's screen-within-the-screen exposes the danger of blind trust in an imagistic culture that appeals to our narcissistic fantasy.

Chen Guofu illustrates the inability of the camera eye to see beyond the surface in an anticlimactic construct of a classic voyeuristic moment. His camera spies on Jiazhen's bathroom manifesto of self-transformation, but is unable or unwilling to penetrate into the private space to offer the audience a more revealing picture (Figure 7.5). Instead, he uses the window frame and foggy mirror to doubly block the audience's intimation of Jiazhen's state of mind and her body image. Despite its intrusive approach, Chen's subjective camera remains a coy observer that presents an obstructed viewpoint of the protagonist's complex emotional reality.

Chen Yuhui likewise conveys the narrator's perspectival limitations. In order to show the framed boundary of seeing and to present opposing viewpoints, she borrows the cinematic stylistic techniques of close-up and shot-reverse-shot. In her first blind date, for example, the narrator's scrutiny of the face of her respondent—a fifty-year-old physician—establishes the tone and visual border of the story. As she sizes him up, she betrays her own biases:

> I looked at him: his neatly combed hair was styled with grease; his face was pale and large. Except for the wrinkles around the corners of his eyes, his face wasn't really marked by years of toil.

> His eyes were small but lively, and this feature made his whole face look rather interesting. (Chen Yuhui 2002: 21)

"I looked at him" introduces a close-up that records the narrator's perspective. The physician's greased hair tags him as part of a passé generation decades removed from the narrator's age group. This age difference anticipates the ideological clash in their subsequent conversation in which the narrator diverts the physician's fatherly criticism with false statements. His look of white-collar patriarchal authority, however, gives the reader very little information about his personality, because the narrator chooses such bland adjectives as "pale and large" to show that his face seems unmarked by either experience or age. Even his "lively" eyes earn him only the vague comment of "interesting." With such an absence of specificity, Chen's "close-up" exposes less of the physician's individuality than his banality.

The physician's unremarkable face prepares us to receive his speech, filled with truisms that are both trite and assertive. Next in a sequence of shot-reverse-shot used as a literary device, Chen Yuhui creates a self-interrupting rhythm of storytelling.

> He didn't talk much, and this was probably why I felt embarrassed. I started explaining that the marriage ads were forced upon me by my family, which was pressuring me to get married sooner rather than later. In fact, I myself really wasn't in a hurry to get married. It wasn't until later that I became conscious of how my explanation sounded more like a vainglorious attempt to validate my sense of superiority.
>
> He asked me if a lot of people had contacted me after the ad appeared. I said not a lot, and the majority of the candidates were not ideal. Your ad was badly written. You didn't use the right rhetoric, he said. Not only did the ad not specify the age of the man you were looking for, it was ambivalent enough to create misunderstandings. I still insisted that it wasn't written by me.
>
> Long silence. (21)

This frustrated conversation shows that the narrator is defensive and discursive, while her interviewee is taciturn but confident. The narrator fears that the physician's silence signals his (and others') disapproval of the ways that she advertises her desire to get married, for it may well appear to be a desperate act of self-marketing. Anticipating accusatory charges, the narrator claims that she is the victim of familial pressures and is acting not on behalf of herself but of others. Yet this self-exonerating preemption, she later confesses, reveals a crisis in her self-confidence, for she is too timid to challenge the mainstream culture's disdain for the modest hope offered by personal ads. Ultimately, she sees herself colluding with the physician/patriarch to solidify the divide between the conventional and the marginal.

Careful analysis of this scene, however, reveals that the narrator's inconsistency does not make her a victim of circumstances. On the contrary, Chen Yuhui construes the protagonist's variance as a form of adaptability that enables her to negotiate with the dialogic construction of the self both as a speaking and spoken subject. This flexibility is most visible in the conversation between the narrator and the doctor where Chen carefully splits the female narrator into first- and second-person pronouns. Their exchange features two competing images of the narrator: the autobiographical voice of "I" appears to be unpredictable and confessional, while the narrated subject "you"—constructed by the direct-speech of the physician—is accused of being incompetent and ambivalent. ("You didn't use the right rhetoric.") A combined picture of "I" and "you" therefore shows the narrator's different relations with the reader and the story. The first-person narrator "I" seeks to disown her personal ad because it is a double failure: not only does it prove her unpopularity in the mainstream social network, but it also, in attracting so few qualified candidates, reveals her lack of communicative skill in the more utilitarian and desperate back-up medium of advertising. De-authorizing the personal ad by insisting that "it wasn't written by me" distances the narrator from the posting's social misstep. It also exposes her hypocrisy as a noncommittal speaker for the marginal culture whose nonconformist vision has generated her writing project.

The fluctuating voice of "I" contrasts with the authoritative steadfastness of the inflexible third-person speech. Addressing her in the second person, the doctor flatly criticizes the narrator: "Your ad was badly written." Chen Yuhui uses "you" without quotation marks in the text to transmit the immediacy of his critique and to create a shared second-person pronoun for the doctor and the reader, whose alliance strengthens the diagnosis of the narrator's presumed rhetorical blunder.[11] In the end Chen's style draws attention to a new auto/biographical voice that conflates different subjects, pronouns, and even tenses. This mélange is both technical and ideological, because the many viewpoints employed by Chen Yuhui's anxious, self-critical narrator express her emotional conflicts and exemplify the kind of narrative that, as critic Mark Currie suggests, aims to create and maintain contradictions rather than reduce them to individual meanings or structures (1998: 40). On a much larger level, produced by the multiplication of scenes like the one between the narrator and the doctor, the democratic implications of a deconstructive story and storytelling are significant. The voiced but unresolved contradictions articulate a pluralistic vision of postmodernity.

Given the cultural context in Taiwan, how does Chen's narrator function *outside* a chauvinistic system that administers the standards of evaluation? I would suggest that her narrator becomes "another" subject by removing the binary framework of ethics. Averting the dualistic and patriarchal judgment of right/true and wrong/false, she presents an evolving emotional reality in which the psychological schism of a modern woman multiplies her subjective viewpoints and consumes other voices. This would help explain the striking way the narrator, throughout *The Personals,* paraphrases her respondents' speeches or quotes their remarks without quotation marks. These men always speak in the third-person "he," never the first-person "I," and the absence of the centralized vertical subject diminishes the authority of their descriptive power. Even when they address the narrator in the second-person "you," their lectures are often cannibalized by the text as a part of the narrator's discursive speech and incorporated into a democratizing dialectic.

Chen Guofu also creates a world without an authoritative masculine subject. He invents and then locates the most significant man in the story—Du Jiazhen's married lover—into an offscreen voice mail that dutifully records Jiazhen's solipsistic speeches. This decisive evacuation of centralized male power allows the film to diversify and democratize its scrutiny of *other* men in the story. Starting from the betel-nut-chewing factory worker, Chen parades a host of Taiwanese men (and one woman) who live on the edge of society. The feminist implication of Chen Guofu's narrative paradigm is apparent: men are now the others of women and the narrator's posture provides a yardstick, however wavering, for "normal" and "mainstream" behaviors. But Chen Guofu recognizes the contradictions involved in simply reversing the hierarchy of sexual difference. Even more explicitly and forcefully than Chen Yuhui, Chen Guofu's adaptation exposes the paradoxes inherent in the way Jiazhen simultaneously embraces and attacks bourgeois class and gender expectations.

Chen presents Jiazhen's conflicts by framing her images in alternating shots of her back and close-ups of her face. Presenting the character's back highlights the contextualization of her body language, because the viewer understands the meanings of the image only by interpreting the body's interaction with its environment. Screening the face alone so isolates the image that it becomes self-representational and autogenetic. As Mary Ann Doane points out: "The scale of the close-up transforms the face into an instance of the gigantic, the monstrous: it overwhelms. The face, usually the mark of

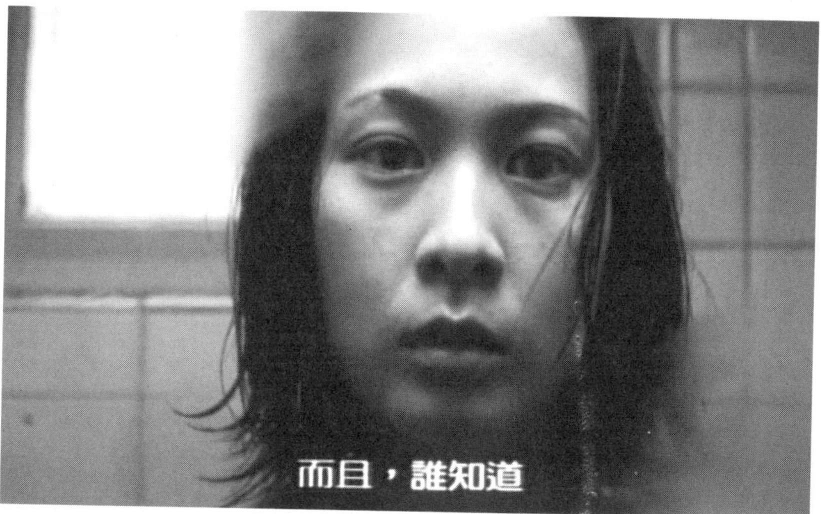

Figure 7.6 Jiazhen takes possession of herself through her image.

individuality, becomes tantamount to a theorem in its generalizability. In the close-up, it is truly bigger than life" (2003: 94).

Chen Guofu juxtaposes these two kinds of presentation to stress the necessary multiplicity of perspectives in examining the relations between individual and society. A case in point is when Jiazhen decides to interview her respondents, and she looks at herself in the mirror in defiance of many requests for her photo (Figure 7.6). This is a picture of a resolute character concluding that her image is her own, not others'. It is also an illustration of her quest for autonomy and freedom to sever herself not only from a "dead" relationship (her lover has already passed away), but also from a constricting professional identity (as an eye doctor) and the constraining social etiquettes of being a single woman. In other words this close-up represents Jiazhen's manifesto of seeing nothing but herself. To a certain extent, we can read such a self-centered vision as a deconstruction of Doane's overall point that sees close-up as an abstract theorem, an etherealizing removal of self from self, for this magnified reflection in the looking glass can be scrutinized as an attempt, perhaps unsuccessful, to reclaim control over the self-abstractive power of the close-up.

Following the close-up of her resolution is a view of Jiazhen's back as she waits at a bus stop to embark on her first blind date (Figure 7.7). Her self-transformation seems to give her a new identity: she has already quit her job at the hospital, cut her hair, and started to explore the new routine of being a full-time marriage seeker. Looking through the divided panels

Figure 7.7 Image of Jiazhen's back at the public bus stop, her ordinariness.

of the glass window in the bus shelter, Chen's camera stays at a distance to show a faceless protagonist whose anonymity is reinforced by her fake identity—Ms. Wu (her lover's surname, which suggestively rhymes with "emptiness" and "mistake")—she uses in the interviews/rendezvous. Her invisible ordinariness makes her indistinguishable from others. She is one of the many who take plebian public transportation. Departing from the self-centered and perhaps elitist individualism of the close-up, her bus-waiting back image conjures up a prosaic picture of anybody everydayness.

Whereas the close-up of Jiazhen's face in the looking glass makes her a larger-than-life figure whose visage embodies the moral compass for the movie, the shot of her back creates an aura of averageness. It further becomes an important lead-in to many more close-ups of herself and her respondents in an evenly divided shot-reverse-shot formation. The contrasting representations of singularity and commonness point up a paradox inherent in democratic societies: to privilege the many over the one is nevertheless to create totalizing standards. Democracy can therefore be seen both as a system that protects the freedom of being different and as an enforcer of one "universal," standardized Truth that suppresses other smaller, inessential truths.

This paradox emerges even more clearly in Jiazhen's blind date with Wang Chaoming, a factory worker, an encounter between a stereotypical Taiwanese male and a modern, educated, class-conscious professional woman (Figures 7.8 and 7.9).

Figure 7.8 Interview with Wang Chaoming; his face and textual information.

Figure 7.9 Fastidious "Ms. Wu" in interview with Wang Chaoming.

The worker's confidence in his social position as a solid wage earner contrasts with Jiazhen's insecurity about being in the company of an uncouth betel-nut-munching individual. In these back-to-back shots, the PC worker jokes about how his name earns him the alias of being "stately" (*wang chao* means "king" and "dynasty") and "manly" (*ma han* means "tough warrior"). He interrupts his self-introduction with repeated chewing and spitting of betel nut, an act socially construed as "earthy," "working-class," and "masculine," but also culturally interpreted as "crude" and "uneducated." Sending him a look of disdain, Jiazhen ignores all of his comments and asks, instead, with condescending feminine charm if he is able to stop chewing. Evenly balancing their images on the screen, Chen's camera neither belittles nor ridicules the worker's habit; if anything it highlights Jiazhen's nervous little laughs and derides her fastidiousness. As a result, the camera is more empathetic than the character; Chen's close-up humanizes the interviewed subject in ways that repudiate Jiazhen's superficial reading of his disembodied visage. Despite her profession as an ophthalmologist and her experience as an interviewer, she proves unable to look beyond the man's appearance.

Although critics differ in how they interpret the meanings of facial close-ups, Jacques Aumont (1992) is of particular relevance to Chen's aesthetic because he underscores the democratic significance of the cinematic representations of average faces. He sees the "ordinary face" as "an attribute of a free and equal subject with rights like all the others but that must ceaselessly exercise its liberty and equality in confronting that of other free and equal subjects. The ordinary face of the cinema is also that of Western democracy, that is to say, American and capitalist. It is a trait of imperialism, its ordinariness is an order" (60; quoted by Doane 2003: 106). But while Aumont believes that filming ordinary faces inevitably establishes a tyrannical standard, Chen Guofu's "comparative" close-ups of Jiazhen and others—a pluralizing technique that allocates equal time, space, and voice to each one—represent important exceptions or modifications to his theory. In fact, Chen Guofu's aesthetic produces a sharp *critique* of Jiazhen's *undemocratic* attitude. The close-ups are documentary evidence of the way she tries to craft and prioritize an elitist, essentialist vision of society.

Just as visible is Jiazhen's moral duplicity in simultaneously defending and destroying the traditional values of marriage. She is involved with a married man but lectures others on the importance of a monogamous relationship. She advocates women's rights but shows little interest in advancing gender equality. In her interview with a lesbian photographer, she reveals her homophobic anxiety and perpetuates stereotypical misconceptions of sexual "deviants."[12] These and other criticisms unmask Jiazhen's stiff resistance to the polyphonic and multifarious faces of a democratic society.

At the end Chen Guofu shows Jiazhen literally and metaphorically turning her back on a dynamic multicultural society. She embraces, instead, a self-limiting, rigid, and otherworldly vision that is confined to the screens of mechanical devices. Figure 7.10 shows that, after one of those long dating interviews, Jiazhen returns to her empty apartment and speaks into her lover's answering machine. Sitting in front of a TV screen, she seems twice removed from reality: the TV box creates a world of illusion that entraps her imagination, while the recording box speaks of a dead man's seduction still monopolizing her confession and her "genuine" self. The view of her back not only conceals her face but also diminishes her "humanity" to the extent

Figure 7.10 Jiazhen boxed in by illusions, her TV, and her married lover's answering machine.

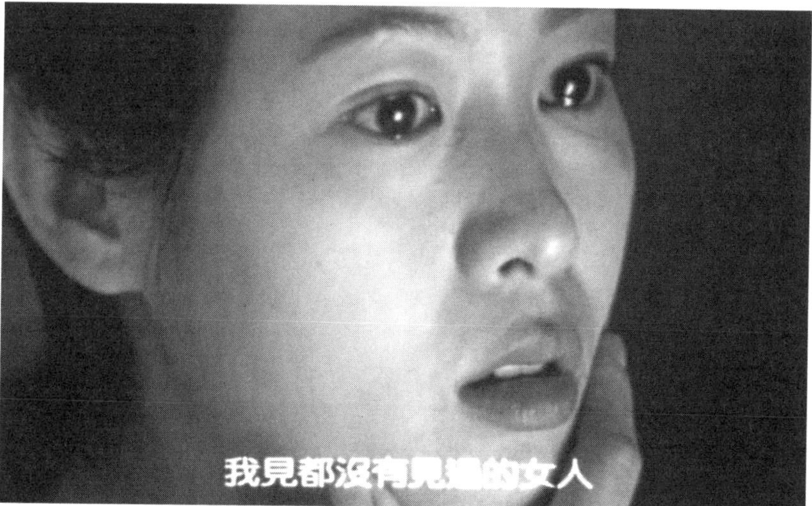

Figure 7.11 Jiazhen learns of her lover's death.

that she is consumed by self-alienating modern machines that dictate her speech and viewpoint.

Contrasting with the depth and ghostly surrealism of her back view is the climactic close-up of Jiazhen's face near the end of the film, when she learns of her lover's death (Figure 7.11). It is a self-reckoning because Jiazhen now realizes that she has been in the dark about the reasons behind his disappearance. Revelation of the truth coincides with the blow-up of her facial features and illustrates the limitation of her (and the viewer's) perspective. Unlike the earlier scene in the bathroom, which crucially involved a mirror, now Jiazhen *is* fully captured and revealed by a camera that projects rather than reflects her face, "that bodily part not accessible to the subject's own gaze" (Doane 2003: 93). We now see that Jiazhen is seen, but not seeing. Moreover, for the first time in the film, the phone becomes an active agent in silencing her narcissistic confession.

In both the literary and film versions, *The Personals* addresses the potentials and the limitations of Taiwan as a democratic polyphonic society. While Chen Yuhui explores the indeterminacy and multiplicity of subjects to project Taiwan's changing identity politics, Chen Guofu draws special attention to the restrictions of perspective and highlights the instability of Taiwan's self-fracturing visions. Both artists emphasize the way gender politics plays an integral part in the dialogues on Taiwan's democratic plurality, and both use cinematic narrative techniques such as close-up and shot-reverse-shots to explore these and other political paradoxes inherent in "equalizing" the relations between Taiwan's mainstream and its margins. Their confessional and self-critical approach complicates their relations with current cultural discourse and treats storytelling as an authentic yet self-parodic medium of representation, one destined to produce fragmentary yet democratic meanings.

Conclusion

Throughout this book I have pulled at many threads in the fabric of Chinese film, literature, and cultural politics. Rather than pursuing the question of "fidelity" in adaptation—a trap in every guise from the political to the philosophical to the technical—I have emphasized individual contexts and meanings, each of which has advanced Chinese cinema and literature in an important way. Looking back, what stands out is a range and diversity—China, Hong Kong, Taiwan, and overseas Chinese communities—that challenge the very idea of geographical or linguistic unity. We saw basic forms as different as cinematic adaptation of literature, literary adaptation of film, self-adaptation, and nonnarrative adaptation, along with an array of genres, including martial arts, melodrama, romance, autobiography, and documentary drama. And so many literary and cinematic movements! The Fifth Generation Movement, Taiwan New Cinema, Taiwan Second New Wave, Hong Kong Second Wave, martial arts fiction, Hong Kong modernism, Chinese experimental modernist fiction, postrealism, realist neonativism, postmodernism, the list goes on. Seven of the most influential contemporary Chinese-language directors—Ang Lee, Zhang Yimou, Stanley Kwan, Wong Kar-wai, Dai Sijie, Hou Xiaoxian, and Chen Guofu—have ascended to the rank of auteur in large part because of their success in reinterpreting Chinese literature. The evidence of this book suggests that we can appreciate the aesthetic philosophies and ideological positions of Chinese cinema only if we take literature into account.

With such diversity in play, general comments seem reductive. Still, in the interest of providing markers for future discussion, a few tentative conclusions may be warranted.

The first one I am tempted to draw is that adaptation succeeds best when the source text inspires complex character psychology. The examples are numerous and striking: Jen's moral ambivalence in *Crouching Tiger,* Lotus's madness in *Raise the Red Lantern,* Jiaorui's composite image as a good-yet-bad-woman in *Red Rose,* Mrs. Chan's ethico-romantic predicament in *In the Mood,* the narrator-protagonist's transcendental and yet down-to-earth third-cultural vision in *Balzac,* Aha's China-Taiwan-Hakka complex in *A Time,* and Jiazhen's first-second-third-person identity crisis in *The Personals.* In each case a literary vocabulary or narrative strategy was extracted and changed in order to articulate the struggles of characters that were simultaneously internal, in the individual mind and body, and external, in a changing world.

Of course, the richness of characterization may be a cornerstone of adaptation in non-Chinese settings, too. As we saw in Chapter 4, such "literary" directors as Alain Resnais and Michelangelo Antonioni are expert at dissecting and visualizing human psychology, and other major filmmakers could be mentioned who share this penchant. Akira Kurosawa in Japan, Satyajit Ray in India, Ousmane Sembène in Senegal, and Luis Buñuel in Spain are a few seminal figures who have brilliantly experimented with literary characters to produce period dramas, social-realist stories, postcolonial tales, and surrealist fantasies.

But perhaps Chinese adaptation features to a special degree a stylistic commitment to dialogue scenes. Again, this is by no means unique on the world stage, but the films we have seen undeniably showcase conversations as one of the richest loci or flashpoints for cine-lit symbiosis. Contemplative or stichomythic, subdued or passionate, conversations of all kinds concretize larger political, symbolic, historical, and aesthetic strata. Recall how Ang Lee, Wong Kar-wai, and Hou Xiaoxian deftly and often radically used shot-reverse-shots to juxtapose words and images in blends of connection and disconnection. In fact virtually every adaptation featured in this book screens multilayered, dialogical mixtures of minds and bodies, with such elaborate mises-en-scène often depending upon the audience to perceive tensions between what is said and unsaid, seen and unseen.

What is the future of Chinese adaptation? This question may be imprudent and difficult, but it is also natural. For my part, I expect to see more successes in the area of cinematic fiction. Zhang Yimou's blockbuster hit *Hero* (2002) was adapted into a novel with the same title by Li Feng in 2002. Taiwanese director Wei Desheng's (Wei Te-sheng) sensational *Cape No. 7* (*Hai jiao qi hao,* 2008) recently broke all box office records in Taiwan and has now been adapted into a best-selling novel with the same title by Lan Gefeng. This two-way street of adaptive exchange will surely continue, extending well beyond feature films and novels. We are already seeing more multimodal adaptations in films, stage plays, folklore, comics, TV dramas, Internet fiction, and other narrative media. Perhaps the most adaptable and adapted tale in the history of Chinese culture, the protean classic *Journey to the West,* shows no sign of losing its ability to inspire new versions in new settings.[1]

In the context of global artistic production, another growth industry is already visible in the cross-cultural and translingual adaptations that bring together different national cultures and subcultures. In *Crouching Tiger* and *The Little Chinese Seamstress* we saw how international collaborations shaped the work of two Chinese directors. More recently, Hou Xiaoxian has adapted Albert Lamorisse's classic 1956 short *The Red Balloon* into the critically acclaimed *Le Voyage du ballon rouge* (Flight of the red balloon, 2008). Joining the lineage of such pioneers of transcultural adaptation as Kurosawa and Sembène are other directors drawing upon the possibilities afforded by newer media. Japanese director Gorō Miyazaki recently adapted Ursula Le Guin's fantasy *A Wizard of Earthsea* into the animated hit *Tales from Earthsea* (2006), a much-anticipated production that crossed boundaries of language, culture, genre, and medium. Similarly, the popular Korean director Boon Joon-ho is currently adapting a French dystopian comic *Le Transperceneige* into a feature film to be released in 2011. As the global circulatory system of film adaptation continues to widen and become more complex, transnational adaptations, including but far transcending Chinese examples, will continue to reshape all national literatures and cinemas.

Notes

Introduction

1. This list of adaptation scholars is by no means exhaustive. Some other very useful references include Robert Richardson (1969); a series of Chinese essays on adaptation published by the editorial department of *Film Art* (1992); William Ferrell (1995); Mikhail Iampolski (1998); Deborah Cartmell and Imelda Whelehan, eds. (1999); Corrigan, Timothy, ed. (1999); Martin Huang, ed. (2004); John Desmond and Peter Hawkes, eds. (2006); and James Welsh and Peter Lev, eds. (2007).

Chapter 1: Wang Dulu and Ang Lee

1. Dudley Andrew. 1984. *The Concept of Film Theory.* Oxford: Oxford University Press. 97.

2. *Crouching Tiger, Hidden Dragon* not only won four Oscars in 2001, including the "Best Foreign Language Film," and seventy-two other film awards, but it is also "the most commercially successful foreign-language film in U.S. history and the first Chinese-language film to find a mass American audience" (Klein 2004: 18). For further references, see Stephen Teo's interview with James Schamus (Teo 2001b); and Christina Klein (2004). The film has also received an unprecedented amount of critical attention. See, for example, Richard Corliss (2000), Felicia Chan (2003), James Schamus (2004), Andrian Martin (2005), Fran Martin (2005), Chris Berry and Mary Farquhar (2006), and L. S. Kim (2006), among others.

3. Although scholars have pointed out Ang Lee's indebtedness to the Chinese *wuxia* cinematic tradition, pioneered by such masters as King Hu and Zhang Che in the 1960s and 1970s (Teo 2005a; Martin 2005), they have not studied Lee's connection to Wang Dulu (1909–1977). This is due in part to the fact that martial arts fiction has not had the same impact on the global market as martial

arts cinema, the popularity of which is evident in the subsequent blockbuster successes of Zhang Yimou's *Hero* (2002) and *House of Flying Daggers* (2004), Chen Kaige's *The Promise* (2005), and Feng Xiaogang's *The Banquet* (2006). Lee is rightly credited with helping reintroduce the *wuxia* genre to the world, but it is important to note that he has also helped redefine the collaborative relations between the two most popular "vernacular" forms of Chinese storytelling, martial arts cinema and martial arts fiction.

4. For studies of martial arts fiction as a narrative genre, see James J. Y. Liu (1967); Chen Yongming and Joseph Liu (1998); and John Christopher Hamm (2005).

5. Jen's relation with her governess Jade Fox is sexually ambiguous. In addition to their intimate daily interaction—hair-brushing and undergarment-making—Jade Fox further proposes to bring Jen with her as she travels around *jianghu*—the anarchistic world of knights-errant and criminals. They will "keep each other company," Jade Fox states several times in the movie.

6. *Jianghu* is a unique term used extensively in Chinese martial arts fiction and film. It literally means "rivers and lakes," but allegorically it means a utopia (or dystopia, depending on the situation) that allows knights-errant and vagabonds to coexist. I will explain in more detail the full significance of the term later in the text.

7. The original novel was published in 1941 as part of a newspaper serial called *Crane Iron Series* (*He tie xi lie*). The series was later republished in five volumes by Shanghai's Li li shu ju in 1948 (Sang 2005: 304). All of my citations are from the 2001 edition published by Yuan jing, and the translations of Wang Dulu's novel from Chinese into English are mine.

8. Given the extensive influence of Freudian theory on the works of Lee and Wang, it seems plausible to suggest that both artists interpret the notion of *yi* in a way that parallels Freud's definition of the superego: both *yi* and the superego function as cultural authorities that exist to consolidate the power of civilization and police wayward, instinctual behavior.

9. There are many other specific associations of *bao* with the lady knight-errant's chivalrous moral function. The Tang tale "The Merchant's Wife" (Gu ren qi) and Pu Songling's seventeenth-century short story "The Lady Knight-Errant" (Xia nü) in *Stories of the Strange* (*Liaozhai zhiyi*) are two of the most famous. More generally, the notion of *bao* is often attributed to Sima Qian (ca. 145–86 BCE)—one of China's greatest historians, who lived in the Han dynasty (206 BCE-220 CE). In Sima's *Biographies of the Assassin Retainers* (*Ci ke lie zhuan*), an assassin, Yu Rang, famously pronounces the meanings of *bao* as follows: "A woman makes herself beautiful for those who appreciate her; a gentleman stands ready to die for those who understand him" (*nü wei yue ji zhe rong, shi wei zhi ji zhe si*).

10. The Four Books and Five Classics (*Si shu wu jing*) are the classical Chinese texts that contain the basics of Confucian teachings. The Four Books

include *The Great Learning* (*Da xue*), *The Doctrine of the Mean* (*Zhong yong*), *The Analects of Confucius* (*Lun yu*), and *The Mencius* (*Meng zi*). The Five Classics comprise *The Book of Changes* (*Yi jing*), *The Book of Poetry* (*Shi jing*), *The Book of Rites* (*Li ji*), *The Book of History* (*Shu jing*), and *The Spring and Autumn Annals* (*Chun qiu*). According to Ang Lee, Xiulian is a traditional and conservative character who generally abides by the Confucian view of a gendered, hierarchical world (2002: 276).

11. In her analysis of Wang Dulu's *Crouching Tiger, Hidden Dragon*, Tze-lan Deborah Sang points out that Wang uses the premodern historical setting in his characterization of Yu Jiaolong (Jen) to dramatize the conflict between a defiant self-liberating woman and the Confucian codes of behavior. "The result of this transposition," Sang suggests, "yields a simultaneously romanticized and radicalized portrait of the unorthodox elite woman fighting to emancipate herself from the restrictive roles of the naïve, cloistered daughter and the housewife. This imaginary portrait is a romanticized image larger than life because the novel grants its heroine undefeatable swordsmanship when faced with adversaries.... This portrait is also a radicalized image because, by choosing the eighteenth century over contemporary times as the novelistic setting, Wang gained license to represent Confucian orthodox as largely intact and its disciplinary power as entrenched—more entrenched than it might have been in the semicolonial, half-Westernized Chinese cities of his day. The temporal shift from the present (that is, the early twentieth century) to a somewhat archaic setting thus renders the conflict between a free-spirited woman and the Confucian gender doctrine all the more acute and, in the eyes of the reader, all the more extraordinary, dramatic, and enthralling" (2005: 288). In short, restrictive Confucianism acts as a cultural superego trying to govern Jen's behavior.

12. Ang Lee's challenge to dualism takes place not only in the context of Wang's fiction but also against a tradition in martial arts cinema. Chinese producers such as Raymond Chow, the head of Golden Harvest, prefer "clear-cut story lines with black presented as black and white presented as white" (quoted in S. Teo, 2005a: 195).

Chapter 2: Su Tong and Zhang Yimou

1. Recent studies of Chinese film and literature have drawn out the importance of rethinking the relationship between gender and Chinese modernity. See, for example, Shih Shu-mei (2001); Zhong Xueping (2000); Yeh Wen-hsin (2000); Margaret Decker (1993); Kristine Harris (1997); Wendy Larson (1998); Sheldon Lu (1997); Rey Chow (1995); Lu Tonglin (1995); Tani Barlow (1993); Yue Ming-bao (1993); Widmer and Wang (1993); and Chow (1991). Other topics of interest include the relations among subjectivity, romanticism, and cultural politics. See Perry Link (1981); Denten (1998); Chi Pang-Yuan and David Wang, eds. (2000); Leo Ou-fan Lee (1973 and 1993).

2. The term *Jiangnan* literally means "south of the Yangtze River," a very prosperous and largely Wu-speaking area that includes such regions as the southern part of Jiangxi province, the southern part of Anhui province, the northern part of Jiangxi province, and the northern part of Zhejiang province.

3. Chen Kaige's famous debut, *Yellow Earth* (1984), for which Zhang Yimou was his cinematographer, is a poignant portrayal of a chance encounter between intellectuals and peasants in a rural farming community. This film was an important breakthrough for the Fifth Generation directors and was well received at the 1985 Hong Kong Film Festival. For critical accounts of the rise of the Fifth Generation directors, see Chris Berry, ed. (1991); Sun Xiandao and Li Duoyu, eds. (2006); Ni Zhen (2002); and Zhang Yingjin (2002 and 2004).

4. Zhang's *Hero* and other martial arts epic films are, of course, controversial because they evoke very polarizing interpretations. They can be exalted as celebrations of traditional Chinese art or criticized as conscious salutes to fascist art. See, for example, Jenny Kwok Wah Lau (2007).

5. Zhang demonstrates his pragmatic marketing instinct in his interview with Ni Zhen: "First, films must be enjoyable, and their deeper meanings must be experienced by the audience through their enjoyment. That's the kind of film I like, and that's why I never was particularly taken with Italian neorealism" (quoted in Ni Zhen 2002: 102). See also Judy Stone (1997).

6. There is a fundamental difference between critical realism and socialist realism. Critical realism, according to Lee (1993) and Anderson (1990), makes a distinction between "I" and "they," and in the context of the May Fourth Movement it "may in fact have been part of a manifestation of individualism" (Lee 1993: 364). Meanwhile, socialist realism signaled a "great return" to the "communal," for its narrative subject is the "collective we." As a result, socialist realism was later transformed into a kind of revolutionary romanticism before and during the Cultural Revolution. Both experimental novelists and the Fifth Generation directors strongly oppose the didacticism of socialist realism.

7. All four of Chen's wives are from different social backgrounds. Chen's oldest wife, Joy, is from a privileged social class; his second wife, Cloud, still has "the appearance of a cultured young woman from a good family" (Su 1993b: 15–16); his third wife, Coral, is a famous opera singer; and his fourth wife, Lotus, comes from the middle class.

8. Suzie Young-Sau Fong offers an interesting analysis of Zhang's title, which she translates as *Big Red Lantern Hanging High*. She comments that the "hanging" suggests an in-medias-res device and introduces spectators to the interruptive violence of the film. See "The Voice of Feminine Madness in Zhang Yi Mou's *Da Hong Deng Long Gao gao Gua* (*Raise the Red Lantern*)" in *Asian Cinema Asian Cinema* 7, 1 (1995): 12–23.

9. Those who see Zhang Yimou's critical-realist approach as lacking in depth include David Edelstein (1988: 64), H. C. Li (1989: 113), and Dai Qing

(1993: 333–337). Those who salute it for showing an understanding of the power of surfaces include Rey Chow (1995: 142–172) and Sheldon Lu (1997).

10. I have made slight modifications to Michael Duke's translation.

11. Zhang's focus on the exploitation of women's bodies is guided by a humanist concern for the production of a critical consciousness. He explains in an interview: "What I want to express is the Chinese people's oppression and confinement, which has been going on for thousands of years. Women express this more clearly on their bodies because they bear a heavier burden than men" (quoted in Sheldon Lu 1997: 110).

12. Although, like Su, Zhang later also reveals Chen's much-discussed impotence, in the film it is not as open and visible a situation as it is in the novel. Chen remains a shadowy figure throughout the movie.

13. Rey Chow mentions that "these tales of gothic and often morbid oppression are marked by their contrast with the sensuous screen design of the films. Zhang's film language deploys exquisite colors in the depiction of "backwardness" (1995: 143). This "backwardness" refers mainly to the deprivation of women's rights.

14. Quoted in Doane (1991: 48).

15. A number of critics have noticed a connection between Lotus and the well. Lu Tonglin writes: "The world of the well is also a metaphor for [Lotus's] subjective world: morbid, lonely, friendless, and, at the same time, mysterious and seductive" (1995: 138). More important in this chapter is the fact that there is an "objective" and "rational" world that exists outside the well and the mind of Lotus. When these two worlds collide in Lotus's consciousness, new visions of the self emerge. It is a self that tries to negotiate a livable space between reality and fantasy, to amend the narrative gap between a concubine's past and future, and to find a path for a woman to resist patriarchal dominance. "Who knew the meaning of that well?" Lotus asks (Su 1993b: 55). The voices of the well and Lotus resist being penetrated by logic, reason, and measurement, and in a sense their imperviousness puts them beyond the patriarch's law. Ultimately Su Tong's narrative makes the well a bewitching pool that projects a self-other fusion: Lotus and the drowned concubines become nearly indistinguishable, "lawbreakers" who strive to make "the voices of some lost souls" surface and be heard (1993b: 73).

16. One of the most important links among power, liberation, and intellectual life is Lotus's possession of a flute that Chen Zuoqian later burns. Lotus's nostalgia for a carefree past is associated with the freedom of learning (Su 1993b: 38).

17. The passivity associated with washing is much different from an earlier episode in which she shows tremendous composure and courage by washing her hair in the same pond where her father has just committed suicide (Su 1993b: 19).

18. Yue Ming-bao offers several interesting examples to substantiate her

critique: Ye Shengtao's *One Life* (*Yi sheng*), Xiao Qian's *The Raining Dusk* (*Yuxi*), Ye Zi's *On the Yangzi Ferry* (*Chang jiang lun shang*). I would add Lu Xun's "New Year Sacrifice" (Xin nian de zhufu).

19. Su Tong's feminist bent is often ignored by critics, who see his writings as an endorsement for "misogynistic tendencies in contemporary China" (Lu Tonglin 1995: 14). My analysis of *Wives and Concubines* suggests instead that the well imagery concentrates precisely the subversive potential that Luce Irigaray expressed through her preferred image of the cave. Critiquing the "twisted, reversed, inverted" phallic theory about gender relations, Irigaray's cave functions like the female body and speaks through a "feminine" language that comprises many voices (1985a: 279). The mystery of this grotto/body, Irigaray writes, is like "a shadow theater where only the shakiest of certainties are produced—phantom presences, dim memories, expectations of something unforeseen—which disappear as fast as they appear and reappear" (1985a: 354–355). The cave's unfathomable nature is similar to Irigaray's controversial definitions of "feminine language" that highlight the discursive and variant characteristics of a woman's speech: "'She sets off in all directions, leaving 'him' unable to discern the coherence of any meaning. Hers are contradictory words, somewhat mad from the standpoint of reason, inaudible for whoever listens to them with readymade grids, with a fully elaborated code in hand" (29). Like the cave/body/well, Irigaray's "feminine language" asserts comparably irregular and illegible signs that defy male linguistic rules. Although aspects of Irigaray's theory are debatable (Silverman 1988: 141–186), her cave specula(riza)tions are a useful counterpoint to Su Tong's elaborations on the well.

20. Su's story shows how women's ambition to "go up" is prohibited. In his attack on Coral's unruliness, Chen Zuoqian characterizes her transgression as follows: "'She wants to climb onto the top of my head.' 'Will you let her?' asked Lotus. Chen Zuoqian waved his hand dismissively, 'Never! Women can never climb onto the top of men's heads'" (Su 1990:165). My translation of this exchange differs from that of Michael Duke. In this dialogue between Chen and Lotus about Coral, Duke removes Su's vertical imagery that points to Coral's aggressive "climbing up" or "ascending to" (*padao*) and therefore diminishes her active challenge to Chen's authority. His translation reads: "'She wants to be more important than I am' 'Are you going to let her?' Chen Zuoqian waved his hand and said, 'Don't be ridiculous! Women can never be more important than men'" (Su 1993b: 16).

21. One of Su's innuendoes that Zhang refuses to entertain is the presence of ghosts. In Su's story, Lotus's repeated "hallucinations" about the concubines murdered in the well successfully creates an aura of cultural mysticism that reveres the existence of another world. But in Zhang's movie the ghost scare in Coral's room after she has been murdered is immediately demystified by the presence of the vengeful, torch-bearing Lotus. Perhaps Zhang eliminates the

ghostliness of Su's story because, in critical-realist fashion, he aims more for clarity and coherence.

Chapter 3: Eileen Chang and Stanley Kwan

1. Publications of Chang's biography abound. See, for example, Zhang Zijing (1996) and Feng Zuyi (2004).

2. My English translations of these titles are tentative since there exist other standard English translations of these two films.

3. Many have studied the representations of Shanghai in Chinese film and literature. See, for example, Zhang Yingjin (1996) and Poshek Fu (2003).

4. A new study of Chang edited by Liu Shu and Wang Gang (2008), for example, offers a very interesting historical account of Chang's relations with the film industry. Other critical studies of Chang include Edward Gunn (1980), Leung Pin-Kwan (1998), Yang Ze (1999), and Lim Chin-chown (2002).

5. Unless noted otherwise, all the translations of Chang's story "Red Rose and White Rose" from Chinese into English are mine.

6. For studies that unite feminism, psychoanalysis, and cinema, see Irigaray (1985a); Cixous (1975); Mulvey (2000); Doane (1991); Zhong (1997); Shiach (1999); and Kaplan (2000).

7. Geoffrey Bennington summarizes the boundary between inside and outside in the narration of the nation: "The idea of the nation is inseparable from its narration: that narration attempts, interminably, to constitute identity against difference, inside against outside, and in the assumed superiority of inside over outside, prepares against invasion and for 'enlightened' colonialism" (1990: 132). See also Homi Bhabha (1990); Wimal Dissanayake, ed. (1994); He Baogang and Guo Yingjie (2000); Maria Hsia Chang (2001); and Chen Xiaomei (2002).

8. Carolyn Thompson Brown's translation (1978).

Chapter 4: Liu Yichang and Wong Kar-wai

1. For characterizations of Hong Kong's Second Wave, see Law Kar (2001) and Hector Rodriguez (2001). Other informative studies of Hong Kong cinema include Lisa Stokes and Michael Hoover (1999); Evans Chan (2000); Esther Yau (2001); and Meaghan Morris et al. (2005).

2. It is important to note that Liu Yichang published two versions of *Intersection:* a novella (1972) and a condensed short-story version (1975). The English translation by Li Wenjing of *Intersection* (1988) is based on the short story. However, Wong's adaptation and my textual analysis are both based on the novella. I use the 2005 edition of Liu's novella for all of my references. All the translations of Liu's story are mine, if not noted otherwise.

3. For Stephen Teo, Wong's romantic melodrama (*wenyipian*) is a kind of "literature and art film," which is akin to soap opera, "a form that assumes

classic expression in the 1960s with the rise of Mandarin pictures from both Hong Kong and Taiwan (particularly adaptations from the literary works of the author Qiong Yao, often starring Brigitte Lin) (2001c: 3). Qiong Yao is undoubtedly one of the most popular female writers of melodramatic novels from the 1960s to the 1980s. Her romance stories have enchanted many coming-of-age teenagers and fashioned a unique style of narrative. Attributing the origin of *wenyipian* to Qiong Yao's novels, Teo's comment explains the origin of Wong's stylized melodrama because it points out two critical traditions in "literature and art film." First, *wenyipian* has a generic relation with popular literature because it often works with literary adaptations to appeal to a certain type of audience. Second, due to the genre's rise in the 1960s, it often evokes "a sense of period and place" (http://archive.sensesofcinema.com/contents/01/13/mood.html.) and inspires nostalgia for a simpler time. For other useful studies on melodrama, see Peters Brooks (1976) and John Mercer and Martin Shingler (2004).

4. Peter Brunette made a very powerful statement about Wong Kar-wai in his 1995 interview with the filmmaker in Toronto. After watching Wong's *Fallen Angels* (1995), Brunette says: "I've just seen the future of cinema" (2005: iii). Many critics share with Brunette this strong affirmation of Wong's impressive achievements. See Juanita Zhou (1998); Tony Ryans (2000); Fiona Villella (2001); Rey Chow (2002); Shelly Kracier (2005); Stephen Teo (2005b and 2005c); and Chen Xiaohong (2006).

5. *Hiroshima Mon Amour* deals with the relationship between a French actress and a Japanese man in Japan. Resnais uses flashbacks to reveal that the French actress also had a German lover during World War II.

6. Bluestone, Cohen, Stam, and Dudley agree that "narrativity is the most solid median link between novel and cinema, the most pervasive tendency of both verbal and visual languages" (Cohen 1979: 92).

7. *Tête-bêche* functions as a metaphor for Wong's vision of adaptation, one that roughly corresponds to what Western scholars call "intersecting adaptation," where, as André Bazin puts it, "the film *is* the novel as seen by cinema" (quoted in Andrew 1984: 99). Wong seems to approve of this ontological identification when he suggests that "intersection" is a language for both literature and cinema.

8. In his discussion of Wong's visual expressivity, Brunette comments: "Objects and body parts are focused on in a new way and with a new intensity in shots with little narrative relevance, like the lingering shots of a woman's hand on the threshold of a door or the railing of a stairway.... Often, when the couple is walking together, the camera will somewhat perversely continue to remain on their midsection rather than, more conventionally, panning up to their faces as quickly as possible to preserve normal-framing. Wong has said that this technique was employed, especially in interiors, to give an impression what things looked like to a five-year-old—in other words, to him as a child—but he also seems to be playing with the viewer's expectations. For what is being

stimulated here, beyond the spectator's own sexual desire, is his or her desire to see, always to see more, an impossible desire linked to the couple's impossible desire for each other" (2005: 90).

9. Ironically, Wong manufactured his "authentic" Hong Kong in a foreign country. He explains in interviews that he had to shoot *In the Mood for Love* in Thailand because he could not find enough old buildings in Hong Kong to give it a 1960s feel.

10. Janet Salaff (1995) offers an interesting sociological study of Hong Kong's economic and social conditions from the 1960s to the 1970s.

11. Wong explains in an interview that the rice cooker is one of the greatest modern inventions for women: "Without the rice cooker you have to spend hours in the kitchen. After we got rice cookers, the women had more time for themselves" (quoted in Brunette 2005: 124).

12. *Ling yi ban* literally means "the other half," but it is often used to mean "one's spouse."

13. This is a consistent practice in Wong's film. In an earlier scene from *In the Mood for Love*, for example, the Shanghainese landlady and her friends speculate on why Mrs. Chan dresses up to go to a noodle stand. Their conversation is overheard over a shot devoid of people, and the vacant screen reinforces the invisible but controlling power of local gossip.

14. Wong said in a question-and-answer session that *In the Mood for Love* is to him "actually like a thriller, a story with a lot of suspense. So we always kept the spouses, the husband and wife, somewhere outside the frame. We can't see them, but there's always a kind of clue. The two [central] characters in the film want to know why, and they want to find out the truth. So it is a very typical Hitchcock story structure" (Brunette 2005:130).

15. This happens literally in one of the sieges that Mrs. Chan and Mr. Chow suffer. Their fear of gossip confines them to Mr. Chow's room for more than twenty-four hours. When Mrs. Chan leaves Mr. Chow's room late the next night, she has to borrow his wife's high heels to pretend that she is just returning from work.

16. During the 1960s and 1970s, Asia saw the Chinese Cultural Revolution, the Vietnam War, and the Cambodian Revolution; in Africa thirty-two countries became independent from their colonizers. In addition there were socialist movements in Europe and the civil rights movement in the United States.

17. Mrs. Suen is played by Rebecca Pan, a famous Shanghainese singer who moved to Hong Kong in 1949 and whose singing career began in 1957. Wong plays one of her famous songs, *Bengawan Solo* (an English rendition of an Indonesian folk song) in *In the Mood for Love*.

18. Liu presents Yubai's moralizing rhetoric ironically in part because Hong Kong in the 1960s did have a policy of censoring popular culture to preserve a conservative social climate. Yao Surong, one of the most acclaimed singers in

Hong Kong at the time, had many of her songs censored: over 80 of her 220 songs were banned by the Hong Kong cultural bureau because they were said to encourage morally ambiguous practices. Among them, the popular "I Am Not Going Home Today" (Wo jintian bu hui jia) was emblematic; its title was even changed to "I Am Going Home Today" to appease Hong Kong's censorship bureau. In the novel this song reminds Yubai about his prodigal Shanghai youth. For the political meanings of Hong Kong's popular music, see Ho Wai-chung (2000).

19. Since Wong plays the whole song in the scene, it is worth noting that its lyrics convey a certain ominous anxiety about life's unpredictability:

> The blooming years, the moonlike spirit
> The crystal clear wisdom
> Beautiful life, loving couple
> Happy family
> Suddenly this lonely island is overshadowed by
> Miseries and sorrows, miseries and sorrows
> Ah, my lovely country
> When can I run into your arms again
> When can I see that clouds dissipate
> And there shine through your light?
> The blooming years, the moonlike spirit.

Zhou's song refers to China's war-torn era in the 1930s and 1940s. The singer herself fled from Shanghai to Hong Kong in 1946, and her song conveys a sense of regret: although these are the best years of one's life, happiness can be flimsy due to the circumstances beyond human control. While Wong evokes the wistful patriotic touch of the song to make reference to the greater political and historical pressures of the 1960s, we also notice that his film focuses mainly on the enclosed space of the two protagonists, whose interactions with the outside world remain marginal in the picture.

Chapter 5: Dai Sijie

1. My characterization of Dai's "third" viewpoint is different from John Brockman's definition of a "Third Culture." Brockman defines the Third Culture as one way of bridging the divide between what C. P. Snow calls the two cultures, that of literary intellectuals and that of scientists. Brockman argues that "the third-culture thinkers are the new public intellectuals" because they are the scientists and thinkers who explain and shape the meanings of life in the empirical world (2006:19). It is also important to differentiate Dai's "third" viewpoint from Ruth Hill Useem's notion of the "Third Culture Kid" (TCK); Useem

defines TCK as children who follow their parents to a foreign culture and integrate their birth culture with their adopted culture into a "third culture." For further references on Useem's TCK, see Useem (1999).

2. In his famous "Talks at the Yan'an Forum on Literature and Art" in 1942, Mao Zedong argued that "literature and art" must "fit well into the whole revolutionary machine as a component part," that they must "operate as powerful weapons for uniting and educating the people and for attacking and destroying the enemy," and, finally, that they must "help the people fight the enemy with one heart and one mind" (quoted in Denton 1996: 459).

3. See Chapter 2 for more discussion of Fifth Generation directors.

4. In an interview with *eNorth* (*Bei feng wang*, 2003), Dai mentioned that studying in Fémis was one of his happiest dreams that came true, because all students at Fémis have a film card that entitles them to watch movies in all French theaters for free. But the entrance exam was extremely competitive. The test was divided into three stages. There were a few thousand people in the first stage, two hundred in the second, and sixty in the third. At the third stage, all students had to stay at the same hotel for three days, were given the same story outline, and had to produce a story of dozens of pages in French. Dai considered himself fortunate because there was no Chinese student at Fémis at that time (one Hong Kong student had graduated some time ago), so he was able to negotiate with the school administration about skipping the final test due to his limited French. Fémis asked Dai to submit instead six recommendations, three from French directors and three from Chinese directors. In the end Dai submitted two French references and two Chinese ones and was admitted. See Dai Sijie (2003a). The translation from Chinese into English is mine.

5. See Dai's interview with *Beijing Youth Journal* (2003). This is Dai's best interview. Two of his other interviews with *Taipei Times* (2002) and *New Beijing Journal* (2007) are also very informative.

6. The difficulties of cross-cultural criticism have been much discussed. Noted feminist film scholar Ann Kaplan examines the issue from the perspective of an Anglophone critic of Chinese cinema: "Cross-cultural analysis is difficult: It is fraught with danger. We are either forced to read works produced by the Other through the constraints of our own frameworks/theories/ideologies; or to adopt what we believe to be the position of the Other—to submerge our position in that of the imagined Other. Yet, cross-cultural work appears increasingly essential in an era when secure national identities are being eroded in the wake of multiple immigrations and other boundary confusions. The challenge is to undertake cross-cultural research in ways that avoid defamiliarizing the alien text, appropriating or "managing" it, with the result of making it subordinate to the imaginary Western "master" discourses; or, worse still, "domesticating" it into dominant Western critical paradigms. Arguably, since all texts conceal their multiple and shifting meanings, it is conceivable that cross-cultural work (from many directions, incidentally: North American-Chinese interchange represents only two of the

desirable exchanges) might uncover strands of a text's multiple meanings different from those found by critics in the originating culture" (Kaplan 1993: 9).

7. See Dai (2003b).

8. Scholars sometimes attribute the "roots of the modern incongruity theories of humor" to Immanuel Kant's *Critique of Judgement.* In *The World as Will and Idea* (1819), Arthur Schopenhauer defines laughter similarly: "The cause of laughter in every case is simply the sudden perception of the incongruity between a concept and the real objects which have been thought through it in some relation, and laughter itself is just the expression of this incongruity" (quoted in Attardo 1994: 48).

9. See Dai (2003a).

10. According to David Wang, Shen Congwen's lyricism can be defined as "a modulation of language that conveys a dreamlike 'associational rhythm' (*Biancheng* [The border town]); a simultaneous perception of the world that brings the chronological flow of time to a halt ("Chun" [Spring]); the bracketing of an ephemeral experience with a personal epiphany or antiepiphany ("Jing" [Quiet]); the adoption of pastoral motifs and figures reminiscent of a primitivist landscape ("Baizi" [Baizi]); *Xiangxing sanji* [Random sketches on a trip to Hunan]); and a yearning for the ancient tribal condition of myth (*Fengzi* [Fengzi]). Through the conscious work of Shen's narrator, objective experience undergoes a process of metamorphosis, crystallizing into a constellation of sensuous pictures and musical patterns" (David Wang 1993: 205).

11. See Dai (2003a; 2003b)

12. Shen's narrative style is closely related to the soldiering experience he had early in his life. Born a Miao ethnic minority in Hunan province, Shen joined a local army as a low-ranking military secretary when he was sixteen. For five years he drifted through the border towns and along the Yuanshui River with the troops and witnessed a great deal of fighting between warlords and the Miao tribesmen. In his autobiography, he describes all kinds of atrocities and tragedies, including beheading, torture, and passion killings.

13. See *Shen Congwen's Autobiography* [Shen Congwen Zizhuan] (Taipei: Lian he wen xue za zhi she, 1987 [1996 printing]).

14. This interview is a part of the 2002 DVD's special collection.

15. For more on Scar Literature, see Yomi Braester (2003).

16. Studies of Lou Ye's *Suzhou River* (2000) abound. See, for example, Silbergeld (2002); and Searls (2001).

17. See Dai (2003a).

18. Despite Dai's intense effort, both the novel and film versions of *Balzac* were ultimately banned in China.

19. Because of the harsh terrain and conditions in Sichuan province, where Dai was sent for re-education, Dai moved the crew to Zhangjiajie in Hunan province and shot the film there. Dai mentions that the Chinese cultural officials had two main problems with his film. One was the portrayal of the village head-

man and "the idea that he represented the ordinary Communist [but] in the film he came across as an idiot." The second was the premise of having "a foreign book" change someone's life. In the end Dai added a couple of Chinese books to those in Four Eyes' stolen suitcase in an attempt to appease the Chinese censors. See Dai 2002 DVD, postproduction interview.

20. In *Madame Bovary* Flaubert confirms the importance of his blind beggar's role when, in the last chapter, the beggar's ditty is the last thing that Emma hears as she dies. The song carries an existential, sexual truth similar to the miller's verse in *Balzac*. At the end of Dai's novel, when the protagonists are burning the books of Western literature in a ritual to mourn the loss of the seamstress, the Flaubert page that "won't burn"—that is, cannot be repressed—is the page where Emma dies while listening to the beggar.

Chapter 6: Hou Xiaoxian and Zhu Tianwen

1. The phrases identifying periods in Hou's career are from Yeh and Davis (2005). Critics such as June Yip have argued that Hou's New Cinema is indebted to the rise of the Nativist Literary Movement (Xiang tu wen xue) in the late 1970s to 1980s, which was committed to "capturing the everyday realities of the Taiwanese socio-historical experience" (Yip 2004: 9). I would add that Hou's cinematic art has evolved to integrate the influences of many other literary movements; most important for this chapter are Shen Congwen's "critical lyricism" and Zhu Tianwen's "urban depravity fiction."

2. There are many studies of Taiwan New Cinema. Douglas Kellner considers Taiwan New Cinema to be "new" in the way it rebels against previous genre cinema. For him, the key is that it produces a "socially critical and aesthetically innovative cycle of films appropriate to explore contemporary Taiwan society" (1998: 101). See also Chris Berry and Lu Feii, eds. (2005); Peggy Chao (1997); Robert Ru-shou Chen (1995); Lu Tonglin (2002); Wu I-Fen (2003); Sheldon Lu and Emilie Yeh (2005); and Lin Wenqi et al., eds. (2005).

3. For studies of the narrative functions of auto/biography in characterizing and contesting Taiwan's mixed cultural identity, see Yeh and Davis (2005: 146–149); and Corrado Neri (2003: 160–166).

4. Zhu's narrative is a mixture of the two genres because it is her recollection of one of her classmates' story. The first-person narrator is featured prominently as the storyteller and participatory observer of how her friend Xiao Bi deals with his transition from being the only child of a Taiwanese prostitute to being the stepson of a Chinese veteran in Taiwan.

5. For a groundbreaking study of Taiwan's Nativist Literature Movement, see Sung-sheng Yvonne Chang (1993). Other useful studies of Taiwanese literature include David Der-wei Wang (1991); Chen Ruoxi (1993); Kao Hsin-sheng, ed. (1993); Li Shifen (1994); William Tay (1994); Sung-sheng Yvonne Chang (2001); Zhou Yingxiong and Liu Zhihui (2004).

6. Zhu's father, Zhu Xining (Chu Hsi-ning, 1926–1998), is one of the most famous anti-Communist writers of his generation. Her mother, Liu Musha, is an important translator of Japanese literature. Her two younger sisters, Zhu Tianxin and Zhu Tianyi, are both well-known writers in their own right. She grew up "in a congenial literary circle and raised in Confucianism, Christianity, Chinese and Japanese literature" (Yeh and Davis 2005: 151).

7. Yeh and Davis explain that when Zhu entered college, "she and her two sisters and close friends founded the Three-Three Society [San san shu fang], which reflected and promoted their captivation by Sun Yat-sen's Three Principles of the People (San ming zhu yi) and the Christian concept of the Holy Trinity (*sanyi*)" (2005: 151).

8. In "The Capital of a Burning Summer" and her critically acclaimed novel *Notes of a Desolate Man,* Zhu uses such filmic techniques as flashbacks, close-ups, jump cuts, montage, dissolves, and tracking shots to create a sequence of "shots" that mimic filmic narrative.

9. Again the Three-Three phrase refers to the names of a series of publishing companies that Zhu and many of her literary cohorts established in the 1970s. Yeh and Davis note that, according to Hwei-cheng Cho, "Zhu and her Three-Three romantic, nationalist idealism was soon to disintegrate because of the changing political conditions in Taiwan. The once solid national identity began to fracture with the U.S. government's normalization of diplomatic relations with China. In 1978 the United States snubbed Taiwan in order to reestablish formal relations with China. This was a national shock, but it prompted people like Zhu to reconsider the long-standing KMT doctrine of national salvation and recovery of the mainland. By the early 1980s, society at large was moving toward a Taiwanese sensibility, as nativist literature had always hoped. And it was during this period, through her involvement in the New Cinema, that Zhu came into contact with a Taiwan previously unknown to her" (2005: 152).

10. For an informative analysis of Hou's staging techniques, see David Bordwell (2005b). Bordwell states that Hou distinguished himself from traditional Taiwanese filmmaking in the 1970s by picking "an uncommon option from the analytical-editing menu, that attenuated approach to continuity editing to which European directors adhered in the 1910s. He favored prolonged establishing shots, with comparatively few cut-ins, thereby producing somewhat longer takes. His average shot length in these early 1980s films (between ten and twelve seconds) is about twice that of the fast-cut films of the 1970s. He is willing to film a conversation in a shot lasting more than two minutes, and he is prone to include more one-take scenes than his contemporaries, especially in interiors" (194). Such a nonintrusive stylistic maneuver makes the actors' performance appear more natural and therefore closer to life.

11. Translations of Zhu's work from Chinese into English are mine.

12. Rey Chow points out that while filmmakers and writers often hope

to locate both innocence and knowledge in representations of "the people," this configuration is problematic. Such fascination with "'the people' suggests an attempt to cling to the beliefs that [lie] at the foundation of modern Chinese national identity. Yet precisely because the turn to 'the people' is nostalgic as much as utopic—a desire for home as much as for change—it inevitably reencounters all the problems that are fundamental to that turn" (1996: 1041–1042).

Chapter 7: Chen Yuhui and Chen Guofu

1. According to a conversation I had with Zhang Fengmei, Chen Guofu's marketing director, *The Personals* was the first Taiwanese movie that experimented with advance ticket sales, and this was a runaway success. They employed other well-executed marketing strategies, Ru-Shou Robert Chen also notes (1999), often targeting specific groups and holding advance screenings, advance ticket sales, question-and-answer sessions, and lectures. See also He Ruizhu (2004).

2. Taiwan's four major political parties are the Democratic Progressive Party (DPP), the Kuomintang (KMT or Nationalist Party), the People First Party (PFP), and the Taiwan Solidarity Union (TSU). For a comprehensive, regularly updated summary of Taiwan's sociopolitical conditions, see http://www.state.gov/r/pa/ei/bgn/35855.htm

3. In 2007 a dispute raged between the Ministry of Education and Taipei's Cultural Bureau concerning the renaming of Chiang Kai-shek Memorial Hall, built in 1980. Denouncing the military rule of the Chiang period, DPP-appointed Minister of Education Du Zhengsheng planned to change the name of the historic building from Chiang Kai-shek Memorial Hall to The Memorial Hall of Taiwan's Democracy. This change was resisted by the Taipei City Government, headed by the KMT's Hao Longbin. In 2008 the new Taiwanese president, a member of the KMT, Ma Ying-jeou (Ma Yingjiu), reversed the policy of the previous president, Chen Shuibian, and reinstituted the name Chiang Kai-shek Memorial Hall.

4. The million-person march in October, 2006, for example, was a tour de force of democratic theater staged by the prominent dissident Shi Mingde (Shih Ming-te). The month-long protest demanded the resignation of President Chen Shuibian, who was implicated at that time but not indicted in a corruption scandal involving his wife and son-in-law.

5. These tensions between centrifugal and centripetal ideologies recall Mikhail Bakhtin's notion of "dialogic utterance." Arguing that all discourses are interdependent and therefore necessarily participate in reinscribing each other's meanings, Bakhtin suggests that each dialogic utterance pronounces the normalizing *and* destabilizing functions of a speech act which serves divergent political purposes of consolidating and dismantling cultural hierarchies between center and periphery. See Bakhtin (1992).

6. Many of Chen Yuhui's writings display a diverse mixture of narrative dictions. See, for example, *My Enormously Hungry Soul* (1996) and *Have You Ever Loved Before* (2001). All translations of the writings of Chen Yuhui and Chen Guofu from Chinese into English are mine, unless noted otherwise.

7. For comparative studies of Taiwan New Cinema and Taiwan Second New Wave, see Yeh and Davis (2005); June Yip (2004); and Chris Berry and Lu Feii, eds. (2005).

8. Between 1989 and 2009 foreign movies have overwhelmed Taiwan's domestic market. In 2006, for example, domestic ticket sales for Taiwan films was 1.62 percent of the total (NT$43,392,928), while sales of tickets for foreign films (excluding films from Hong Kong and China) totaled 94.68 percent (NT$2,535,874,266). For further information, see Taiwan's movie database at http://tc.gio.gov.tw

9. To some extent it may be productive to understand Chen Guofu's moral ambivalence through Fredric Jameson's Marxist interpretations of postmodern cultural logic. See Jameson (1992 and 1998).

10. All of my references to *The Personals* are from the 2002 edition.

11. Chen Yuhui's self-conscious equivocation mimics a kind of feminine discourse inspired by her extensive study of Western art, philosophy, and literature. From Freud to Sabina Spielrein, Chen has shown an intense interest in psychoanalysis and feminism in her essays (2006: 223–235), and Luce Irigaray's ideas of *écriture feminine* are one useful lens through which to examine Chen's revision of women's speech. For Irigaray, women's writing often adopts a kind of gendered, rhetorical strategy that underscores the multivalence of words. Such uses of language give the woman speaker at least two advantages: not only does it secure her narrative mobility, so she can "avoid becoming fixed, immobilized" by patriarchal logic and truism, but it also gives her a distinct sexual identity, one that is different from that of the male subject (Irigaray 1985a: 103). Chen's stylistic decision to juxtapose the narrator's evasive speech—her deconstructive confession—with the physician's assertive criticism accentuates the equitable and parallel, rather than hierarchical, differences in their rhetoric. Chen reinforces this with a shot-reverse-shot dialogic composition that refuses to privilege one version of truth over another. In this sense the narrator is able to tell, in her own way and with her own words, her side of the story and therefore avoids becoming a mimic of the male subject or, in Irigaray's words, "an other of the same and not an actual other" (Irigaray 1995: 10).

12. Jiazhen's genteel demeanor, visible vulnerability, and sense of guilt have led critics to consider her a nostalgic construct that reaffirms, as Nick Kaldis states, "a patriarchal desire for [a return to] a traditional type of gender ideal" (2004: 41) Her conservatism is most noticeable in her class and sexual biases. However, Chen carefully differentiates her position from that of the film by

exposing and ridiculing her prejudices: her actions are constantly watched and documented by others.

Conclusion

1. A 2006 Japanese adaptation of *Journey to the West* is controversial because it makes the leading character, Priest Xuanzang, into a woman who falls in love with "her" student Monkey. This plot alteration has enraged many Chinese viewers.

Bibliography

Abbas, Ackbar. 1997. *Hong Kong: Culture and the Politics of Disappearance.* Minneapolis: University of Minnesota Press.

Anderson, Benedict. 1991. *Imagined Communities.* London: Verso.

Anderson, Marston. 1990. *The Limits of Realism: Chinese Fiction in the Revolutionary Period.* Berkeley: University of California Press.

Andrew, Dudley. 1984. *Concepts in Film Theory.* Oxford: Oxford University Press.

———. 1998. "Adaptation from *Concepts in Film Theory.*" In *Film and Literature: An Introduction and Reader,* ed. Timothy Corrigan. Upper Saddle River, NJ: Prentice-Hall, Inc.

Ang, Ien. 1998. "Can One Say No to Chineseness? Pushing the Limits of the Diasporic Paradigm." *Boundary 2.* 25, no. 3 (Autumn): 223–242.

———. 2001. *On Not Speaking Chinese.* New York: Routledge.

Assayas, Olivier, ed. 1999. *Hou Hsiao-hsien.* Paris: Editions Cahiers du cinéma.

———. 2000. *Hou Hsiao-hsien (Hou Xiaoxian).* Trans. Lin Zhiming et al. Taipei: Cai tuan fa ren dian ying zi liao guan.

Attardo, Salvatore. 1994. *Linguistic Theories of Humor.* New York: Mouton de Gruyter.

Auerbach, Erich. 1991. *Mimesis.* Trans. William Trask. Princeton: Princeton University Press.

Aumont, Jacques. 1992. *Aesthetics of Film.* Trans. Richard Neupert. Austin: University of Texas Press.

Bakhtin, Mikhail. 1984. *Rabelais and His World.* Trans. Hélène Iswolsky. Bloomington: Indiana University Press.

———. 1992. *The Dialogic Imagination: Four Essays.* Trans. Caryl Emerson and Michael Holquist. Austin: University of Texas Press.

Barlow, Tani, ed. 1993. *Gender Politics in Modern China: Writing and Feminism.* Durham: Duke University Press.

Bazin, André. 2000. "Adaptation, or the Cinema as Digest." In *Film Adaptation,* ed. James Naremore, 19–27. New Brunswick: Rutgers University.

———. 2005. *What Is Cinema?* Trans. Hugh Gray. Berkeley: University of California Press.

Bei Feng Wang. 2003. "Dai Sijie: 'The Little Seamstress changed and I did, too'" (Dai Sijie: Xiao caifeng bian le, wo ye bian le). *eNorth* (*Bei feng wang*). September 9. http://ent.enorth.com.cn/system/2003/09/09/000630164.shtml. Accessed November 16, 2007.

Beijing Youth Journal (*Beijing qing nian bao*). 2003. "Dai Sijie: 'One thing that really moves people is emotion'" (Zhen zheng tao hao ren de shi qing gang). September 1. http://www.guxiang.com/others/others/xinwen/200309/200309010001.htm. Accessed November 16, 2007.

Bennington, Geoffrey. 1990. "Postal Politics and the Institution of the Nation." In *Nation and Narration,* ed. Homi Bhabha, 121–137. New York: Routledge.

Berry, Chris, ed. 1991. *Perspectives on Chinese Cinema*. London: British Film Institute Publishing.

———, ed. 2003a. *Chinese Films in Focus: 25 New Takes*. London: Institute Publishing.

———. 2003b. "*Wedding Banquet:* A Family (Melodrama) Affair." In *Chinese Films in Focus: 25 New Takes*, ed. Chris Berry, 183–190. London: British Film Institute Publishing.

———. 2004. *Postsocialist Cinema in Post-Mao China: The Cultural Revolution after the Cultural Revolution*. New York: Routledge.

———, ed. 2005. *Island on the Edge: Taiwan New Cinema and After.* Hong Kong: Hong Kong University Press.

Berry, Chris, and Mary Farquhar. 2006. *China on Screen*. New York: Columbia University Press.

Berry, Michael. 2005. *Speaking in Images: Interviews with Contemporary Chinese Filmmakers.* New York: Columbia University Press.

Bhabha, Homi, ed. 1990. *Nation and Narration*. London: Routledge.

———. 1994. *The Location of Culture*. London: Routledge.

Bloom, Michelle. 2005. "Contemporary Franco-Chinese Cinema: Translation, Citation and Imitation in Dai Sijie's *Balzac and the Little Chinese Seamstress* and Tsai Ming-Liang's *What Time Is It There?*" *Quarterly Review of Film and Video* 22, no. 4: 311–325.

Bluestone, George. 1957. *Novels into Film*. Baltimore: The Johns Hopkins Press.

———. 2000. *Planet Hong Kong: Popular Cinema and the Art of Entertainment*. Cambridge, MA: Harvard University Press.

———. 2005. "Hou, or Constraints." In his *Figures Traced in Light*, 186–237. Berkeley: University of California Press.

Bordwell, David, and Kristin Thompson. 2005. *Film Art: An Introduction*. New York: McGraw-Hill.

Braester, Yomi. 2003. "Disjointed Time, Split Voices: Retrieving Historical Experience in Scar Literature." In his *Witness Against History*, 146–157. Stanford: Stanford University Press.

Brockman, John. 1996. *The Third Culture: Beyond the Scientific Revolution.* New York: Simon & Schuster.

Brooks, Peters. *The Melodramatic Imagination.* 1976. New Haven: Yale University Press.

Brown, Carolyn. 1978. "Eileen Chang's 'Red Rose and White Rose': A Translation and Afterword." Ph.D. diss. The American University.

———. 1993. "Woman as Trope: Gender and Power in Lu Xun's 'Soap.'" In *Gender Politics in Modern China,* ed. Tani E. Barlow, 74–89. Durham, NC: Duke University Press.

Brunette, Peter. 2005. *Wong Kar-wai.* Urbana: University of Illinois Press.

Burdeau, Emmanuel. 1999. "Interview with Hou Hsiao-hsien." In *Hou Hsiao-hsien,* ed. Olivier Assayas, 79–132. Paris: Editions Cahiers du cinéma.

Cai Rong. 2005 "Gender Imaginations in *Crouching Tiger, Hidden Dragon* and the *Wuxia* World." *positions* 13, no. 2: 441–471.

Cartmell, Deborah, and Whelehan, Imelda, eds. 1999. *Adaptations: From Text to Screen, Screen to Text.* London: Routledge.

Chan, Ching-kiu Stephen. 1993a. "The Language of Despair: Ideological Representations of the 'New Woman' by May Fourth Writers." In *Gender Politics in Modern China,* ed. Tani E. Barlow, 13–32. Durham, NC: Duke University Press.

Chan, Evans. 2000. "Postmodernism and Hong Kong Cinema." *Postmodern Culture* 10, no. 3 (May). http://muse.jhu.edu/journals/pmc/v010/10.3chan.html. Accessed January 26, 2008.

Chan, Felicia. 2003. "*Crouching Tiger, Hidden Dragon:* Cultural Migrancy and Translatability." In *Chinese Films in Focus: 25 New Takes,* ed. Chris Berry, 56–64. London: British Film Institute Publishing.

Chan, Kenneth. 2004. "The Global Return of the *Wu Xia Pian* (Chinese Sword-Fighting Movie): Ang Lee's *Crouching Tiger, Hidden Dragon. Cinema Journal* 43, no. 4 (Summer): 3–17.

Chang, Eileen. 1991. "Red Rose and White Rose." In *Collection of Eileen Chang's Short Stories* (*Zhang ailing xiaoshuo ji*), 57–108. Taipei: Huang guan chu ban she.

Chang, Maria Hsia. 2001. *Return of the Dragon: China's Wounded Nationalism.* Boulder, CO: Westview Press.

Chang, Sung-sheng Yvonne. 1993. *Modernism and the Nativist Resistance: Contemporary Chinese Fiction from Taiwan.* Durham, NC: Duke University Press.

———. 2001. *Change of Literary Fields* (*Wenxue chang yu de bian qian*). Taipei: Lianhe wen chong.

Chao, Peggy. 1997. *Taiwan New Cinema* (*Taiwan xin dianying*). Taipei: Shi Bao.

Chen Guofu. 1985. *Partial Reflections* (*Pian mian zhi yan*). Taipei: Dianying tushuguan.

———. 1997. *The Personals* (*Zheng hun qi shi*). Taipei: Xin wen ju.

Chen Ruoxi. 1993. "Prologue: Chinese Overseas Writers and Nativism." In

Nativism Overseas, ed. Hsin-sheng Kao, 9–19. Albany: State University of New York.

Chen Ru-shou (Ruxiu) Robert. 1995. *Movie Empire* (*Dianying diguo*). Taipei: Wan Xiang.

———.1999. "Marketing *The Personals:* New Strategies Pay New Dividends." *Cinemaya* 45: 38–39.

Chen Xiaohong. 2006. "As Beautiful as a Flower: On Nostalgia and Object-Fetish in *In the Mood for Love*" (*Ru hua mei juan: Lun <huayang nianhua> de niandai jiyi yu lianwu qingjie*). *Dangdai wenhua yanjiu wang* (Contemporary cultural studies) (www.cul-studies.com/community/shenshaohong/200602/3475.html). Accessed on August 23, 2007.

Chen Xiaomei. 2002. *Occidentalism: A Theory of Counter-Discourse in Post-Mao China*. Lanham, MD: Rowman & Littlefield Publishers.

Chen Yong-ming, and Joseph S. M. Liu, eds. 1998. *Essays on Chinese Martial Arts Fiction* (*Wuxia xiaoshuo lun juan*). Hong Kong: Mingho Publishers, Ltd.

Chen Yuhui. 1992. *The Personals: Forty-two Men and I* (*Zheng hun qi shi: Wo yu shi shi er ge nan ren*). Taipei: Yuan Liu.

———. 1996. *My Enormously Hungry Soul* (*Wo de linghun gandao juda de e*). Taipei: Lianhe wenxue.

———. 2001. *Have You Ever Loved Before* (*Ni shi fou ai guo*). Taipei: Lianhe wenxue.

———. 2002. *The Personals* (*Zheng hui qi shi*). Taipei: Er Yu.

———.2006. *Selections of Chen Yu-hui's Writings* (*Chen yuhui jing xuan ji*). Taipei: Jiu Ge.

Chi Pang-Yuan, and David Wang, eds. 2000. *Chinese Literature in the Second Half of a Modern Century.* Bloomington: Indiana University Press.

Chow, Rey. 1991. *Woman and Chinese Modernity: The Politics of Reading between West and East.* Minneapolis: University of Minnesota Press.

———. 1995. *Primitive Passions: Visuality, Sexuality, Ethnography, and Contemporary Chinese Cinema.* New York: Columbia University Press.

———. 1996. "We Endure, Therefore We Are: Survival, Governance, and Zhang Yimou's *To Live*," *South Atlantic Quarterly* 95.4 (Fall): 1039–1064.

———. 1998. "Introduction: On Chineseness as a Theoretical Problem." *Boundary 2.* 25, no. 3 (Autumn): 1–24.

———.1999. "Seminal Dispersal, Fecal Retention, and Related Narrative Matters: Eileen Chang's Tale of Roses in the Problematic of Modern Writing." *Differences* 11, no. 2: 153–176.

———. 2002. "Sentimental Returns: On the Uses of the Everyday in the Recent Films of Zhang Yimou and Wong Kar-wai." *New Literary History* 33: 639–654.

———. 2007. *Sentimental Fabulations, Contemporary Chinese Films: Attachment in the Age of Global Visibility.* New York: Columbia University Press.

Chow Tse-tsung. 1960. *The May Fourth Movement: Intellectual Revolution in China.* Cambridge, MA: Harvard University Press.

Chun, Allen. 1996. "Fuck Chineseness: On the Ambiguities of Ethnicity as Culture as Identity." *Boundary 2.* 23, no. 2 (Summer): 111–138.

Cixous, Hélène. 1975. "The Laugh of the Medusa." Trans. Keith Cohen and Paula Cohen. *Signs* 1, no. 4: 875–893.

Cohen, Keith. 1979. *Film and Fiction: The Dynamics of Exchange.* New Haven, CT: Yale University Press.

Corliss, Richard. 2000. "Martial Masterpiece." In *Crouching Tiger, Hidden Dragon: A Portrait of the Ang Lee Film*, ed. Linda Sunshine. 8–13. New York: Newmarket Press.

Corrigan, Timothy, ed. 1999. *Film and Literature: An Introduction and Reader.* Upper Saddle River, NJ: Prentice-Hall, Inc.

Cui Shuqin. 2003. *Women through the Lens: Gender and Nation in a Century of Chinese Cinema.* Honolulu: University of Hawai'i Press.

Currie, Mark. 1998. *Postmodern Narrative Theory.* New York: St. Martin's Press.

Dai Qing. 1993. "Raised Eyebrows for *Raise the Red Lantern.*" Trans. Jeanne Tai. *Public Culture* 5, no. 2. 333–337.

Dai Sijie. 2000. *Balzac et la petite tailleuse chinoise.* Paris: Gallimard.

———. 2002a. *Balzac and the Little Chinese Seamstress.* Trans. Ina Rilke. New York: Anchor Books.

———. 2002b. *Balzac and the Little Chinese Seamstress* (*Ba er zha ke yu xiao cai feng*). Trans. Wei Chixiu. Taipei: Huang guan.

———. 2003a. Interview with *Beijing Youth Journal* (*Beijing qing nian bao*). http://www.guxiang.com/others/others/xinwen/200309/200309010001.htm. Accessed November 16, 2007.

———. 2003b. Interview with *eNorth* (*Bei fang wang*). http://ent.enorth.com.cn/system/2003/09/09/000630164.shtml. Accessed November 16, 2007.

———. 2003. *Le complexe de Di.* Paris: Gallimard.

———. 2005. *Mr. Muo's Traveling Couch.* Trans. Ina Rilke. New York: Knopf.

Decker, Margaret. 1993. "Political Evaluation and Reevaluation in Contemporary Chinese Fiction." In *Gender Politics in Modern China,* ed. Tani E. Barlow, 290–303. Durham, NC: Duke University Press.

Denton, Kirk A., ed. 1996. *Modern Chinese Literary Thought: Writings on Literature, 1893–1945.* Stanford: Stanford University Press.

———. 1998. *The Problematic of Self in Modern Chinese Literature: Hu Feng and Lu Ling.* Stanford: Stanford University Press.

Desmond, John, and Peter Hawkes, eds. 2006. *Adaptation: Studying Film and Literature.* Boston: McGraw-Hill.

Ding Ling. 1989. *I Myself Am a Woman: Selected Writings of Ding Ling.* Eds. Tani E. Barlow and Gary J. Bjorge. Boston: Beacon Press.

Dissanayake, Wimal, ed. 1993. *Melodrama and Asian Cinema.* Cambridge: Cambridge University Press.

———, ed. 1994. *Colonialism and Nationalism in Asian Cinema.* Bloomington: Indiana University Press.

Doane, Mary Ann. 1991. *Femmes Fatales: Feminism, Film Theory, Psychoanalysis.* New York: Routledge.

———. 2003. "The Close-up: Scale and Detail in the Cinema." *Differences* 14, no. 3: 89–111.

Duan Zhensu. 1995. "*Red Rose and White Rose:* The Joy of Man and the Sorrow of Woman." *Yingxiang Film Magazine* 57 (January): 68–70.

Edelstein, David. 1988. "The Corn Is Red." *Village Voice.* October 11: 64.

Eisenstein, Sergei. 1988. *Selected Works: Writings, 1922–1934.* Eds. and trans. Richard Taylor and Michael Glenny. London: British Film Institute Publishing.

Elliot, Kamilla. 2003. *Rethinking the Novel/Film Debate.* Cambridge: Cambridge University Press.

Feng Zuyi. 2004. *The Century of Eileen Chang's Family* (*Bainian jiazu Zhang Ailing*). Taipei: Tuxu.

Ferrell, William. 1995. *Literature and Film as Modern Mythology.* Westport, CT: Praeger.

Film Art Editorial Department. 1992. *Re-creation: Essays on the Problem of Film Adaptation* (*Zai chuangzuo: Dianying gaibian wenti taolunji*) Beijing: Zhongguo dian ying chu ban she.

Flaubert, Gustave. 1992. *Madame Bovary.* Trans. Geoffrey Wall. New York: Penguin Books.

Fong, Suzie Young-Sau. 2000. "The Voice of Feminine Madness in Zhang Yi Mou's *Da Hong Deng Long Gao Gao Gua* (*Raise the Red Lantern*)." *Asian Cinema* 7, no. 1: 12–23.

Freud, Sigmund. 1989. *Civilization and Its Discontents.* Trans. James Strachey. New York: W.W. Norton & Company.

Fu Lei. 1944. "On the Fiction of Eileen Chang." (Lun Zhang Ailing de xiaoshuo). *Wanxiang,* No. 11 (May).

Fu, Poshek. 1997. *Palimpsests: Literature in the Second Degree.* Trans. Channa Newman and Claude Doubinsky. Lincoln: University of Nebraska Press.

———. 2003. *Between Shanghai and Hong Kong: The Politics of Chinese Cinemas.* Stanford: Stanford University Press.

Gomes, Catherine. 2005. "Crouching Women, Hidden Genre: An Investigation into Western Film Criticism's Reading of Feminism in Ang Lee's *Crouching Tiger, Hidden Dragon.*" *Limina: A Journal of Historical and Cultural Studies* 11: 47–56.

Gunn, Edward M. 1980. "Antiromanticism." In his *Unwelcome Muse: Chinese Literature in Shanghai and Peking 1937–1945,* 193–263. New York: Columbia University Press.

Hamm, John Christopher. 2005. *Paper Swordsmen: Jin Yong and the Modern Chinese Martial Arts Novel.* Honolulu: University of Hawai'i Press.

Harris, Kristine. 1997. "*The New Woman* Incident: Cinema, Scandal, and Spectacle in 1935 Shanghai." In *Transnational Chinese Cinema: Identity, Nationhood, Gender*, ed. Sheldon Hsiao-peng Lu, 277–302. Honolulu: University of Hawai'i Press.

Harvey, David. 1990. *The Condition of Postmodernity.* Cambridge: Blackwell Publishers.

Hasumi, Shigehiko. 1995. "An Oblivion of Archaeology: On Hou Hsiao-hsien's *City of Sadness.*" (Kaoguxue de huanghu: Hou hsiao-hsien de beiqing chengshi) Trans. Zhang Changyen. *Film Appreciation* 13, no. 1.

He Baogang and Guo Yingjie. 2000. *Nationalism, National Identity and Democratization in China.* Aldershot, England: Ashgate.

He Ruizhu. 2004. "Chen Guofu's Evolution and Sorrow" (Chen guofu de bian dong he aichou). http://movie.cca.gov.tw/Case/Content.asp?ID=134&Year=2007. Accessed August 6, 2008.

Ho Wai-chung. 2000. "The Political Meaning of Hong Kong Popular Music: A review of Sociopolitical Relations between Hong Kong and the People's Republic of China since the 1980s." *Popular Music* 19, no. 3: 341–353.

Hsia C.T. 1961. *A History of Modern Chinese Fiction.* Bloomington: Indiana University Press.

Hsieh, Yvonne. 2002. "Splendeurs et miseres des mots: *Balzac et la petite tailleuse chinoise* de Dai Sijie." *Etudes francophones* 17, no. 1: 93–105.

Huang, Martin W., ed. 2004. *Snakes' Legs: Sequels, Continuations, Rewritings, and Chinese Fiction.* Honolulu: University of Hawai'i Press.

Hutcheon, Linda. 2006. *A Theory of Adaptation.* New York: Routledge.

Iampolski, Mikhail. 1998. *The Memory of Tiresias: Intertextuality and Film.* Trans. Harsha Ram. Berkeley: University of California Press.

Irigaray, Luce. 1985a. *This Sex Which Is Not One.* Trans. Catherine Porter, Ithaca: Cornell University Press.

———. 1985b. *Speculum of the Other Woman.* Trans. Gillian Gill, Ithaca: Cornell University Press.

———. 1995. "The Question of the Other." *Yale French Studies.* No. 87. *Another Look, Another Woman: Retranslations of French Feminism.* 7–19.

Jameson, Fredric. 1992. *The Geopolitical Aesthetic: Cinema and Space in the World System.* Bloomington: Indiana University Press.

———. 1998. *The Cultural Turn.* London: Verso.

Jones, Kent. 1999. "Cinema with a Roof over Its Head: Kent Jones on the Latterday Films of Hou Hsiao-hsien." *Film Comment.* September/October. http://www.filmlinc.com/fcm/9-10-99/hou.htm. Accessed November 7, 2006.

Kaldis, Nick. 2004. "Monogamorphous Desires, Faltering Forms: Structure, Content, and Contradictions in *The Personals* (*Zhenghun Qishi*) (Taiwan, 1998)." *Asian Cinema* 15, 1 (Spring/Summer): 37–56.

Kao Hsin-sheng, ed. 1993. *Nativism Overseas: Contemporary Chinese Women Writers.* Albany: State University of New York.

Kao, Karl. 1989. "*Bao and Baoying:* Narrative Causality and External Motivations in Chinese Fiction." *Chinese Literature: Essays, Articles, Reviews (CLEAR)* 11: 115–138.

Kaplan, E. Ann. 1993. "Melodrama/Subjectivity/Ideology: Western Melodrama Theories and Their Relevance to Recent Chinese Cinema." In *Melodrama and Asian Cinema*, ed. Wimal Dissanayake, 9–28. Cambridge: Cambridge University Press.

———. 2000. "Is the Gaze Male?" In *Feminism and Film*, ed. E. Ann Kaplan, 119–138. Oxford: Oxford University Press.

Kar, Law. 2001. "Overview of Hong Kong's New Wave Cinema." In *At Full Speed*, ed. Esther Yau, 31–52. Minneapolis: University of Minnesota.

Kellner. Douglas. 1998. "New Taiwan Cinema in the 80s." *Jump Cut* 42 (December):101–115. http://www.ejumpcut.org/archive/onlinessays/JC42folder/80sTaiwanCinema.html. Accessed November 8, 2006.

Kim, L. S. 2006. *"Crouching Tiger, Hidden Dragon:* Making Women Warriors—A Transnational Reading of Asian Female Action Heroes." *Jump Cut* 48. www.ejumpcut.org/currentissue/womenWarriors/index.html. Accessed November 16, 2007.

Klein, Christina. 2004. "*Crouching Tiger, Hidden Dragon:* A Diasporic Reading." *Cinema Journal* 43, no. 4 (Summer): 18–42.

Kraicer, Shelly. 2005. "Tracking the Elusive Wong Kar-wai." *Cineaste.* http://www.cineaste.com/Kraicer.htm. Accessed August 23, 2007.

Kwan, Stanley. 2002. Interview with Fiona Ng. "Love in the Time of Tiananmen; Stanley Kwan's *Lan Yu.*" In IndieWire. http://www.indiewire.com/article/interview_love_in_the_time_of_tiananmen_stanley_kwans_lan_yu/. Accessed August 15, 2006.

Lai Sufen. 1999. "From Cross-Dressing Daughter to Lady Knight-Errant: The Origin and Evolution of Chinese Women Warriors." In *Presence and Presentation: Women in the Chinese Literati Tradition*, ed. Sherry J. Mou, 77–107. New York: St. Martin's Press.

Larson, Wendy. 1993. "The End of 'Funü Wenxue.'" In *Gender Politics in Modern China*, ed. Tani E. Barlow, 58–73. Durham, NC: Duke University Press.

———. 1998. *Women and Writing in Modern China.* Stanford: Stanford University Press.

Lau, Jenny Kwok Wah, ed. 2003. *Multiple Modernities: Cinemas and Popular Media in Transcultural East Asia.* Philadelphia: Temple University Press.

———. 2007. "*Hero:* China's Response to Hollywood's Globalization." *Jump Cult* 49 (Spring). http://www.ejumpcut.org/currentissue/Lau-Hero/text.html.

Lee, Ang. 2002. *Ten Years of a Movie Dream* (*Shi nian yi jiao dian ying meng*). Ed. Zhang Jingpei. Taipei: Shi bao wen hua chu ban.

Lee, Leo Ou-fan. 1973. *The Romantic Generation of Modern Chinese Writers.* Cambridge, MA: Harvard University Press.

———. 1990a. "In Search of Modernity: Some Reflections on a New Mode of Consciousness in Twentieth-Century Chinese History and Literature." In *Ideas Across Cultures: Essays on Chinese Thought in Honor of Benjamin I. Schwartz,* eds. Paul Cohen and Merle Goldman, 109–135. Cambridge, MA: Council on East Asian Studies, Harvard University.

———. 1990b. "Beyond Realism: Thoughts on Modernist Experiments in Contemporary Chinese Writing." In *Worlds Apart: Recent Chinese Writing and Its Audiences,* ed. Howard Goldblatt, 64–77. New York: M. E. Sharpe.

———. 1993. "Afterword: Reflections on Change and Continuity in Modern Chinese Fiction." In *From May Fourth to June Fourth: Fiction and Film in Twentieth-Century China,* eds. Ellen Widmer and David Der-wei Wang, 361–383. Cambridge, MA: Harvard University Press.

———. 1999. *Shanghai Modern: The Flowering of a New Urban Culture in China, 1930–1945.* Cambridge, MA: Harvard University Press.

Leung Pin-Kwan. 1998. "Two Discourses on Colonialism: Huang Guliu and Eileen Chang on Hong Kong of the Forties." *Boundary 2.* 25, no. 3 (Fall): 77–96.

Li H. C. 1989. "Color, Character, and Culture: On *Yellow Earth, Black Cannon Incident,* and *Red Sorghum.*" *Modern Chinese Literature* 5, no. 1 (Spring): 91–119.

Li Shifen. 1996. *Love and Marriage: Study of Contemporary Taiwanese Female Writers* (*Aiqing yu hunyin: Taiwan dangdai nü zuojia xiaoshuo yanjiu*). Taipei: Wenshizhe chu ban she.

Lim Chin-chown. 2002. "Castration Parody and Male 'Castration': Eileen Chang's Female Writing and Her Anti-patriarchal Strategy." In *Critical Studies: Feminism/Femininity in Chinese Literature,* eds. Peng-hsiang Chen and Whitney Crothers Dilley, 127–144. Amsterdam: Rodopi Press.

Lin Wenqi. 1997. "The Postmodern Style. The Postcolonial Hong Kong: The Allegory of Nation in Stanley Kwan's Films" (Hou xian dai de feng ge. Hou zhi min de xiang gang: Guan jin peng dian ying zhong de (fan) guo jia yu yan). In *Identity, Difference, and Subjectivity* (*Ren tong cha yi zhu ti xing*), ed. Jian Yingying, 175–216. Taipei Hsien: Li xu wen hua.

Lin Wenqi, Shen Xiaoyin, and Li Zhenya, eds. 2005. *Drama Loves Life: Studies of Hou Hsiao-hsien's Films* (*Xi lian Ren sheng: Hou Hsiao-hsien dian ying yian jiu*). Taipei: Mai tian chu ban she.

Lin Yü-sheng. 1979. *The Crisis of Chinese Consciousness: Radical Antitraditionalism in the May Fourth Era.* Madison: University of Wisconsin.

Link, Perry. 1981. *Mandarin Ducks and Butterflies: Popular Fiction in Early Twentieth-century Chinese Cities.* Berkeley: University of California Press.

Liu, James J.Y. 1967. *The Chinese Knight-Errant*. Chicago: University of Chicago Press.

Liu, Joyce Chi-Hui. 2002. "Filmic Transposition of the Roses: Stanley Kwan's Feminine Response to Eileen Chang's Women." In *Feminism/Femininity in Chinese Literature*, ed. Peng-hsiang Chen and Whitney Crothers Dilley, 145–158. Amsterdam: Rodopi.

Liu Kang. 1993. "Subjectivity, Marxism, and Cultural Theory in China." In *Politics, Ideology, and Literary Discourse in Modern China*, eds. Liu Kang and Xiaobing Tang, 232–255. Durham, NC: Duke University Press.

Liu, Lydia. 1993. "Invention and Intervention: The Female Tradition in Modern Chinese Literature." In *Gender Politics in Modern China*, ed. Tani E. Barlow, 33–57. Durham, NC: Duke University Press.

———. 1995. *Translingual Practice: Literature, National Culture, and Translated Modernity—China, 1900–1937*. Stanford: Stanford University Press.

Liu Shu, and Wang Gang, eds. 2007. *Eileen Chang's Space of Light and Shadow* (*Zhang Ailing de guang ying kong jian*). Beijing: Shijie zhishi chu ban she.

Liu Yichang 1972. *Dui Dao*. In *Xing dao wan bao* (*Sing tao wan pao;* Xindao evening daily). Novella version.

———. 1975. "Dui Dao." *Si Ji* (Four seasons). Condensed short-story version.

———. 1988. "Intersection." Trans. Li Wenjing (Nancy Li). *Renditions* 29–30: 84–101

———. 2005. *Dui Dao* (Intersection). Hong Kong: Huo yi chu ban she, Ltd.

Lu, Sheldon Hsiao-peng. 1997. "National Cinema, Cultural Critique, Transnational Capital: The Films of Zhang Yimou." In *Transnational Chinese Cinema: Identity, Nationhood, Gender*, ed. Sheldon Hsiao-peng Lu, 105–137. Honolulu: University of Hawai'i Press.

——— et al. 2005. *Chinese-Language Film*. Honolulu: University of Hawai'i Press.

Lu Tonglin. 1995. *Misogyny, Cultural Nihilism, and Oppositional Politics: Contemporary Chinese Experimental Fiction*. Stanford: Stanford University Press.

———. 2002. *Confronting Modernity in the Cinemas of Taiwan and Mainland China*. Cambridge: University of Cambridge Press.

Lu Xun. 1972. *Selected Stories of Lu Hsun*. New York: W. W. Norton and Company.

———. 1999. *Collection of Lu Xun's Fiction* (*Lu xun xiaoshuo ji*). Taipei: Hongfan.

Ma Ning. 1993. "Symbolic Representation and Symbolic Violence: Chinese Family Melodrama of the Early 1980s." In *Melodrama and Asian Cinema*, ed. Wimal Dissanayake, 29–58. Cambridge: Cambridge University Press.

Martin, Andrian. 2005. "Wuxia Redux: *Crouching Tiger, Hidden Dragon* as a Model of Late Transnational Production." In *Hong Kong Connections: Transnational Imagination in Action Cinema*, eds. Meaghan Morris, Siu Leung Li, and Stephen Chan Ching-kiu, 191–204. Durham: Duke University Press.

Martin, Fran. 2005. "The China Simulacrum: Genre, Feminism, and Pan-Chinese Cultural Politics in *Crouching Tiger, Hidden Dragon.*" In *Island on the Edge: Taiwan New Cinema and After*, eds. Chris Berry and Feii Lu, 149–160. Hong Kong: Hong Kong University Press.

McCall, Ian. 2006. "French Literature and Film in the USSR and Mao's China: Intertexts in Makine's *Au temps du fleuve amour* and Dai Sijie's *Balzac et la petite tailleuse chinoise.*" *Romance Studies* 24, no. 2: 159–170.

McFarlane, Brian. 1996. *Novel to Film: An Introduction to the Theory of Adaptation.* New York: Oxford University Press.

Mercer, John, and Shingler, Martin. 2004. *Melodrama: Genre. Style. Sensibility.* London: Wallflower.

Morris, Meaghan, Li, Siu Leung, and Chan, Stephen Ching-kiu, eds. 2005. *Hong Kong Connections.* Hong Kong: Hong Kong University Press.

Mulvey, Laura. 2000. "Visual Pleasure and Narrative Cinema." In *Feminism and* Film, ed. E. Ann Kaplan, 34–47. New York: Oxford University Press.

Naremore, James, ed. 2000. *Film Adaptation.* New Brunswick, NJ: Rutgers University Press.

Neri, Corrado. 2003. "*A Time to Live, A Time to Die:* A Time to Grow." In *Chinese Films in Focus: 25 New Takes,* ed. Chris Berry, 160–166. London: British Film Institute Publishing.

New Beijing Journal (Xin jing bao). 2007. "Dai Sijie: 'I wanted to prove that I was smart.'" March 24. http://www.gmw.cn/content/2007–03/24/content_577287.htm. Accessed November 16, 2007.

Ni Zhen. 2006. *Memoirs from the Beijing Film Academy: The Genesis of China's Fifth Generation.* Trans. Chris Berry. Durham: Duke University Press.

Pu Songling. 2002. "The Lady Knight-Errant." Trans. Lorraine S.Y. Lieu and the editors. In *Traditional Chinese Stories: Themes and Variations*, eds. Y. W. Ma and Joseph S. M. Lau, 77–82. Boston: Cheng & Tsui Company, Inc.

Raban, Jonathan. 1998. *Soft City.* London: Harvill Press.

Rayns, Tony. 1991. "Breakthroughs and Setbacks: The Origins of the New Chinese Cinema." In *Perspectives on Chinese Cinema*, ed. Chris Berry, 104–113. London: British Film Institute Publishing. 104–113.

———. 2000. "In the Mood for Edinburgh." *Sight and Sound* (August). http://www.bfi.org.uk/sightandsound/feature/55. Accessed November 17, 2007.

Richardson, Robert. 1969. *Literature and Film.* Bloomington: Indiana University Press.

Riding, Alan. 2005. "Artistic Odyssey: Film to Fiction to Film." *New York Times.* July 27. http://www.nytimes.com/2005/07/27/movies/MovieFeatures/27balz.html. Accessed October 10, 2007.

Rodriguez, Hector, 2001. "The Emergence of the Hong Kong New Wave." In *At Full Speed,* ed. Esther Yau, 53–72. Minneapolis: University of Minnesota Press.

Salaff, Janet. 1995. *Working Daughters of Hong Kong: Filial Piety or Power in the Family?* New York: Columbia University Press.

Sang, Tze-lan Deborah. 2005. "Women's Work and Boundary Transgression in Wang Dulu's Popular Novels." In *Gender in Motion,* eds. Bryna Goodman and Wendy Larson, 287–308. Lanham, MD: Rowman & Littlefield Publishers.

Schamus, James. 2004. "Aesthetic Identities: A Response to Kenneth Chan and Christina Klein." *Cinema Journal* 43, no. 4 (Summer): 43–52.

Searls, Damion. 2001. "Suzhou River." *Film Quarterly* 55, no. 2 (Winter): 55–60.

Shen Congwen. 1981. "Three Men and One Woman." Trans. Kai-yu Hsu. In *Modern Chinese Stories and Novellas: 1919–1949,* eds. Joseph S. M. Lau, C. T. Hsia, and Leo Ou-fan Lee, 253–265. New York: Columbia University Press.

———. 1987. *Shen Congwen's Autobiography.* Taipei: Shan wu chu ban she.

Shiach, Morag. 1999. *Feminism and Cultural Studies.* Oxford: Oxford University Press.

Shih Ruite. 1995. "The Vile Thing—*Red Rose and White Rose.*" *Ying xiang Film Magazine* 57 (January): 190.

Shih Shu-mei. 2001. *The Lure of the Modern: Writing Modernism in Semicolonial China, 1917–1937.* Berkeley: University of California Press.

Silbergeld, Jerome. 2002. "Hitchcock with a Chinese Face: Lou Ye's *Suzhou River.*" *Persimmon* 3, no. 2 (Summer): 70–73

Silverman, Kaja. 1988. *The Acoustic Mirror: The Female Voice in Psychoanalysis and Cinema.* Bloomington: Indiana University Press.

Stam, Robert. 2005. *Literature through Film.* Malden, MA: Blackwell Publishing.

Stam, Robert, and Alessandra Raengo, eds. 2005. *Literature and Film.* Malden, MA: Blackwell Publishing.

Stewart, Susan. 1984. *On Longing: Narratives of the Miniature, the Gigantic, the Souvenir, the Collection.* Baltimore, MD: Johns Hopkins University Press.

Stokes, Lisa, and Michael Hoover. 1999. *City on Fire.* London: Verso.

Stone, Judy. 1997. "Zhang Yimou." In *Eye on the World: Conversations with International Filmmakers.* 116–120. Los Angeles: Silman-James Press.

Su Tong. 1990. *Wives and Concubines* (*Qiqie chengqun*). Taipei: Yuanliu.

———. 1993a. *Decadence of the South* (*Nanfang de duoluo*). Taipei: Yuanliu.

———. 1993b. *Raise the Red Lantern: Three Novellas.* Trans. Michael S. Duke. New York: Penguin Books.

———. 1996. *Rice* (*Mi*). Taipei: Yuan liu chu ban shi ye gu fen you xian gong si.

———. 1997. *Angel's Food* (*Tianshi de liangshi*). Taipei: Maitian.

———. 2001. *My Life as an Emperor* (*Wo de di wang sheng ya*). Taipei: Mai tian chu ban she.

Sun Xiandao, and Li Duoyu, eds. 2006. *One Hundred Years of Chinese Cinema* (*Zhong guo dian ying bai nian*). Beijing: Zhong guo guang bo dian shi chu ban she.

Tay, William, ed. 1994a. *From the Modern to the Contemporary* (*Cong xiandai dao dangdai*). Taipei: Sanmin.

———. 1994b. *The World of Eileen Chang* (*Zhang ailing de shijie*). Taipei: Yunchen.

Teo, Stephen. 2001a. "Love and Swords: The Dialectics of Martial Arts Romance." *Senses of Cinema.* http://www.sensesofcinema.com/contents/00/11/crouching.html. Accessed August 15, 2006.

———. 2001b. "We Kicked Jackie Chan's Ass! An Interview with James Schamus." *Senses of Cinema.* http://www.sensesofcinema.com/contents/01/13/schamus.html. Accessed August 15, 2006.

———. 2001c. "Wong Kar-wai's *In the Mood for Love:* Like a Ritual In Transfigured Time." *Senses of Cinema.* http://archive.sensesofcinema.com/contents/01/13/mood.html. Accessed April 30, 2007.

———. 2002. "King Hu." *Senses of Cinema.* http://www.sensesofcinema.com/contents/directors/02/hu.html.

———. 2005a. "*Wuxia* Redux: *Crouching Tiger, Hidden Dragon* as a Model of Late Transnational Production." In *Hong Kong* Connections, eds. Meaghan Morris, Siu Leung Li, and Stephen Ching-kiu Chan, 191–204. Hong Kong: Hong Kong University Press.

———. 2005b. *Wong Kar-wai.* London: British Film Institute Publishing.

———. 2005c. "*2046:* A Matter of Time, A Labour of Love." *Senses of Cinema.* http://www.sensesofcinema.com/contents/05/35/2046.html. Accessed September 8, 2007.

Tu Wei-ming, ed. 1994. *The Living Tree: The Changing Meaning of Being Chinese Today.* Stanford: Stanford University Press.

Useem, Ruth Hill. 1999. "Third Culture Kid (TCK)." http://www.iss.edu/pages/kids.html. Accessed on November 18, 2007.

Villella, Fiona. 2001. "The Cinema of Wong Kar-wai: A Writing Game." *Senses of Cinema.* http//www.sensesofcinema.com/contents/01/13/wong-symposium.html. Accessed January 26, 2008.

Wang, David Der-wei. 1991. *Reading Contemporary Fiction* (*Yuedu dangdai xiaoshuo*). Taipei: Yuanliu chu ban she.

———. 1992. *Fictional Realism in Twentieth-Century China: Mao Dun, Lao She, Shen Congwen.* New York: Columbia University Press.

———, ed. 1993. *From June Fourth to May Fourth: Fiction and Film in Twentieth Century China.* Cambridge, MA: Harvard University Press.

———. 1997. "Decadence and Seduction of the South" (Nanfang de duoluo yu youhuo). In *Angel's Food* (*Tian shi de liang shi*), Su Tong, 11–36. Taipei: Maitian.

Wang Dulu. 1941. *Crane Iron Series.* (*He tie xi lie*). In *Qingdao Daily Journal* (*Qing dao ri bao*). Published as a serial.

———. 1948. *Crane Iron Series.* (*He tie xi lie*). Vols. I-V. Shanghai: Li li shu ju.

———. 2001. *Crouching Tiger, Hidden Dragon* (*Wo hu cang long*). Vols. I, II, and III. Taipei: Yuan jing.

Wang Huiling. 2006a. "A Conversation with Ang Lee's Script Writer Wang Huiling" (Bian ju wang hui ling yan li de li an). *Sina Entertainment* (*Xin lang yu le*). http://ent.sina.com.cn/s/h/37006.html. Accessed July 17, 2007.

———. 2006b. "Xie xie ni ceng jing ai guo wo: Wang huiling tan yu li an he zuo" (Thank you for having had loved me: Conversation with Wang Huiling about her collaboration with Ang Lee). http://ent.sina.com.cn/v/m/2006–07–17/16291161512.html. Accessed September 15, 2007.

Wang Yuejin. 1991. "*Red Sorghum:* Mixing Memory and Desire." In *Perspectives on Chinese Cinema*, ed. Chris Berry, 80–103. London: British Film Institute Publishing.

Welsh, James, and Peter Lev, eds. 2007. *The Literature/Film Reader.* Lanham, MD.: Scarecrow Press.

Widmer, Ellen, and David Der-wei Wang, eds. 1993. *From May Fourth to June Fourth: Fiction and Film in Twentieth-Century China.* Cambridge, MA: Harvard University Press.

Wilson, Emma. 2006. *Alain Resnais.* Manchester: Manchester University Press.

Wong Kar-wai. 2005. "Preface to the Photo Collection of *Duidao*" (*Duidao* xie zhen ji qian yan). *Duidao.* Hong Kong: Huoyi chu ban.

Wu I-Fen. 2003. "Looking for Nostalgia: Memory and National Identity in Hou Hsiao-Hsien's *A Time to Live, A Time to Die.*" *CineAction!* 60: 45–51.

Xu Sinian. 2001. "Looking for Teacher Wang Dulu: Preface to the Taiwanese Edition of *The Works of Wang Dulu.*" In Wang Dulu, *Crouching Tiger, Hidden Dragon* (*Wo hu cang long*), vol. 1. Taipei: Yuanjing.

Yang, Mayfair Mei-hui. 1993. "Of Gender, State Censorship, and Overseas Capita: An Interview with Chinese Director Zhang Yimou." *Public Culture* 5, no. 2: 300–307.

Yang Ze, ed. 1999. *Yue du Zhang Ailing* (Reading Eileen Chang). Taipei: Maitian.

Yau, Esther C. M., ed. 2001. *At Full Speed: Hong Kong Cinema in a Borderless World.* Minneapolis: University of Minnesota Press.

Yeh, Emilie Yueh-yu, and Darrell William Davis. 2005. *Taiwan Film Directors: A Treasure Island.* New York: Columbia University Press.

Yeh Wen-hsin. 2000. *Becoming Chinese: Passages to Modernity and Beyond.* Berkeley: University of California Press.

Yip, June. 2004. *Envisioning Taiwan: Fiction, Cinema, and the Nation in the Cultural Imaginary.* Durham, NC: Duke University Press.

Yu Sen-lun. 2002. "Romantic Boyhood Memories of a Chinese Filmmaker." *Taipei Times.* May 20. http://www.taipeitimes.com/News/feat/archives/2002/05/20/136866. Accessed on October 13, 2007.

Yue Ming-bao. 1993. "Gendering the Origins of Modern Chinese Fiction." In *Gender and Sexuality in Twentieth-Century Chinese Literature and Society,* ed. Lu Tonglin. 47–65. Albany: State University of New York Press.

Zhang Yingjin. 1996. *The City in Modern Chinese Literature & Film: Configurations of Space, Time, and Gender.* Stanford: Stanford University Press.

———. 2002. *Screening China.* Ann Arbor: University of Michigan.

———. 2004. *Chinese National Cinema.* New York: Routledge.

Zhang Zhen. 2002. "Building on the Ruins: The Exploration of New Urban Cinema of the 1990s." In *Reinterpretation: A Decade of Experimental Chinese Art: 1990–2000,* eds. Wu Hung, Wang Huangsheng, and Feng Boyi. 113–120. Guangzhou: Guangzhou Museum of Art.

Zhang Zijing. 1996. *My Sister Eileen Chang* (*Wo de jiejie Zhang Ailing*). Taipei: Shibao.

Zhong Hui-ling. 1997. *Feminism and Chinese Literature* (*Nuxing zhuyi yu zhonggu wenxue*). Taichung: Li ren.

Zhong Xueping. 2000. *Masculinity Besieged? Issues of Modernity and Male Subjectivity in Chinese Literature of the Late Twentieth Century.* Durham, NC: Duke University Press.

Zhou, Juanita Huan. 1998. "Ashes of Time: The Tragedy and Salvation of the Chinese Intelligentsia." *Asian Cinema* 10, no. 1 (Fall): 62–70.

Zhou Yingxiong, and Liu Zhihui, eds. 2004. *Writing Taiwan: Literary History, Postcolonialism, and Postmodernity* (*Shu xie taiwan: Wen xue shi, hou zhi ming yu hou xian dai*). Taipei: Maitian chu ban she.

Zhu Tianwen. 1991a. "The Story of Little Bi" (Xiao bi de gu shi). In *Collection of Zhu Tianwen's Movie Stories* (*Zhu tian wen dian ying xiao shuo ji*), 9–21. Taipei: Yuan liu chu ban gong si.

———. 1991b. "A Time to Live, A Time to Die" (Tong nian wang shi). *Collection of Zhu Tianwen's Movie Stories* (*Zhu tian wen dian ying xiao shuo ji*), 131–164. Taipei: Yuan liu chu ban gong si.

———. 1991c. *Collection of Zhu Tianwen's Movie Stories* (*Zhu tian wen dian ying xiao shuo ji*). Taipei: Yuan liu chu ban gong si.

———. 1994. *The Capital of a Burning Summer* (*Yan xia zhi du*). Taipei: Yuan liu chu ban gong si.

———. 1997. *Fin-de-siècle Splendor* (*Shi ji mo de hua li*). Taipei: Yuan liu chu ban gong si.

———. 1999. *Notes of a Desolate Man.* Trans. Howard Goldblatt and Sylvia Li-chun Lin. New York: Columbia University Press.

———. 2006. *Remembering the Flower's Previous Life* (*Hua yi qian shen*). Taipei: Mai tain chu ban she.

Zhu Tianwen, and Wu Nianzhen. 1989. *Dust in the Wind* (*Lianlian fengchen*). Taipei: San san shu fang.

Zhu Tianwen et al. 1992. *Topics for an Afternoon Tea* (*Xia wu cha de hua ti*). Taipei: Mai tian Chu bain.

Selected Filmography

Chen Guofu: as director

1989. *High School Girls* (*Guozhong nüsheng*). Hao Ke Record Production.
1998. *The Personals.* (*Zhen hun qi shi*). Central Motion Pictures Corporation.

Dai Sijie: as director

1989. *China, My Sorrow* (*Niu peng*). Centre National de la Cinématographie (CNC).
1994. *The Moon Eater* (*Le mangeur de lune*). Les Films du Losange.
1998. *The Eleventh Child* (*Tang le onzième*). REZO Films.
2002. *Balzac and the Little Chinese Seamstress* (*Balzac et la petite tailleuse chinoise*). Les films de la Suane.
2006. *The Chinese Botanist's Daughters* (*Les filles du botaniste*) Fayolle et Sotela Films.

Hou Xiaoxian (Hsiao-hsien): as director

1983. *Boys from Fenggui* (*Feng gui lai de ren*). Central Motion Pictures Corporation.
1983. *The Sandwich Man* (*Er zi de da wan ou*). Central Motion Pictures Corporation.
1984. *A Summer at Grandpa's* (*Dong dong de jia qi*). Central Motion Pictures Corporation.
1985. *A Time to Live, A Time to Die* (*Tong nian wang shi*). Central Motion Pictures Corporation.
1986. *Dust in the Wind* (*Lian lian feng chen*). Central Motion Pictures Corporation.
1987. *Daughter of the Nile* (*Ni luo he de nü er*). Central Motion Pictures Corporation.

Kwan, Stanley: as director

1985. *Women* (*Nü ren xin*). Zhou li ying shi.
1987. *Rouge* (*Yan zhi kou*). Golden Harvest Company.
1992. *Center Stage*. (*Ruan Lingyu*). Golden Way Films Ltd.
1994. *Red Rose/White Rose* (*Hong meigui, bai meigui*). Golden Flare Films Company.
1996. *Yang & Yin: Gender in Chinese Cinema*. British Film Institute.
2001. *Lan Yu*. Kwan's Creation Workshop.
2005. *Everlasting Regret* (*Chang he ge*). JCE Entertainment Ltd.

Lee, Ang: as director:

1991. *Pushing Hands* (*Tui shou*). Central Motion Pictures Corporation.
1993. *The Wedding Banquet* (*Xi yan*). Central Motion Pictures Corporation.
1994. *Eat Drink Man Woman* (*Yin shi nan nü*). Central Motion Pictures Corporation.
1995. *Sense and Sensibility*. Columbia Pictures.
1997. *The Ice Storm*. Fox Searchlight Picture.
1999. *Ride with the Devil*. Good Machine.
2000. *Crouching Tiger, Hidden Dragon* (*Wo hu cang long*). Columbia Pictures.
2001. *The Hire: Chosen*. Anonymous content.
2003. *The Hulk*. Universal Pictures.
2005. *Brokeback Mountain*. Good Machine.
2007. *Lust, Caution*. Hai Sheng Film Production Company.

Wong Kar-wai: as director

1988. *As Tears Go By* (*Wang jiao ka men*). Kino International Corp.
1991. *Days of Being Wild* (*A feng zheng zhuan*). Mega Star Video Distribution.
1994. *Ashes of Time* (*Dong xie xi du*). Sony Pictures Classics.
1995. *Fallen Angels* (*Duo luo tian shi*). Kino International Corp.
2000. *In the Mood for Love* (*Hua yang nian hua*). Mei Ah Entertainment.
2004. *2046*. 20th Century Fox.
2007. *My Blueberry Nights*. The Weinstein Company.

Zhang Yimou: as director

1987. *Red Sorghum* (*Hong gao liang*). Xi'an Film Studio.
1990. *Ju Dou*. China Film Co-Production Corporation.
1991. *Raise the Red Lantern* (*Da hong deng long gao gao gua*). Century Communications.
1992. *The Story of Qiu Ju* (*Qiu ju da guang si*). Sil-Metropole Organization.
1994. *To Live* (*Huo zhe*). ERA International.
1999. *Not One Less* (*Yi ge dou bu neng shao*). Beijing New Picture Distribution Company.

2000. *Happy Times* (*Xing fu shi guang*). Guangxi Film Studio.
2002. *Hero* (*Ying xiong*). Beijing New Picture Film Company.
2004. *House of Flying Daggers* (*Shi mian mai fu*). Beijing New Picture Film Company.
2005. *Riding Alone for Thousands of Miles* (*Qian li zou dan qi*). Beijing New Picture Film Company.
2006. *Curse of the Golden Flower* (*Man cheng jin dai huang jin jia*). Beijing New Picture Film Company.

Index

About the Author

Hsiu-Chuang Deppman is associate professor of Chinese at Oberlin College. She has published widely on Chinese literature and film in a variety of books and journals including *positions: east asia culture critique*, *Journal of Narrative Theory*, *Modern Chinese Literature and Culture*, *Journal of American Chinese Studies*.

Production Notes for Deppman | *Adapted for the Screen*

Cover design by University of Hawai'i producton staff

Text design by Santos Barbasa Jr. with display type in Post Antiqua and text type in Bembo Hawn

Composition by Terri Miyasato

Printing and binding by The Maple-Vail Book Manufacturing Group

Printed on 60# Maple Recycled Opaque, 408 ppi